# Leadership
## A Critical Text

## Simon Western

Los Angeles • London • New Delhi • Singapore • Washington DC

First published 2008

Reprinted 2008

SAGE Publications Ltd
1 Oliver's Yard
55 City Road
London EC1Y 1SP

SAGE Publications Inc.
2455 Teller Road
Thousand Oaks, California 91320

SAGE Publications India Pvt Ltd
B 1/I 1 Mohan Cooperative Industrial Area
Mathura Road
New Delhi 110 044

SAGE Publications Asia-Pacific Pte Ltd
33 Pekin Street #02-01
Far East Square
Singapore 048763

**Library of Congress Control Number: 2007922335**

**British Library Cataloguing in Publication data**

A catalogue record for this book is available from the British Library

ISBN 978-1-4129-2304-0
ISBN 978-1-4129-2305-7 (pbk)

Typeset by C&M Digitals (P) Ltd., Chennai, India
Printed in Great Britain by TJ International Ltd, Padstow, Cornwall
Printed on paper from sustainable resources

**FSC**
**Mixed Sources**
Product group from well-managed
forests and other controlled sources

Cert no. SGS-COC-2482
www.fsc.org
© 1996 Forest Stewardship Council

76

# Contents

This book is dedicated to the memory of Mike Broughton, a great friend, whom I miss. Also, to my son Fynn, who has sparkling spirit and surely will be a leader in the future.

# Website guides

For lecturer resources and guidance on how to use this book, go to
**www.sagepub.co.uk/western**

For further information on *Leadership: A Critical Text*, go to
**www.simonwestern.com**

This site contains up-to-date leadership development activity, training support, research, keynote speeches, seminars and other associated activity. On this website you will also find a Leadership Discourse Indicator. This offers individuals and organizations feedback on their leadership assumptions.

# Acknowledgements

Thanks to all of my family and friends for their sustenance over the years. Especially to my parents, brothers Jon and Mark and my son Fynn.

Thanks to Chris Hart for his idealism and knowledge, during hundreds of much needed coffee breaks between sharing writing. We use our local café in the traditional fashion, a place for political and social debate, a place of community where I learn more than from attending academic conferences. To Sonya Sharma for reading chapters and being so encouraging.

Also thanks to Mary, Laura, Anne and Elizabeth Simpson who have provided great friendship and conversation. Thanks to Simon Massey, Norman, Marion, Kieran and Liam Warden, Alex Massey, Nick Jenkins and Deborah O' Sullivan, Terry Burgin and Su, Louise Davey, Hester Speirs, Calla Thompson, Mary Gleeson, Rachel, Peter, Wendy and Joe Dixon for continuity of friendship. For the worldwide Quaker movement, an extended family and community which I value, and also to the kind friends in the Pacific School of Religion, California, where I stayed and wrote the first draft of this book.

To all of my colleagues; especially Jonathan Gosling for his friendship, creativity and for introducing me to the world of leadership development. Colin Brown for supervising my PhD and telling me I needed to publish this book, without his confidence in my work, this book would not have been conceived. To Lynne Sedgmore with whom I have enjoyed collaborating on exciting leadership initiatives and who shares a special interest in spiritual leadership. To Cameron Findlater for reading the text and offering very helpful comments. To John Mackness who is always encouraging and a good friend and to Sally Watson, Norman Scott, Scott Ehrens and Miguel Fernandez–Arias.

And finally to all those leaders who have led me well, and to those who have led me dreadfully. I have learnt much from you all.

# Introduction

This book sets out to promote a critical and curious stance in the reader's mind when thinking about leadership in the workplace. This book is written from my broad practical experience rather than from the confines of academic life. I have been heavily influenced by my own experiences of leadership and followership, in a wide variety of settings (see Box 1). My work as a coach and therapist has also given me unusual and privileged access to the psychological and emotional experiences of others, giving me insights into them and how work, organizational culture and leadership have impacted on them.

---

### Box 1   Simon Western: Work and leadership experiences

I began work at the age of 17 as an office boy in a factory, witnessing 'scientific management' techniques on production lines and controlling leadership. Strong unionized labour, women spending all day packing paper bags which tumbled off clattering machines, men labouring to keep the machines working 24 hours a day and fed with heavy rolls of paper and ink, this mundane work (now exported to Asia) was brutalizing. I remember tough men and women, with a fierce humour to cope. I left at the age of 18 to enter the nursing profession. I worked with the sick and dying, becoming aware of the existential issues of mortality and of the concept of embodiment, how our emotions and thinking are situated in the body. Long shifts working with primitive human emotions, set in a rigid matriarchal nursing system that had echoes of the military, a commander in chief (the matron), uniforms denoting rank, strict authority, no first names on the ward. The organizational structures were geared as social defences against facing the emotional pain of working with illness and death (Menzies Lyth, 1960). No counselling if you worked with a traumatic death, just a coffee break and gallows humour in the bar after work. I loved the work, made great friends, learnt buckets about life and myself but struggled in this constraining organizational culture. Nursing leadership was predominantly female, from ward sister to hospital matron, in contrast to the medical leadership that was predominantly male. This dual leadership created a symbolic structure replicating a 'heteronormative' parental structure; father leading with technical expertise,

*(Continued)*

*(Continued)*

mother being the carer. This raised my awareness of gender issues, of power, responsibility and pay differentials. I was a male on the female team and often in my life have found myself in the position of experiencing 'otherness' from a very close proximity.

Within this archetypal parental leadership model, Daddy Doctor and Mummy Nurse, the patients were symbolically childlike in their dependency. The contemporary rhetoric of individual choice, and the omnipotence of our wanting to always be in control, are confronted by Freud's 'reality principle' when in hospital and facing major surgery or death. For some patients, the dependency culture was wholly appropriate, as it helped them give up their autonomy for a period of time to enable the surgeon's knife to be wielded and to allow themselves to be bed-bathed and toileted as an infant would be. For others in rehabilitation, the dependency culture was completely wrong and hindered their attempts to regain autonomy. Dependency culture can be very damaging and undermine innovation and dispersed leadership or it can be a useful culture when thoughtfully utilized to free individuals from the need to be in control in certain situations (Obholzer and Roberts, 1994; Western, 2005).

I then trained as a psychiatric nurse working, finding liberty in a more relaxed uniform-free setting, and finding myself totally engaged in human psychology, and finding my passion for the 'talking cure'. I worked with the obsessive, neurotic, depressed, schizophrenic and psychotic in Victorian-built asylums which Goffman (1961) describes as total institutions. I witnessed electro-convulsive therapy and worked on some wards where 70 men slept in long dorms without curtains or any privacy. The system of 'token economy' was used on long-term wards, filled with institutionalized patients. Patients received tokens which were exchanged for cigarettes to reinforce good behaviours, e.g. for getting out of bed, and had tokens taken away for 'bad behaviour'. Institutionalization had an impact on staff and patients (sometimes it was hard to tell the difference!), and the concept of asylum has stayed with me. At one level, it provided a safe and caring space, a refuge from the terrors of the world, and at the same time it could be an oppressive and totalizing space. I also learnt counselling skills, group facilitation skills and, most importantly, how to manage my own and others' anxiety when facing psychotic disturbance and distress. Learning how thin and blurred the line is between madness and sanity was another lesson, I witnessed some quite disturbing undiagnosed pathology in the workplace. Reflecting back, both token economy and the culture control I witnessed in these total institutions still resonate with me when I experience transformational leadership advocating culture control. I am now very alert to ethics and the question, 'Does this leadership stance and the culture it supports, enhance or diminish our humanity?'

During this period I was a skilled rugby player and at the age of 18 captained my local club, experiencing leadership in the combative and very collaborative world of rugby. Rugby provided me with the opportunity to learn motivational skills, team-work, and it was probably the most honest and

*(Continued)*

*(Continued)*

egalitarian community I ever participated in. Our club consisted of lawyers, entrepreneurs, business leaders, unemployed, ex-convicts, and all were treated with respect, and anybody pulling ego or rank over another was teased mercilessly – it was a levelling experience. Team-work, having the courage to have a go, and being able to laugh at myself were lessons I learned from leading the rugby club.

At the age of 23, I was promoted taking a Charge Nurse role in a regional residential unit run as a therapeutic community unit for emotionally disturbed adolescents. The unit's philosophy was to devolve leadership to the young people themselves, empowering them to find their voices and to learn how to take responsibility for themselves and others, through experimenting in a safe environment. I was given a huge amount of responsibility at very young age, working with young people who had serious problems such as anorexia or who had been suicidal and abused. Working closely with the boss, we radicalized the unit to make it fully self-catering, and the medical input was marginalized. This was to remove the dependency culture and the stigma of being given a medical diagnosis and treated as a patient. The dynamic of learning to take responsibility for each other was the most therapeutic environment I have experienced. I learnt two key lessons here: (1) my idealism that if you remove leadership and deny power relations, that pure democracy will flourish was crushed. Actually chaos and fear flourish; and (2) devolving power and decision-making responsibly and enabling dispersed leadership within safe boundaries works wonderfully. Our so-called 'disturbed' young people were able to run the unit, making important decisions together and work on their emotional selves at the same time. They helped us to interview and appoint new staff, took control over their own destinies and supported their peers with great skill and empathy. This experimental community, set in the NHS, marginalized the medical model and gave power back to the client group. I am indebted to this intense learning experience.

From here, in my mid-twenties, I spent three years as a single parent on welfare (that too was work) and again found myself challenging gender stereotypes, wandering into mother and toddler groups and struggling with the responses I received. I loved the freedom of being a home-parent, each day being thrown back to my own resources to make ends meet and create the day; this was a time of adventures!

On return to work, I spent ten years training and working as a Family Therapist and psychotherapist, mainly with the urban underclass, and was a Clinical Manager of a community-based multi-professional healthcare team. I loved Family Therapy as it gave me the opportunity to be hugely creative in therapy sessions and gain insights into how systems impact on individuals; this has hugely influenced my leadership work since. I also decided to get a university education for the first time (I had no A-levels or Bachelors degree) and I studied for a Masters in Counselling at Keele University. I finally left this community team, under the pressure of working with emotionally disturbed families and suicidal teenagers in an under-resourced provision.

*(Continued)*

*(Continued)*

This was still within a health setting, with a leadership dominated by the hegemony of medical power, which allowed little room for constructive dissent and change, particularly if it came from a nurse. The medical model provided the wrong leadership, wrong culture and wrong treatment for this client group. For the most part, my clients were not ill but suffered from the emotional, social and mental strains of living in poverty and unemployment. They required therapeutic and emotional support, more resources and structural-political change rather than medical diagnosis, labels and medicines. This experience taught me how the systemic power structures and culture of an institution can dominate and impair potential positive change. My attempts to make changes as a nurse manager were partly successful, and ideas of more collaborative work are now in place. However, they also met with structural resistance from medical and managerial power. The NHS on the whole had an institutional leadership culture that was powerfully totalizing, there was little room for innovation or creativity, and I found the leadership of the National Health Service in the 1980s and 1990s to be dogmatic and rigid.

I then took another Masters degree to better understand organizational culture and studied psychoanalytic approaches to Organizational Consultancy at the internationally renowned Tavistock Centre. My interest was to promote partnerships and collaborative working across the boundaries of health, education and social services in order to better serve families who found that institutions worked in silos. Developing an understanding of the unconscious processes that underpin organizational culture was a huge learning experience for me, which I been able to apply to my work ever since.

In the past decade, I have also worked in real estate, working closely with the building trade observing how the leadership is transient, moving between trades on the same building job. The building trade is interesting as it is both highly competitive with a harsh culture but also depends wholly on collaboration. Designing and altering physical spaces is a passion of mine, which comes through in my work when I think about a leader's role as an organizational architect. Place, location and spatial understanding of organizational life form an under-researched leadership area.

Another experience, which has informed my understanding of leadership and organizational culture, is my religious affiliation. I have been a Quaker (Religious Society for Friends) for 15 years, which has an unusual organizational structure without a formal leadership. It does not appoint church ministers but believes in a 'priesthood of all believers' abolishing *not* the idea of priests but abolishing the laity. The business meetings are run (and have been for 350 years) by spiritual consensus, which can mean up to 1,000 Quakers at a yearly meeting deciding on Quaker 'policy' (http://www.quaker.org.uk). Quaker meetings are structured around the idea of equality. Sitting in a circle, in silence, anyone moved to speak can 'minister' to those present. The Quakers' history was an important part of my PhD research,

*(Continued)*

*(Continued)*

leading me to examine how their informal leadership and organizational structure have changed over the centuries, to accommodate social change, while holding onto the central experience and structures. My experience of leadership has been further informed by engaging with social movements: trade unions, feminist, anarchist and green activist movements.

In the past nine years I have worked in academia, studying for a PhD and working in leadership development in executive education. Academic leadership is an interesting model, it is underpinned by a dependency culture that replicates educational models of teacher–student dynamics, and tends towards a frustrating bureaucratic leadership. However, it also has an adolescent rebellious nature, maybe due to very bright individuals, expert in their own fields, resisting external control. Maybe because it employs adults, many of whom just never left school!

My current role is Director of Coaching at Lancaster Management School where I have established a critical approach to coaching, drawing heavily on psychoanalytic and systems thinking. I have also been designing and delivering leadership development to international senior leaders in corporate life and across different sectors. I have worked in corporate America, with multi-national mergers in Europe and I have also visited Sudanese refugee camps and Kosovo, working with leaders in the not-for-profit sector. These diverse opportunities to study leadership first hand, in such varied contexts, have been a privilege and a revelation. Moreover, as Director of Coaching at Lancaster Management School, I gain intimate access as a coach to many leaders and I supervise and teach a diverse range of coaches who work closely with leaders. This gives me an unusual and personal perspective on leadership from the inside.

This book emerges from the culmination of this lived experience, and follows from my doctoral studies on leadership at Lancaster University Management School.

I have questioned the notion of leadership and tested my early utopian ideals of leaderless groups, I have been a leader, and experienced leadership in many forms and in many professions, organizations, trades, sectors and social movements. I have experienced excellent leadership, mediocre leadership and leadership that has made me despair. However, it is from this breadth of experience that I totally affirm leadership as a necessity. I am not one of the critical thinkers who denigrates individual leaders or leadership. I am certain that leadership is vital for healthy organizations. Organizations can be extremely dysfunctional with poor leadership, but without it they would cease to function altogether. Leadership can be many things: it can be formal or informal, hierarchical or democratic, explicit or hidden. Leadership can be found in many places, the debates as to where it is situated, the individual, a collective group, or a process, depends as much on where you look for it as to where it is actually situated or being enacted. My work experience has further taught me that a critical approach is vital to reveal the hidden discourses of leadership to get beneath the surface of what is really going on.

Taking a critical approach is the starting point of finding sustainable approaches to improving leadership in practice. Box 1 gives a brief summary of my work experiences, which formed my own leadership approach and provides the context for this book.

I am writing this leadership biography to identify myself first of all with leadership in practice (a task I often ask leaders to do in order to help them locate themselves). The aims of the book are not to deconstruct leadership using an overly academic or post-modern, post-structuralist approach, nor to attempt to scrutinize every aspect of the leadership debate. The aim is to establish a critical framework to help the reader through her or his own process of inquiry into the theory and practice of leadership.

The book briefly reviews some of the main contested leadership issues and analyses these to demonstrate two parallel processes. First, how the leadership issues in question can be understood in multiple ways, demonstrating that there is more than is revealed in popular texts and mainstream understandings. Second, by taking a critical stance, dominant ideas in organizations and in wider society are illuminated, from which new options become available to the leader practitioner. To achieve this, new resources are required to support the search for new ways of seeing.

The book brings new resources from different disciplines to illuminate contemporary leadership in organizational life. For example, drawing on theory from new social movements and anarchism to shed light on self-managed teams and the ideas around dispersed leadership. Psychoanalysis helps reveal the undercurrents and unconscious processes for leaders and followers and within organizational life itself. Analysis of new organizational forms, taken from outside the usual management literature, offers the opportunity to 'look awry' at leadership, of particular interest are the Christian Fundamentalist leaders in the USA. Closer analysis and understanding of this movement show how it both mimics and informs corporate leadership and organizational life in the West, particularly through the influential 'transformational leadership' theories (Bass, 1985; Burns, 1978). These new resources help to situate different leadership processes and patterns within historical and socio-cultural frames. The book identifies three main discourses of leadership in the past century, and these discourses underpin how leadership is perceived and practised. Using these discourses as a heuristic tool, leadership is seen through a different prism that exposes new nuances in how leadership is enacted on the organizational stage.

The aim of this book is to illuminate theory and to offer readers insights and skills to enable them to take a critical perspective in order to become reflexive practitioners. Critiquing one's personal leadership practices and the leadership encountered within our organizations and workplaces liberates us from being trapped within the dominant normative discourses and enables emancipatory change to occur.

Chapter 1 will explain why a critical approach to leadership is important and then outlines the critical approach (theoretical methodology) this book takes. Chapters 2 and 3 set out some key debates within leadership theory, applying critical theory approaches (this process will continue through other chapters as I work through each leadership discourse). Chapter 4 looks at leadership and the issues of diversity. In Chapter 5, 'Asymmetric leadership' will set out seven leadership stances analysed from within a single social movement, identifying leadership as asymmetric in that it is not easily definable, and cannot be reduced to fit neatly into a single category or dual categories.

Chapters 6, 7 and 8 and 9 then focus on the leadership discourses. Through developing an understanding of these discourses, it is possible to critically analyse the leadership assumptions and norms that are encountered in organizational life. These leadership discourses are not exclusive of each other and they can overlap and converge, however, one is usually dominant in any organizational-departmental culture. The third and latest dominant leadership discourse 'the messiah discourse' will be examined in some detail, as it underpins the contemporary populist and mainstream ideas of leadership such as the 'transformational leader'.

Chapter 10 looks at religious fundamentalism and its relationship to leadership, before moving onto Chapter 11 that describes how Christian Fundamentalism in the USA has influenced the contemporary transformational leadership model. The cultures arising from fundamentalist leadership teach us much about leadership success and also about the dangers of the totalizing cultures formed under certain conditions which are espoused through transformational leader literature. Chapter 12 summarizes the discourse chapters and Chapter 13 then takes a look at what's new in leadership and identifies a new emergent leadership discourse that I have called 'Eco-leadership'. Chapter 14 is the final chapter that I use to briefly reflect on the book. From my reflections I raise a question as to whether a process I call 'leadership formation' might be a more apt way to develop the next generation of leaders rather than focus on individual leadership development.

# 1

# Why a Critical Theory Approach to Leadership?

The aim of this book is to establish a critical theory framework to help the reader through her or his own processes of inquiry into the theory and practice of leadership. Chapter 1 will unpack what it means to take a critical approach and will then define the specific critical framework taken in this book. Finally, we discuss critical theory and its application to the practice of leadership.

## Critical thinking and critical theory

Critical thinking and critical theory are overlapping terms that require to be differentiated and clarified for the purpose of this book. Critical thinking or a critical approach are generic terms which are often used loosely and at times indiscriminately and interchangeably with critical theory, but, as Johnson and Duberley identify, there is more to critical theory than being reflective and critical:

> Whilst many researchers of management may consider themselves to be critical, in that they attempt to stand back from their work and interrogate their findings with a critical eye, this does not mean they are operating within a critical theory perspective. (Johnson and Duberley, 2000: 124)

To be critical can be to take a more radical, reflective and marginal stance, in contrast to taking a more mainstream, positivistic or rationalistic perspective. Fulop and Linstead write in the opening of their book *Management: A Critical Text*:

> This introduction outlines a critical approach to management that enables us to reflect on how we learn about management. It is designed to help us develop the intellectual rigour and knowledge to deal with the complex and multi-faceted issues that arise in everyday work situations. (1999: 4)

The key element in their position is to be reflective and reflexive, which they expand on in their discussion of a critical approach. Reflexivity is one element of a critical stance but there is more, for example, Calhoun (1995: 35) offers his perspective on critical theory:

1 Critical Theory critiques the contemporary social world looking for new possibilities, and positive implications for social action.

2　Critical Theory gives a critical account of historical and cultural conditions.
3　Critical Theory gives a continuous critical re-examination of the conceptual frameworks used (including the historical construction of these frameworks).
4　Critical Theory confronts other works of social explanation, analyzing their strengths and weaknesses, as well as their blind spots, but then demonstrates the capacity to incorporate their insights for stronger foundations.

These examples illustrate a use of a critical theory which brings into play critical thinking from a social, historical and cultural perspective, taking a social constructionist approach, i.e. how reality is constructed and made sense of through processes of socialization and past historical influences. Finally, there is another tradition of critical theory that goes beyond the objectives of revealing the underlying trends. In this tradition, critical theory aims to use its insights to take an explicitly ethical position. Its aims are to improve the human condition by making ethical and value judgements on what it is to be a free, autonomous, human subject, and revealing what hinders or supports the Enlightenment aims of liberty and emancipation. The aim is to work towards a theory which improves collective and individual autonomy and well-being. This critical theory stance contrasts sharply with a post-modern position, which claims that all values are relative and therefore values judgements which work towards social improvement cannot be made.

Critical theory aims to achieve its emancipatory goals through revealing and exposing political, cultural and social structures, discourses and practices which impinge on the liberty of individuals and reduce collective agency. Going beyond critiquing, a key aspect of critical theory is to link theory to practice and to find constructive ways of emancipating subjects from social, political and cultural constraints. Using knowledge to create new social structures and to find ways of communicating and organizing society and human relations that minimize oppression and maximize autonomy and liberty are the ethical aims of this critical theory approach. It is from this tradition that this book is written.

## The critical stance of this book

In this book I aim to critique current leadership theory and practice and offer new insights into leadership, but, more importantly and ambitiously, the aim is to provoke critical thinking about leadership. The intention is not simply to impart knowledge but to stimulate an ongoing learning process, an ability to think critically. Critical thinking skills are the pre-requisite leadership skills required to promote sustainable emancipatory change within organizations. This is because critical theory aims to reveal how and why certain leadership ideas, discourses and knowledge forms become privileged and dominant while others become marginalized. The assumption that knowledge promotes progress, new thinking and learning is not always true; knowledge can also be used to reproduce the status quo, supporting existing power elites or worse, knowledge can be used knowingly and unknowingly to limit and oppress. Throughout this book I develop a particular critical theory framework that has been influenced by contemporary critical theorists with the explicit ethical aim of emancipation at its core.

## *Theoretical stances*

In order to understand contemporary leadership within organizations from a critical perspective, I have developed a framework of four key critical lenses:

- Emancipation
- Depth analysis
- Looking awry
- Systemic praxis.

I will now discuss each of them in turn.

## *Emancipation*

This book draws upon the post-Marxist ideas of the Frankfurt School (for example, Max Horkheimer, Theodor Adorno and Jürgen Habermas) and others such as the post-structuralist Michel Foucault, who attempt to develop emancipatory agendas through their work.

### *The Frankfurt tradition: an emancipatory critical approach*
The underlying principles of critical theory from the Frankfurt School were to challenge the dominant positivistic theories that produced 'instrumental reason' (Horkeimer, 1987) which they claimed was an oppressive use of knowledge and rationality. They maintained that the theory-neutral language of science ignored power relationships and the effects of moral and socio-cultural interests. Science and rationality had become the dominant discourse, with dangerous secondary effects and few checks and balances. Jürgen Habermas a second generational member of the Frankfurt School wrote about the dominance of scientific-rationalism, 'we no longer understand science as one form of possible knowledge but rather identify knowledge with science' (1971: 4). John Ralston Saul describes the dominant figure of rationality as the modern technocrat whose 'talents have become the modern definition of intelligence' (1992: 106–7). Saul goes on to say how positive claims of rationality and reason have been used by technocrats, social scientists, orientalists, race scientists, social-Darwinists and imperialists which have led to many wars (see Farish Noor, 1997). Zygmunt Bauman argued in his renowned book, *Modernity and the Holocaust* (1989) that the Holocaust, rather than being a specific German problem, was a result of modernity and bureaucracy, which had created unintended conditions which led to a demise in moral responsibility: the Holocaust is 'fully in keeping with everything we know about our civilization, its guiding spirit, its priorities, its immanent vision of the world' (Bauman, 1989: 8). He points to the example of how eugenics was not restricted to being a Nazi idea but was given scientific credibility in other countries such as the USA and Scandinavia. Habermas has observed that increasingly the public sphere is administered remotely from individual citizens, diminishing their freedom and agency. He described this as the 'colonisation of the lifeworld' (Habermas, 1984) whereby the individual subject is surrounded by bureaucracy, which uses the ideology of efficiency and rationality to justify this.

The post-9/11 anti-terrorist drives are a contemporary example of how 'life-worlds' can become colonized within the public sphere, through increased surveillance. The explicit and rational aim of increased surveillance is efficiency in the battle to defeat terrorism. Critics, however, point to the by-product of surveillance which further diminishes the freedom of the individual by colonizing public spaces through physical intrusion, i.e. searches, CCTV security cameras, phone and computer surveillance, identity cards, etc. Britain is particularly fond of surveillance: 'The two worst countries in the 36-nation survey are Malaysia and China, and Britain is one of the bottom five with "endemic surveillance". There are up to 4.2m CCTV cameras in Britain – about one for every 14 people' (BBC News, 2006).

This rational effort to stop crime, and to defeat terrorism using technology, has other unwanted effects; trust between individual citizens and also between diverse communities is undermined, particularly racial and religious communities, and it increasingly adds to a culture of fear (Furedi, 2003). This fear culture of 'terrorists are lurking everywhere' is more pervasive than the physical intrusions of surveillance, as it creates a mindset where by individuals and social groups self-manage and police themselves and their peers (Foucault, [1977] 1991). Foucault discusses this process referring to 'the panopticon'. For Habermas, communication was a key inhibitor of freedom and therefore a key tool of emancipation. Understanding how language and discourses were limiting freedom was a shift in emphasis from the Marxist focus on structural change through economic and class struggle. McCarthy states that the Habermasian goal of critical theory is 'a form of life free from unnecessary domination in all of its forms' (McCarthy, 1978: 273).

However, unlike post-modernists who decried rationality and reason, identifying it as 'the problem', the Frankfurt School believed rationality was always part of the Enlightenment project, which they believed was an unfinished project. Their aim was to recover the link between rationality, liberty and freedom, and find contemporary ways to use knowledge and rationality to support progress.

In short, human freedom was the Frankfurt School's main concern and in order to fulfil the emancipatory aims they worked to make transparent and to challenge concealed power relations and structures, including those hidden in discourse and communication. To achieve this, the Frankfurt School claimed rationality and knowledge had to be understood subjectively and they recognized that it was not a neutral source of good, independent of power and elites, but that it was socially embedded.

### Summarizing the Frankfurt School's approach to critical theory

- Rationalism and knowledge must be linked to values and interests to enable it to be used as a force for emancipation. Critical theory challenges the privileging of a theory-neutral positivism (instrumental reason), claiming it to be covert, pervasive and undermining of individual and social autonomy.
- Critical theory challenges the post-modern turn, particularly its relativist stance that claims all points of view are of equal value. Elitist groups reproduce their hold on power, making their views privileged while less privileged groups are silenced. These hidden power relations ensure that not all views are

of equal value. Critical theory links politics, values and interests to knowledge, to undermine relativism.

- Critical theory has a clear ethical aim to work towards an emancipatory agenda. It aims to achieve this by revealing power relations that exist within social structures and within discourses and symbolic practices. It then focuses on how to change practices which undermine liberty and to find new ways to promote human agency and freedom.

This book uses this approach and draws on others that take an emancipatory Critical theory approach as a core ethical position.

## Depth analysis

Depth analysis describes a method of analysis derived from psychoanalysis. This book draws on psychoanalytic theorists such as Sigmund Freud, Jacques Lacan, Melanie Klein, Wilfred Bion and Slavoj Žižek. Psychoanalysis is characteristic of and perhaps the earliest example of a critical theorist method, as explained by Johnson and Duberley:

> Perhaps the prototype for critical science is psychoanalysis because it involves 'depth-hermeneutics' [Habermas, 1971: 218] in which the distorted texts of the patient's behaviour become intelligible to them through self-reflection. In this fashion emancipation occurs as the patient becomes liberated from the terror of their own unconscious as previously suppressed and latent determinants of behaviour are revealed and thereby lose their power. (Johnson and Duberley, 2000: 120)

The psychoanalytic framework I develop throughout the book attempts to under-take this same emancipatory task, not for a patient but for an organization through its leaders and the organizational cultures they establish. Depth analysis uses psychoanalysis but also takes in other critical theory methods which investi-gate what happens beneath the surface in organizational life (discourse analysis, narrative analysis, etc.), and particularly in this book what happens between leaders and followers. Understanding how the dynamics of power, control and influence are internalized by individuals and groups and lived out in the workplace through overt policies, behaviours and structures (the conscious) but also through unconscious behaviours and assumptions which become norms and translate into hard systems and structures, or simply are 'the way things are done around here', supporting certain values, assumptions and organizational cultures, which are not openly recognized. To see beyond the established 'natural order of things' and to achieve a critical position on leadership and organizational systems and struc-tures, new resources are required to help 'unmask' what is hidden.

Different psychoanalytic approaches provide frameworks and tools to achieve this. For example, the classical clinical psychoanalytic method, the analyst, the client (the analysand) and the couch, provides a classical model of containment that enables the therapist to explore the individual unconscious. The use of the 'self-as-tool', reading our emotional responses as a way of understanding the self and other, is another Freudian technique (based on the theories of projection, introjection, transference and counter-transference), these translate well as a critical theorist's action-research methodology and are under-used. They are all essential to the practice of leadership itself.

Many of these techniques pioneered by Freud have been developed over the past century and while much scepticism is aimed at psychoanalysis, much of Freud's work has become mainstream and many of his central ideas have become the commonplace language as frames for understanding human behaviour. Psychoanalysis as clinical practice has become a diminishing and marginal activity, partly because of medical insurance refusing to fund psychoanalysis, as it is too expensive a treatment method, partly because the psychoanalytic community became inward-looking, factional and elitist and marginalized itself. However, in media, critical, feminist and cultural studies there is something of a psychoanalytic renaissance, with a particular interest in Jacques Lacan. It seems as if the basic premise of Freud's the 'talking cure' has won the day, through counselling, psychotherapy, coaching and the personal growth and the self-help explosion. The American psychologist Philip Rieff announced in 1966 'The Triumph of the Therapeutic' and Furedi updates this prediction by citing an 'ever widening definition of psychological distress … . In a NEWSWEEK Poll, nearly 20 percent of American adults say they have had some form of therapy or counseling' (Furedi, 2003: 111). Therapy culture pervades our world in a way Freud could not have imagined. Oprah Winfrey and other TV shows and magazines encapsulate how the 'therapeutic culture' has become dominant in our thinking. The multitude of personal growth media offerings and the abundant self-help manuals can all be traced back to Freud's ideas of reflecting on oneself to gain a deeper self-understanding which aims to enable us to live more fulfilling lives. Freud's theories went beyond individual analysis and he felt his most important contribution would be to deepen an understanding of society and culture. In his book *Civilization and its Discontents* ([1930] 2002), Freud identifies the frustrations of being part of a social group:

> [N]oting that the human animal, with its insatiable needs, must always remain an enemy to organized society, which exists largely to damp down sexual and aggressive desires. At best, civilized living is a compromise between wishes and repression — not a comfortable doctrine. It ensures that Freud, taken straight, will never become truly popular, even if today we all speak Freud. (Gay, 1999: 3)

Advertising and marketing campaigns now have integrated Freudian concepts into their thinking by relying on the unconscious to attract new customers through linking their brands to individual identity (Klein N., 2000). Subliminal advertising is common, drawing on Freud's links between sex and power and his understanding of unconscious fantasy; hence the stereotypical advert of fast cars being linked to glamorous women, to appeal to the male desires and fantasises of having more phallic power. Psychoanalysis, however, remains marginal within leadership, management and organizational studies partly due to the positivistic and rationalist bias in management, which discounts complex understandings in favour of measurable outcomes.

Psychoanalysis is employed in this text as a key critical theoretical method to help reveal how social unconscious processes become internalized, embodied and enacted by individuals, social groups and organizations. Leadership always raises issues of the individual and the group; leadership and followership, power and authority, manipulation and control and therefore depth analysis is vital to understand the processes which help develop models of successful leadership.

## Looking awry

Žižek (1992, 2003) uses a Lacanian psychoanalytic approach as a cultural critical methodology. He claims that a frontal view of an object or text does not offer the best view but a distorted and a limited perspective. To really see what is happening, he suggests the need to *look awry* and take a 'distorted' view: 'The object assumes clear and distinctive features only if we look "at an angle", i.e. with an interested view, supported permeated, and "distorted" by *desire*' (Žižek, 1992: 12). Here, Žižek argues that the observer needs to bring their *desire*, or their subjectivity to the viewing rather than trying to understand from an objective neutral stance (again, this challenges Cartesian dualism, the subject–object, observer–observed, knower–known dichotomy). In *Looking Awry* (Žižek, 1992), Žižek describes how a change in the angle of a camera during filming can give a whole different perspective on the scene. It also means to bring something more from within ourselves to the act of observing. We all become familiar with the normative discourses which surround us in our own script or narrative so that we cannot 'see the wood for the trees'. When we are 'liberated' from a particular way of seeing, new options then become available. This is not only an intellectual exercise but can be a powerful change agent. As a Family Therapist, 'reframing' proved a useful way for individuals and families to find new options to change patterns of behaving they found destructive:

> In Family Therapy, Reframing is a technique developed by the Palo Alto Group. The therapist offers a description that gives the client a different way to look at their actions, hoping that this will enable them to see their problem differently and develop new options for actions as a result. (Weakland et al., 1974: 147)

Likewise, within leadership training and coaching, reframing opens up new options for leaders so that they view their role and can see different options and ways to act or intervene. Žižek describes a process he calls short-circuiting, to bring new resources from different traditions in order to see something new or hidden:

> Is not short-circuiting, therefore, one of the best metaphors for a critical reading? Is not one of the most effective critical procedures to cross wires that do not usually touch: to take a major text and read it in a short-circuiting way, through the lens of a minor (marginalised) author, text or conceptual apparatus? ... such a procedure can lead to insights which completely shatter and undermine our

common perceptions. ... The aim is to illuminate a standard text or ideological formation, making it readable in a totally new way. (Žižek, 2003: Foreword)

Bringing new resources to bear on an object and taking a historical and contextual perspective allows the object to be viewed in new ways, it adds depth to what is seemingly straightforward. To see beyond the obvious requires both new resources and also the ability to look and observe in new ways. This dual process of *short-circuiting* and *looking awry* provides options to reveal what was previously concealed within a dominant discourse. Hidden power structures within the pervasive 'natural order of things' become known.

Apart from utilizing psychoanalysis as a resource to short-circuit, I have also drawn on new social movement (NSM) theorists such as Alberto Melucci and Alain Touraine whose work with other anthropologists, ethnographers and sociologists theorize how NSMs form and differ from traditional social movements. In NSMs leaders are marginalized, and the movements focus on 'identity' and are de-centralized. This has huge implications for new organizational forms trying to work with new methods of organizing and leading such as networked and dispersed leadership or organizational matrix structures, for example. Management and leadership theorists have largely neglected this particular sociological and anthropological literature.

I also draw lightly upon the post-modern and post-structuralist theorists such as Michel Foucault as a theoretical resource to counter the positivist discourses. Post-modernists challenge the modernist ideas of meta-narratives and notions of universality, hierarchies of values and binary opposition favouring deconstruction, relativism and partiality.

The book finds some of the post-modernists' critique of power and their views on culture, discourse, language and symbolic power useful but is also wary of their abandonment of the gains and goals of the Enlightenment project. The danger of post-modern relativism becomes obvious, if all truth is relative, then dictatorship and fascism are of equal moral value to social democracy. Racism is of equal value in promoting diversity. This post-modern denial of the ability to choose one value over another perversely itself becomes a grand narrative of relativism, which, it is argued, can be a very dangerous grand narrative. Another critique is that language and linguistics are of particular interest to post-modernists, to reveal hidden powerful discourses, and yet the language they use can often be impenetrable to the non-academic, which makes the work elitist and difficult when applying post-modern theories to leadership practice. Best and Kellner challenge the populism of the post-modern: 'Post-modernism ... fails to provide a language to articulate what are arguably indispensable concerns with autonomy, rights and justice; it is individualist in its emphasis on desire and pleasure; it is irrationalist in its rejection of theory and rational critique' (Best and Kellner, 1991: 290).

Deconstructing leadership and followership can be useful, but academics should be wary of being seduced by the 'fetish of the new'. Just because post-modern and deconstructivist theoretical approaches are in vogue doesn't mean they should become uncritically accepted as a 'new norm'. M. Parker (1992) claims that post-modernism is problematic when defining the role of business companies in society and so it is with defining the role of leadership in society. Lyotard (1984) suggests that legitimate knowledge is only valid locally, and therefore no universal set of shared norms and assumptions can be applied. When discussing leadership, this provides insights as to the limitations of being able to apply universal competency frameworks for example, but it also poses problems for leadership practice as post-modern theories deconstruct but do not reconstruct. The possibility of creating any grand narrative or any practically useful political or social theory to build on leadership and organizational theory is negated by the theories themselves (Parker 1992; Wilmott 1998).

Using these deconstructive and post-modern approaches heuristically to understand leadership is useful, but let us not throw the 'baby out with the bathwater', a discerning approach is required, and approaches that can induce change in practice are also needed.

Some post-modernists or post-structuralists (particularly some of the new French philosophers such as Foucault) do strive to be read as emancipatory and their texts which deconstruct grand narratives and power can be useful when taken further and harnessed to other theories:

> Foucault ...   taught us to be wary of the institutions through which we are governed. We must always beware of the possibilities that our own institutional arrangements will encourage the rise of new destructive forces inimical to the possibilities of our being free. (Dumm, 1996: 153)

For example, post-structuralism is useful in that it problematizes leadership as a singular identity regarding the self as multiply constructed and negotiable. The leader is not leadership. This means that the constructions of identity, are not fixed but are characterized by fluidity, plurality and contradiction. In her study of a family-owned Japanese firm, Kondo (1990) contends that actors should be seen as multiple, gendered selves whose lives are shot through with contradictions and creative tensions. Arguing that identities are open, negotiable, shifting, and ambiguous, Kondo suggests that multiple selves are 'crafted' not least through ambiguity, paradox, and contradiction (Collinson, 2006: 182).

This perspective helpfully deconstructs the non-negotiable ideas of leadership as belonging to an individual self. Leadership is a social construction rather than (or I would argue as well as) a fixed identity. This means that it is important to realize that the individual leader is socially constructed by those 'followers' around them. In essence, we are all part of the history, culture and norms that surround us and we make sense of ourselves and each other through these frames or discourses. The challenge for post-structuralism is to use these insights to improve leadership. However, that is problematic with theories which denounce the emancipatory agenda as another grand narrative. NSMs and post-modern theory will be used in this book with other short-circuiting resources, to help look awry at leadership, giving new insights into the art and practice of leadership.

## Systemic praxis

I use the term systemic praxis to add a systemic perspective to the idea of praxis. Praxis is the application of, and relation between, theory and practice, which is fundamental to critical theory. To repeat Marx's famous quote in his 'Theses on

Feuerbach': 'The philosophers have only interpreted the world, the point is to change it' (Marx, [1845] 1978: 45).

'Without sustained commitment to praxis, critical theory restricts itself to becoming a self-indulgent academic effort and thus risks losing its emancipatory potential (Prasad and Caproni, 1997: 3, in Johnson and Duberley, 2000: 125). Systems theory, in brief, is to aim to take a holistic perspective, to take an ecological view and attempt to understand the connectiveness and networks that support living systems, whether they are human, social systems as in organizations or natural eco-systems. There are many key theorists, to name but a few: Von Bertalanffy (1968), Bateson (1972), Maturana and Varela (1980, 1987), Churchman (1968, 1979). In the contemporary leadership and management literature Peter Senge is best known for his use of systems thinking.

I use the term systemic praxis to describe the bringing of theory to practice but ensuring that it situates leadership practice within a systemic and critical framework which holds in mind the whole system, *and* the power relations that impact on and in that system. C. West Churchman defines how important systemic thinking is to a critical approach. He refers to ethics, efficiency and effectiveness as the outcomes of a critical systemic approach; 'First, ethical alertness comes from thinking systemically. Second, efficiency and effectiveness come from thinking about the total relevant system' (Flood, 1999: 63).

Any critical engagement leadership theory and practice require one to be vigilant of the wider impact of any leadership intervention taken and conversely to realize how leadership is influenced by other phenomena within a systemic framework. Using systemic praxis as a framework is an attempt to address the complex social, political, economic and environmental challenges which are present in all contemporary multiple-stakeholder organizations. While many critical theorists refer to context as being hugely important, the bridge between the theory and practice, of linking the individual, the team and the wider social context is hugely problematic. I draw upon my experience as a Family Therapist and systemically informed organizational consultant to apply systems thinking to the practice of leadership. The professional expertise developed through reflexive learning in 'real practice' by Family Therapists and systemic consultants offers a transferable and adaptable knowledge base to further develop the bridge between systemic theory and leadership practice.

In Box 1.1 are the four key Critical Lenses from which organizational leadership is viewed within this book.

---

## Box 1.1   Four critical lenses

1  **Emancipatory aims**
   The ethical aim of applying critical theory to leadership is to help create the structural and symbolic conditions where individual and collective agency can flourish, thus allowing subjects to maximize their ability to self-create, be autonomous and to be creative in order to pursue the greater good for all within an organizational, communal and social context.

*(Continued)*

*(Continued)*

2    **Depth analysis**
     This means taking a hermeneutic or interpretative stance. In this book,
     depth analysis is derived mainly from psychoanalytic theory with the aim
     of revealing what is beneath the surface. It is concerned with the under-
     lying assumptions that lie beneath conscious awareness, within dis-
     courses and within individual and group behaviours. Psychoanalytic
     theory and practice focus on the unconscious and the emotional life,
     accounting for the symbolic and irrational processes within organiza-
     tional life as well as the rational, the material and structural aspects
     which are privileged in management and leadership theory and practice.
     This approach advocates using the self-as-an-instrument; engaging with
     one's emotional and cognitive responses and then using these responses
     as data from which to learn and act. This self-reflective ability to observe
     the self while interacting with others is central to the critical approach
     taken in the book and to anybody who takes up a leadership role.
     Leaders are encouraged to mirror the reflexivity of the psychoanalytic
     approach, to become aware of the emotional and unconscious cultures
     in organizational settings. A key leadership task is to create a shared
     sense-making process, which raises awareness of the unconscious and
     emotional life of an organization; and allows interventions to be made
     which to act on this awareness.

3    **Looking awry**
     To be a critical theorist means looking at an object or idea from different
     angles and also from a different place from within ourselves. This entails
     drawing upon new resources from different traditions and short-circuiting
     this knowledge to 'unmask' discourses and power relations. It also means
     situating knowledge and assumptions in historical, political and cultural
     contexts. The critical theorist must also observe the world differently not
     only from an external position but also from within themselves, drawing on
     their emotions and personal experience. Curiosity and self-awareness are
     key attributes that enable the use of subjectivity in a reflexive way. It is not
     possible to take a critical stance or to look awry unless one's own assump-
     tions are acknowledged and open to challenge.

4    **Systemic praxis**
     Praxis is to link theory to practice, and practice to lived experience. It
     means a commitment to the application of theory rather than creating
     knowledge for its own sake. I use the term systemic praxis to describe
     taking account of the connected nature of the world and its power rela-
     tionships when practising leadership. It means applying critical theory to
     the ecology of leadership, as opposed to focusing on the leader as an
     individual atomized figure or object to be studied in isolation of the envi-
     ronment or context in which the leadership is situated.

# Critical theory and leadership

The application of critical theory to leadership demands that we identify some of the undercurrents, the subtleties and historical and social trends in which leadership operates. To achieve this we must look beyond the management and leadership literature that draws too heavily on an 'insider view'. Leadership research, theory and knowledge dissemination are dominated by big business schools, which reproduce their own power elites. Their power is built on the rationalistic and functionalist ideas from management theory, which is still dominated by the MBA. Henry Mintzberg critiques this approach in his book, *Managers Not MBAs*: 'Considered as education for management, conventional MBA programs train the wrong people, in the wrong ways, with the wrong consequences' (Mintzberg, 2004a: 6). Mintzberg goes on to cite Sheldon Zalaznick from *Fortune* Magazine in 1968: 'The idea that the graduate school of business is the principal source of top executive talent has been allowed to flourish, unexamined' (Mintzberg, 2004a: 7). Business schools are reproducing the forms of management and leadership training, at great profit, which serve their own agendas (Western, 2005). This narrow view not only maintains the status quo but can also be commercially dangerous, for example, when new forms of management and production in Japan took car manufacturing into new realms, the USA reproduced old forms of management and production on the premise that the US model (Fordism) had been successful and remained superior. It was only when they were commercially forced to look beyond their own internal world that change occurred. Looking beyond the citadels of the business schools and corporate westernized ideas of leadership styles becomes ever more necessary to find solutions to the challenges of contemporary leadership of new organizational forms.

In the past 20 years, leadership has become an ever-increasing area of interest and influence in organizational life and organizational/management theory. Leadership now challenges the dominant stature of the 'efficient manager' who for the previous century was the unsurpassable figure within the organizational discourse.

The Frankfurt School identified how 'technocratic-rationality' and 'instrumental reason' resulted in the 'logic of efficiency and control'. One of the most identifiable sites for the 'administered society' that results from this worldview is the workplace. This was clearly identified by Whyte who, in his classic 1956 book *The Organization Man*, observed the psychological surrender of the individual to the logic of the efficiency and control of the organization. Management theory (from which leadership theory arises) takes a predominantly functionalist approach to management and the privileging of management knowledge, presented as management science, obscures the political and power aspects of organizations.

Alvesson and Wilmott (1992, 1996) claim that management is treated as a neutral activity and that an overriding mistaken assumption is that management is holistic in its effect and works on behalf of everybody in an organization. The classic manager is an essential, component part of the rational system of contemporary organizations, an administrator of efficiency (MacIntyre, 1985) hence the continued popularity of the MBA, the Master of Business Administration, which has a functionalist format dating back to its conception in 1908 (Mintzberg, 2004a).

Alvesson and Wilmott (1996) attempt to reinstate the political and social into management theory, challenging the technocratic and functionalist tendency, which they argue undermines the emancipatory potential within the workplace. Critiques of this approach argue that if humanistic approaches or critical theory attempts to improve workers' 'micro emancipation', the outcome is that the dominant elite simply get more out of the workers (Sotorin and Tyrell, 1998; Johnson and Duberley, 2000). Others argue that to change a system, managers are key to this process. Critical theorists would agree that a humanist approach can be a cynical and manipulative attempt to improve efficiency and output. They would also argue that the critical theorist approach acknowledges the different interests and power relations and therefore is alerted to this danger. The leadership literature found within mainstream management and organizational literature is born out of and therefore follows the technical-rationalist and positivist agenda described through the dominant management discourse.

Critical theory applied to leadership aims to demonstrate how underlying assumptions and structural features influence organizational life and how leadership plays its part in this scenario. At worse, organizations become instruments of social domination (Morgan, 1986: 275). Morgan believes 'there is often an element of domination in all organizations' (1986: 275). I would go further and say there are always elements of domination in all organizations, which are socially coercive to individuals, groups and sub-groups. The modern organization replaces guilds, religious organizations and other public and social institutions that historically held this institutional socializing role. Therefore organizations themselves have become one of modernity's most powerful tools of social coercion and domination. However, the socializing role of the modern organization is by no means only negative, indeed it is absolutely necessary. Social cohesion and social solidarity cannot take place without socializing processes that include power relations (Melucci, 1989; Etzioni, 1993, 2002). Within organizations, power relations can produce coercive, harmful and dangerous cultures or they can produce healthy open and adaptive cultures. It is the task of critical theorists to focus on creating the latter.

## Conclusion

The emancipatory aim of applying critical theory to the study of leadership in organizational life is specifically to maximize individual and collective autonomy and agency. These gains are transferable to wider society because organizations impact on society and vice versa. At an individual level, employees do not leave their identities and agency at the workplace entrance but the self is carried across the home–work divide and perhaps more than ever individual and collective identity are informed by the workplace experience (Casey, 1995). This emancipatory critical approach is significant as it challenges the fundamental aims of what it means to work towards developing successful leaders. In spite of claims that leadership differs from management, the normative approach to leadership development relies on the same underlying managerial premise that better leaders produce better outputs through increased efficiency (MacIntyre, 1985). The fundamental aim of normative leadership development and leadership success is to improve one object, a person in role called a leader, in order to improve the efficiency of another object, the organization. The critical theory approach to leadership does not attempt to change an object or increase efficiency but focuses instead on subjectivity, i.e. the individual and the collective well-being. In essence, it aims to increase collective human agency and autonomy in order to fulfil human potential. This means accepting responsibility for the other as well as the self. It means accepting responsibility for the power relations which impact on the dispossessed and the marginalized, it means taking responsibility for society, community and the environment.

However, this shift in emphasis also has an impact on organizations and leaders, but only as a by-product of the critical aims will organizations and leaders become more energized, ethical, adaptive and hopefully more successful as a result.

It is the task of this book and other critical theorists to create theoretical frames to identify ways in which 'leadership in practice' can minimize organizational power relations that rely on control and coercion. Coercive leadership, however camouflaged, hidden and subtle, may in the short term lead to profit and commercial or output success. However, any leadership that diminishes individual and collective autonomy in the search for the holy grail of homogeneity, unity of purpose and corporate alignment, risks becoming a totalizing organization with conformist employees taking on 'fundamentalist mindsets'. Western's (2005) doctoral thesis found that such organizations had similar organizational cultures to religious fundamentalist movements. To avoid these 'fundamentalist cultures', critical theorists should apply their core ethic of emancipation to the challenge of how to lead contemporary complex organizations. Recent catastrophic failures such as the huge energy firm Enron and its accountants Arthur Anderson demonstrate the dangers well. In spite of Enron being named by *Fortune* Magazine as America's most innovative company for six successive years, it was the failure of the leadership to create an organizational culture that encouraged individual agency, transparency and autonomy and which demanded organizational success at any cost that led to the collapse of Enron. The leadership was characteristically transformational, which encouraged a blind faith from the employees. The list of organizational, political and commercial failures that did not heed the warnings when poor and unethical leadership create cultures of unquestioning conformity and 'group think' (Janis, 1972) is endless and yet remains common.

Critical leadership theorists must go beyond identifying 'bad leadership practice' and aim to create and support successful ethical frameworks for leadership in practice. This means helping leaders identify organizational structures, processes and forms of communication to promote individual agency and autonomy alongside collective solidarity. This aim should comfortably align itself with progressive and now mainstream contemporary organizational aims, which include corporate responsibility, sustainability, clarity of vision and strong values, non-exploitation of employees and outsourced workers, and ethics as integral to commercial and output success. These are now growing trends throughout companies and organizations, partly due to external pressure from activist groups and partly for pragmatic reasons, as it also makes commercial and organizational sense to have engaged workforces who are making decisions at grassroots levels and feel they are able to be their authentic selves at work. There is a long way to go and finding the right leadership is part of the struggle.

# What Is Leadership?

Chapter 2 will briefly look at how leadership is defined. To begin, let's look at this piece by Woody Allen describing an imaginary letter from Van Gogh to his brother Theo, taken from 'If the Impressionists Had Been Dentists: A fantasy exploring the transposition of temperament':

> Dear Theo, Will life never treat me decently? I am wracked by despair! My head is pounding! Mrs. Sol Schwimmer is suing me because I made her bridge as I felt it and not to fit her ridiculous mouth! That's right! I can't work to order like a common tradesman! I decided her bridge should be enormous and billowing, with wild, explosive teeth flaring up in every direction like fire! Now she is upset because it won't fit in her mouth! She is so bourgeois and stupid, I want to smash her! I tried forcing the false plate in but it sticks out like a star burst chandelier. Still, I find it beautiful. She claims she can't chew! What do I care whether she can chew or not! Theo, I can't go on like this much longer! ... – Vincent. (Allen, 1976)

Leadership is often constructed as a beautiful and rarified idea, but this 'idealized' leadership has about as much use as the 'beautiful teeth' as designed by Van Gogh in this letter. Leadership is often described in a tone which suggests a heroic beauty. Take this example from Bass:

> Leaders are authentically transformational when they increase awareness of what is right, good, important and beautiful, when they help to elevate followers' needs for achievement and self-actualisation, when they foster in followers higher moral maturity and when they move followers to go beyond their self interests for the good of their group, organisation or society. (Bass, 1990a: 171)

Leadership is portrayed as something that is a golden chalice, a most sought-after object, yet it seems always just beyond our reach. Annie Pye suggests 'The continuing search for the Holy Grail, which seems to characterize interest in leadership, implies that research efforts are perhaps being directed at "solving the wrong problem"' (2005: 31). There are many answers on the bookshelves, journals and internet, if we apply this formula, that prescription, these seven steps, then we can reach leadership nirvana! Unlike the leadership texts offering idealized images of leaders, Van Gogh at least acknowledges his lack of concern for the practical application of his beautiful creation.

Leadership is portrayed in this seductive manner, to sell leadership books and training courses, and to meet the demand for easy answers and quick solutions. However, at best, these easy solutions are fairly useless in practice, and can be harmful and misleading (Gemmil and Oakley, 1992). To move beyond the idealistic, this chapter will try to get beneath the surface of the question, what is leadership?

> There are almost as many different definitions of leadership as there are persons who have attempted to define the concept. (Stodgill, 1974: 259)

> Dubrin (2000) estimates there are 35,000 definitions of leadership in academic literature. (Pye, 2005: 32)

Leadership is a common term but it has many diverse meanings, it has been said that, like beauty, you will know leadership when you see it. This, however, means that leaders and leadership are defined in the eye of the beholder. If this is the case, then there is a multitude of definitions and understandings of what it means to be a leader or to witness leadership. Barnard ([1938] 1991: 81) identified that 'lead' is both a noun and a verb and therefore has a double meaning. The noun could mean 'to guide others, to be the head of an organization', while the verb could mean 'to excel and to be in advance'. Likewise, leadership is used to describe a certain type of social interaction between people and the term leader is used to denote a person (or sometimes a group/company) who has influence over others (Yukl, 2002; Northouse, 2004). The term leadership is also used to describe personality traits, behaviours and also to denote the roles of individuals and collectives. Leadership is inherently complex and is not easily definable; in fact, it is unlikely that any consensus on the term will be found (Grint, 1997). However, leadership does have shared meanings, depending on the social group you are discussing it with. Most commonly, the term leadership refers to an individual's role or their traits and behaviours as in 'she or he showed leadership'.

When leadership is restricted to this populist meaning, it has limitations that create difficulties when attempting to change organizations. When one tries to implement leadership and change, it soon becomes clear that leadership does not simply belong to any one individual and that to understand how leadership works in practice a broader and more in-depth view of leadership must be taken. Northouse (2004: 3) reviewing leadership theory identified four common themes:

1 Leadership as a process.
2 Leadership involves influence.
3 Leadership occurs in a group context.
4 Leadership involves goal attainment.

Keith Grint identifies a similar four-fold leadership typology of Person, Results, Process and Position (Grint, 2005).

The relationship between leadership and followership and the process of leadership as a social interaction has become a focal point for critical theorists to explore (Grint, 2005; Collinson, 2006). This is in contrast to the main-stream focus on leaders as individuals and their behaviours, traits and competencies using positivist theoretical frameworks.

Leadership styles and types comprise an ever growing list as the search for the ideal leader continues unabated. Box 2.1 gives some examples of the leadership styles currently in circulation.

---

## Box 2.1   Leadership styles

| | |
|---|---|
| Action-centred | Patriarchal |
| Adaptive | Post-modern |
| Authoritarian | Post-heroic |
| Collective | Primal emotional |
| Consensual | Principle-centred |
| Connected | Relational |
| Contingency | Servant leader |
| Charismatic | Situated |
| Democratic | Spiritual |
| Dictatorial | Strategic |
| Distributive | Technical |
| Emergent | Thought leaders |
| Expert | Transactional |
| Feminized | Transformational |
| Matriarchal | Values-based |
| Participative | |

---

Leadership has increasingly become the focus of attention of management literature and executive education in recent years, pushing management into its shadow. Everybody, it seems, wants to be a leader rather than a manager. Kets de Vries notes that in the leadership bible *Stogdills Handbook of Leadership*, an increase in articles on effective leadership studies has grown since 1974, 'from 3000 to 5000 in seven years, a pace of publication that has accelerated ever since' (in Grint, 1997: 250). Kets de Vries then describes the contents of these articles as 'plodding and detached, often far removed from the reality of day-to-day life' (1997: 251). Smith (1997) cites a survey of 250 British Chief Executives who were asked to identify the most important management skills for ensuring business success, and leadership emerged as the top ranked item. The question then is, what do they mean by leadership? While the leadership literature gains increasing popularity and momentum, it is also problematical in many areas. Much of what is regarded as new leadership literature simply recycles previous management/leadership theories. A great deal of leadership theory is critiqued as over-simplistic, reductionist and offering unrealistic solutions to complex problems:

It may make good politics eventually, here and there, for a leader to say out loud 'Those who claim to know what to do are either fools or liars and, by gratuitously claiming certainty about cause and effect, they foreclose experimenting with additional options.' (Judge, 1994: 78)

This also applies to leadership research: 'Despite all the hype about a "new paradigm" for studying leadership, most of the research uses the same superficial methods that have been prevalent for decades' (Yukl, 1999: 42).

Calas and Smircich critique Peters and Waterman's (1982) so-called innovative text, *In Search of Excellence*, and their celebrated transcendent leader: 'Under the guise of "newness" the authors do no more than articulate some empty discourses from the 1980s, while returning to the beginning of the circle' (1991: 589). They refer to the transcendent leader being a reinvention of the popular 'Transformational leadership' (Burns, 1978) which they consider to be 'empty discourses' and the full circle they refer to is Chester Barnard's work 'The Functions of the Executive', written in 1938. This is a common trend in the leadership literature where a subtle rewriting of existing theory takes place with new nuances and a different terminology applied. For example, the 'great man' theory, or hero leader of the classic tradition becomes in the populist leadership press (there are important differences which will be explored later in the book) the exciting and new Transformational leader of the 1980s. The Transformational leader then mutates into Peters and Waterman's Transcendental leader. The main body of leadership literature focuses on solo-actors and individual leadership traits and competencies. This is widely critiqued by a small minority of critical and systems management thinkers, for example, Barley and Kunda (1992), Casey (1995), Calas and Smircich (1995), Tourish and Pinnington (2002). A variety of critiques and potential solutions are offered in an attempt to make sense of how globalization and technological change impact on the workplace, with some new and interesting drawing on post-modern and deconstructionist theories from the new philosophers, for example, Lyotard (1984), Derrida (1982). Other critiques, like their counterparts in the mainstream literature, recycle 'radical' theories in an attempt to recover past ideologies. The post-war social democratic and the social movements of the 1960s are the most common source drawn upon, which pursued greater democratic and collectivized leadership or leaderless organizations and linked them with identity politics.

To summarize: leadership is a growth industry and remains a 'sexy concept' and a buzz word in Business Schools, organizations and social/political arenas. However, much of the mainstream literature is adapted and recycled theory; old news under a new headline. Another of the main problems when reading the leadership literature is that of reductionist theorizing. There appears to be two main reasons for this. First, the mainstream leadership literature is dominated by work from US Business Schools where there is traditionally a focus on positivistic, scientific approaches to management and leadership that creates a reductionist tendency (Mintzberg, 2004a). Second, the huge business of executive education creates a reductionist pressure; simple solutions are simply an easier sell. A Google search of leadership and executive education courses, consultancy interventions on leadership, or a look at airport bookshops will all provide testimony to the love of the easy answer and the quick fix solution. Leadership is thus 'dumbed down' for the commercial and consumer society in which we live. This reductionism has had a limiting impact on leadership thinking and its most common manifestation is to reduce the complexity of leadership to its most easily understood form: the leader as a solo actor, i.e. the leader as individual. The consequence is that the dominant focus of leadership research and development is the traits and competencies an individual must have to become a better leader. As the book will demonstrate, this marginalizes attempts to problematize leadership, to ask important but difficult questions and to embrace complexity and uncertainty. However, by taking the more challenging critical approach to leadership, there is the hope that we may find more sustainable and realistic leadership solutions, which are greatly needed in our institutions. To take this route we must accept that the solutions we find will be partial, and acknowledge that our work will be part of an ongoing learning process rather than finding a concrete and finite answer.

## Leaders and leadership: individuals, collectives or process?

As already highlighted, there is much confusion and debate within the literature as to what constitutes leadership. Leadership is most commonly referred to and researched as the property of an individual actor, where a leader demonstrates leadership through their personal characteristics and how they behave or act. This view of leadership is culturally coherent, a westernized understanding of individuals where society is viewed as an aggregation of individuals (Luke, 1998); it also fits our heroic narratives seen in history, stories and films. The individual leader is the commonest representation of leadership mainly because it simplifies a complex phenomena. However, as the following statements show, leadership is much more:

- She was a courageous leader.
- The board showed great leadership.
- Scandinavia takes a lead on social welfare.
- Apple consistently demonstrate leadership in innovation and design.
- The Arab league showed leadership in the talks and the tensions subsided.
- An innovative leadership culture flourished in the company.

As these examples show, leadership can be situated within individuals, groups, whole organizations, nations and even within company culture, suggesting a dispersed leadership process.

Leadership is regarded within the critical literature as a process based on interactions and social relations between people (Senge, 1990; Yukl, 1998; Alvesson, 2002; Burgoyne and Pedler, 2003). Leadership cannot exist solely within an individual, as at least one other person (a follower) is required for leadership to be enacted. It is this relationship between the individual and the follower that establishes leadership, it takes two (or more) to tango, as the saying goes. This is not to deny the influence and agency of an individual who can show leadership qualities, for example, Nelson Mandela, Ghandi and Margaret Thatcher, Jack Welch, Steve Jobs, are widely cited as such leaders. Individuals are also elected and given authority as leaders to make decisions. Leadership is sometimes consciously held up as a collective act for example: a government representing a nation may show leadership to other nations over some contested issue, such as world debt relief. A political party can show leadership, a cabinet within government or a board of directors can take collective decisions and show leadership. Some theorists claim that all leadership is essentially collective leadership, Senge (1990), has defined leadership as 'the collective capacity to create useful things' and Collinson states, 'In effect, leadership is the property and consequence of a community rather than the property and consequence of an individual leader' (2006: 183). Burgoyne and Pedler sum up the common view taken by those advocating a more critical and collective approach to leadership, which they call a 'new view of leadership':

Our approach is based on three core beliefs; leadership should be more:

- Focused on challenges rather than upon the person.
- Collective and less individualised.
- Various and less one-size-fits all.

However, like the criticisms of Transformational leadership re-inventing 'Great Man' theory, much of the collective leadership literature re-visits democratic and collectivist theories that arose from social liberation movements, which often had an anti-leadership stance (emerging from Nazi Germany, Stalinism, and other examples of leaders abusing their power). This becomes problematic when discussing what is good leadership, if there is an underlying distrust of all leadership.

Critical theorists now interpret leadership in a more complex way, which extends the idea of leadership beyond the individual, adding breadth to the debate. This breadth can work both ways, it can broaden the view of leadership in a useful way but at the same time leadership can appear to be everywhere, as the panacea for all problems. Alvesson argues that the current popularity of leadership means that it colonizes social and personal life:

There is a tendency for 'leadership' to colonise a wider spectrum of social and personal life. At least in Sweden, leadership is increasingly viewed as a solution also in work areas and professions where self-governance is – or used to be seen as – the norm, like in schools, universities and the church. (Alvesson, 2003: 13)

The popularity of leaderism can also lead to the colonization of the discourses which in the past have been about teamwork, communication, group dynamics, self-management and self-governance etc. This is true of mainstream and critical theorist perspectives.

There are many diverse assumptions made about leaders; the most common perception that persists is the leader as a heroic individual, with male attributes – the 'Great Man' theory, who now appears in many theoretical guises. A minority, but important, view is that leadership is socially constructed or regarded as a process (Douglas, 1983; Grint, 1997). Both arguments have their merits but the debate can easily become polarized, one side (the mainstream) researching and debating individuals as leaders, the other side advocating a social-process leadership theory. There is little clarity in the literature, and, in my experience, even less in practice, as to how individual leaders and collective actors relate or how the role of the individual leader fits into the social process of leadership.

One of the key themes from the literature is that, in the past, leadership has been seen as an elitist activity related to power and to hierarchy. Today it is commonly agreed that leadership is needed at all levels of organizations. Distributive or dispersed leadership are very popular concepts and relate to the changing post-industrial work conditions that cannot be managed in a top-down, expert, command and control structure. Daniel Goleman describes this distributive leadership as 'every person at entry level who in one way or another, acts as a leader' (2002: 14).

Elmore agrees, '[in] knowledge intensive enterprises like teaching and learning there is no way to perform these complex tasks without widely distributing the responsibility for leadership among roles in the organization' (2000: 14). The aim is to maximize the human potential of an organization (Western, 2005). However to achieve an understanding of leadership, one of the key issues which is under-researched and hugely problematic is the relationship between the individual and the group. Turning to psychoanalytic theory, Wilfred Bion, a Tavistock psychoanalyst, describes the difficulty individuals have in managing their relationship to groups, describing the internal tension an individual has between the self and being a 'group animal': 'The individual is a group animal at war, not simply with the group, but with himself for being a group animal and with those aspects of his personality that constitute his "groupishness"' (Bion, 1961: 131).

Sigmund Freud in *Civilisation and its Discontents* (1930) identified the struggle individuals face to maintain autonomy and be part of a social and civilized group which always limits this autonomy. Civilization (group living) demands limits on our unconscious and primitive drives and emotions, for example, our innate biological sexual and aggressive drives. These are both essential and dangerous for group survival. These tensions are played out very much through leadership that represents an active element in this struggle. The leader or leadership of any social group; team, community or nation, often becomes the focal point, the object which represents this boundary between the individual and the group. Perhaps this is why leadership is such an emotive and important issue to each of us, why we love to criticize or idealize leaders. It is rarely that we do not have an emotional response to George Bush, Tony Blair, the national sports coach, or the boss at work.

Bion cites Freud (1921: 3) who points out that individual and group psychology cannot be absolutely differentiated because the psychology of the individual is itself a function of the individual's relationship to another person or object. Bion continues: 'The individual cannot help being a member of a group even if his membership of it consists in behaving in such a way as to give reality to the idea that he does not belong to a group at all' (1961: 131). A monk living in a solitary cell is an example of this; while physically isolating himself, he remains very prominent (a powerful symbol) in the minds of the community he has left and vice versa. He is also connected to his monastic community in spite of his choice of being alone. It is a common preference for theorists to reduce the relationship between the individual and the group to either/or scenarios. A major task in my work as a leadership developer, and leadership coach is to continuously find ways to help HR Directors and Senior executives to think beyond developing individual leaders through coaching or competency frameworks, and to link individual development to organizational development and culture change. There is a huge block in making this link, and either/or scenarios are much too common: 'Should we put our efforts into O.D (organisational development) and culture change or personally develop the high potential leaders?' Individual approaches to leadership such as traits, behaviours and competencies ignore the dynamics and emotions of the role of followers, i.e. they ignore the group. Social construction and collective approaches to leadership focus on the process, and the group, minimizing the role of the individual. This book will attempt to work across the boundaries of leadership, understanding how it is both a process and also how individual leadership is very real and a necessary part of the leadership process.

## Defining leaders by their traits and competencies

One of the most common ways to define leadership is through observing individual leaders and analysing their internal personality traits which make them successful leaders. This approach fits within the individualistic leadership camp. Today the multi-million dollar business of leadership development tends to focus on developing leadership traits and competencies. There has been a long search historically to try and define what aspects of the personality (what traits) make a good leader. Observations and studies of different exceptional leaders try and identify what aspects of their personality enabled them to be 'great men' (as the studies were usually on male heroic figures) and examples such as courage, charisma, vision, fortitude were identified as traits to be exemplified. This focus on the innate personality of leaders was known as 'Great Man' theory. Another approach which closely relates to, and often arises from, behavioural and cognitive behavioural psychology attempts to identify what leaders do, rather than what their personalities consist of. This approach has an individualistic and functionalist approach in that it isolates component parts of an individual's behavioural repertoire with the aim of being able to modify and develop potential leader's behaviour, in order to improve their leadership skills and abilities. This approach is reductionist as it attempts to reduce leadership to a finite set of behaviours. Having identified the traits and competencies that good leaders have, individuals are trained and tested against this list to improve these competencies. I will briefly summarize and critique the trait and competency approach, in order to address the complexity of leadership.

A classic piece of trait theory in management came from McGregor in the 1960s and perhaps best sums up trait theory; it is very over-simplistic focusing on the individual and dividing humanity into two main camps: Theory X and Theory Y (Box 2.2). This approach is still taught in many business schools and can be found in many MBA texts.

---

## Box 2.2   Theory X or Theory Y type manager

From Maslow's work on self-actualization came Douglas McGregor's (1960) Theory X or Theory Y type manager which offers a polemic over-simplification, yet is still cited in much of the management literature: 'Many managers still easily identify with the Theory X and Y distinction and its normative view of good and bad leadership' (Fulop and Linstead, 1999: 165).

McGregor's theories present a philosophical stance and are therefore difficult to validate. McGregor stated that Theory X management/leadership was based on the assumption that:

1   The average human being has an inherent dislike of work and will avoid it if at all possible.
2   Because of this, most people must be coerced, controlled, directed and threatened with punishment to put adequate effort into the achievement of organizational objectives.
3   The average human being prefers to be directed, wishes to avoid responsibility, has relatively little ambition and wants security above all else.

Theory Y of management/leadership represents the other view that:

1   Work is natural.
2   People will exercise self direction.
3   Satisfaction and self-actualization are the most important rewards for individuals.
4   Individuals seek responsibility and development and the average person's potential is not being fully used.

(McGregor, 1960: 33–4)

*(Continued)*

*(Continued)*

McGregor did say that Theory X was an acceptable style at certain times, perhaps during economic recession, for example, but in general there was one best way of management and that was Theory Y. Theory X led to a more autocratic leadership style because of the need to control and coerce unwilling workers whereas Theory Y built relationships and encourages a participative leadership style.

This example of trait theory shows how people are divided into functional groups, in this case, you are an X or Y type. There are numerous examples in the leadership literature of competency and trait approaches. There are thousands of tests: personality tests, psycho-metric tests and frameworks, which attempt to assess leaders. The tests give a pseudo-scientific empirical legitimacy to this approach to understanding leadership and leader development. The popularity of the tests and this approach rely on two fundamental observations:

1  People seem inherently curious about themselves and simplistic answers to the complex problems of personality grab the attention of the individual. Check any magazine rack and the internet for tests to show what type of person you are, and you will be inundated with results. I am always amazed how a buzz enters the university lecture theatre when groups are asked to undertake and discuss their Myers Briggs Test or their Enneagram. As a trainer, it is an almost failsafe way to have a successful seminar, these tests engage immediately with our ego states and our narcissism! Personality tests are used as sales tools because of their popularity, which helps explain the growth in leadership testing.

2  Companies and organizations get a formulaic simplistic quasi-scientific and measurable solution (always popular in the rational-positivist world of management) to the very difficult and complex challenge of leadership development.

Manfred Kets de Vries finds the literature on leadership traits overwhelming and confusing but identifies some commonality in the findings: 'conscientiousness, extroversion, dominance, self-confidence, energy, agreeableness, intelligence, openness to experience and emotional stability' (Kets de Vries, 1994). As Kets de Vries points out, these traits are very open-ended and, when discussed, they open up a heated polemic as to the nature of what they really mean. He goes on to say how individuals' characters need to be assessed using clinical methodologies (Kets de Vries is a psychoanalyst and Director of Insead Global Leadership Center, Insead Business School, France). Many of the traits identified are the obvious traits which could be applied to anybody who is successful in multiple dimensions beyond the idea of leadership. Gemmil and Oakley (1992) identify a resurgence in the

1990s of the 'traitist' approach, identifying charisma as an embodiment of this approach, 'Charisma is the leadership trait most often examined by members of the "leadership mafia"' (in Grint, 1997: 277). Gemmil and Oakley's anti-leadership polemic names Bennis and Nanus (1985), Zaleznik (1989) and Tichy and Devanna (1986) as part of the new wave of leadership theorists drawing on the trait approach. They link the resurgence of leadership and the trait approach in partic- ular as part of a Great Leader Myth which undermines autonomy and creates dependency (this will be revisited later in the book in some depth). Having worked with leadership tests in executive education, one of the real strengths of this approach is that although the focus is on an individual and is reductionist, it can act as a catalyst for a broader discussion about leadership and can offer a common language for a group or organization to discuss some of the leadership issues it faces. Too often, however, this strength is overlooked as individuals are encouraged to focus on their own performance.

The most common criticism of the trait/competency approach is that they are one-size-fits-all approaches. Defining leadership by a set of given competencies or traits suggests a preferred leadership style which all individuals must have if they are to be successful leaders. These approaches are limited in two important areas: first, from a critical theorist perspective, they represent a hegemonic approach. This refers to an elite powerful group, i.e. the senior management team, agreeing on the leadership traits and competencies necessary for success and then demanding, testing, training and measuring these traits in potential leaders in the company. This in itself is a homogenizing approach to leadership that has totalitarian overtones: 'Our leaders will demonstrate to followers these specific personality traits and these competencies ... which the followers will embrace and then mirror these behaviours.' This approach does not embrace per- sonal difference or gender, racial and other aspects of cultural diversity. Where do creative mavericks find a space to experiment in an organization that limits leadership to traits and competencies? Where does the quiet introverted leader who builds success through teamwork, fit into a competency framework that embraces only extrovert qualities? Some more advanced uses of these psycho- metrics are designed to put together teams with different personal qualities, but these still rely on unsound science and are mechanistic and formulaic in their approach.

The second major concern is that a trait or competency approach is a one-size-fits-all approach which ignores context. For example, a National Health Service Quality framework for leadership provided a competency framework for its leaders (see www.nhsleadershipqualities.nhs.uk). From a critical theorist perspective, these frameworks reinforce the underlying assumption that leadership resides in the individual. These frameworks identify standard competencies such as self-belief, self-awareness, personal integrity etc. which are generic traits of any successful person. How these are developed in individuals is another question. The contextual problem is that there is the assumption that a Medical Surgeon, a Charge Nurse running a community psychiatric project and a Health Service Financial Officer, all require the same leadership competencies. To embrace this diversity, the compe-tencies are so open-ended and they become so generic as to be fairly useless: for example, 'leading change through people' begs the question, how else would one lead change? 'Empower others', 'drive for results', 'seizing the future'. Discussing slogans of leadership with many NHS executives and managers/leaders, I hear over and over that there is widespread cynicism about these leadership slogans and mantras and the training programmes which are in place to deliver them. The cynicism I hear reflects the literature that critiques this approach, they are too generic and they conflict with the context and the reality at work where structural, process and resource issues undermine the stated goals of collaboration and empowerment.

This approach ignores the context of a situation and the complexity of running very challenging and diverse workplaces. The experience on the ground may be that there is little room for *seizing the future* and *empowering others* when the context feels disempowering due to a production-line atmosphere where success is meas-ured against meeting targets and deadlines. In practice, there is little evidence that the naming and defining of leadership competencies translate into training or behaviour modification which has had a significant impact on improving leader-ship and change in organizations.

## Situational leadership: leaders to fit the context

Fred Fiedler's Contingency approach (1967, 1974) attempted to rescue management theory from the simplistic notion of the 'one-best-fit' manager/ leader for all situations. Fiedler proposed that the leadership style would need to be different to fit different situations, i.e. it had to be situational and contingent. He attempted to find the optimal match between leadership style and situation. Critics challenge his research claims of success on the grounds that there has been a failure to replicate results and some of the results conflict with subordinates' accounts of leaders (Bryman, 1986). Contingency approaches challenge the notion of the one-best-style leader for different situations and they have focused on the two-factor model of *Relationship- or Task-Centred* leader. Task-Centred leaders focus on the task rather than people and are more directive. This approach suits certain situations, for example, in hierarchical organizations with unstructured tasks, whereas Relationship-Centred leaders are favoured in the majority of situations as they focus on people and participation. Unfortunately this offers yet another dualistic model, 'relational or task', that does not account for the complexity of understanding relationships, power and leadership from multiple perspectives.

The contingency approach attempts to address some of the social context issues faced by leaders and managers but tries to package it into over-simplistic assumptions. Much more work is required in this area as a one-best-fit leadership style or an over-simplified contingency approach to leadership is still common practice. There are many factors requiring further research in the area of understanding how leaders address context and situational difference, for example:

1   *Organizational size:* How different leadership approaches may be required within different size organizations. Can we talk about a single leadership approach and refer to a small start-up company and a global institution?
2   *Leading people: One-one, a small team, a large group and unseen masses in a global organization:* People skills and relational skills are not universal skills that can be applied to all situations. The leadership skills and relational/ communication skills differ hugely when working with different size groups. A leader of a large multinational company will have to lead individuals on a one–one basis, in teams, large groups, and she/he will have to communicate and influence unseen masses of employees in diverse contexts. This has implications for communication and leadership skills which cannot be accounted for through the dualistic contingency model. It implies that leadership needs to intrinsically be diverse in nature which would usually imply that this would not reside in any single person. There are unusually gifted communicators. Bill Clinton is such a leader, who is renowned for his ability to communicate across these groupings and have a leadership impact in individual, team, large group and global situations. However, even with an exceptionally gifted individual, a leadership team and a dispersed leadership are required to meet the multitude of demands of leading organizations.
3   *The social context of an organization:* Different organizations have diverse organizational structures and cultures depending on the wider environmental, social and political context. This must take into account the geography, political interests, the multiple stakeholder interests and the product or output of the organization. All this impacts on the leadership requirements and needs of that organization and how it functions. For example: leadership of a public sector hospital differs from leading McDonald's food chain or a global weapons manufacturer. Multinationals have found to their cost through the failure rate of mergers and acquisitions that under-estimating diverse cultures can have a huge impact on success and failure. The output of the organization impacts on the technical and structural aspects of organizational life and also on the environmental, political and the psycho-social dynamics of the organization. Within organizations there is a diversity of outputs depending on the department or part of the organization one works. Outputs can conflict within an organization or can appear to. As different skills, training and cultures are required in different departments, so also are different leadership styles, structures and processes.

There will be some consistent features and universalities of leadership within each scenario but also major differences. These approaches need problematizing from a critical perspective as they are too often presented in a solution-focused way, providing answers to leadership problems. In the search for good leadership, the problems and questions asked are too often the wrong questions, framed because they can be answered rather than because they are the difficult questions which need answering. As this chapter has identified, the answers given, i.e. a set of leadership competencies, have limited impact on leadership development and leading organizational change. In leadership studies, contingency and situational leadership theory are discussed under social constructionist theory whereby the influence of the social relates to how an individual leader will behave and how their leadership will be received. This is in contrast to the functional/behaviourist trait models of leadership. However, these approaches should not be polarized, as is sometimes the case, because of the different theoretical camps, as they do not compete with each other. Both are important and complementary and both contribute to the wider leadership narrative.

## Managers and leaders

The terms 'management' and 'leadership' can be used interchangeably and both management and leadership are words which evoke multiple meanings. Managers can demonstrate leadership and likewise a leader can have managerial skills. In recent times leadership has been rediscovered and reconstituted to take a newly elevated position in the world of management theory and practice, as pointed out by Bennis and Nanus.

> Management typically constitutes a set of contractual exchanges ... What gets exchanged is not trivial: jobs, security, and money. The result, at best, is compliance; at worst you get a spiteful obedience. The end result of leadership is completely different: it is empowerment. Not just higher profits and wages ... but an organisational culture that helps employees generate a sense of meaning in their work and a desire to challenge themselves to experience success. (1985: 218)

Leaders and leadership have become a very sought-after commodity. Bennis states that many American companies are 'over-managed and under-led' saying, 'I tend to think of the differences between leaders and managers as those who master the context and those who surrender to it' (1986: 45). This shift in focus, which elevates leadership from the pitfalls of managerialism, is now common. Leadership has been rediscovered, apparently, as an attempt to address the contemporary social and economic conditions faced by organizations. Leadership and leaders are thought to possess more of the qualities to address the contemporary organizational challenges than management and managers. There are many articles discussing the managers versus leadership debate (Barker, 1997; Kotter, 1990; Zaleznik, 1992), but the general tone is similar; managers are more scientific, rational, controlling, they relate to structure stability and bureaucracy whereas leadership is about passion, vision, inspiration, creativity and cooperation rather than control. Burgoyne and Pedler (2003) note: 'Leadership is often defined as being about "voluntary" obedience and there are assumptions of harmony and convergence of interest, seldom the leader uses formal authority or means of rewards/punishment in order to accomplish compliance [Barker, 1993; Zaleznik, 1992]'.

Another take on the rise of the leader is that a leader creates change while a manager creates stability. Alvesson and Svenginsson sum up their reading of the leadership literature:

> Contemporary writings usually frame leadership in terms of the visionary and heroic aspects, it is the leader's abilities to address [by talking and persuading] the many through the use of charisma, symbols and other strongly emotional devices, the ambition being to arouse and encourage people to embark upon organizational projects. (2003: 4)

Zaleznik (1992: 126) separates leadership and management neatly, perhaps too neatly:

> A managerial culture emphasises rationality and control. Whether his or her energies are directed toward goals, resources, organisation structures, or people, a manager is a problem solver ... It takes neither genius nor heroism to be a manager, but rather persistence, tough-mindedness, hard work, intelligence, analytical ability and perhaps most important, tolerance and goodwill.

Zaleznik sees managers as conservative folk who work towards conflict resolution, who are ambiguous in an attempt to blur things to avoid offending others, but are better team players. The managers' conservative nature leads them to work hard to defend institutions whereas leaders are more likely to be loners, to inspire creativity that may create conflict and to challenge the status quo, changing institutions. Whereas Leaders:

> Leaders work from high-risk positions; indeed, they are often temperamentally disposed to seek out risk and danger, especially where the chance of opportunity and reward appears promising' (ibid.)

Others see the leaders very much as network builders, integrators, communicators and much more wedded to the ideas of cooperation (Alvesson, 2002). Bryman (1996) says that leaders have an integrative role: creating change and organizational culture through the transmission of cultural values. A key difference, which seems agreed, is that contemporary leaders seldom use formal authority or means of rewards/punishment in order to accomplish compliance (Zaleznik, 1992).

## Management as the 'Other' to leadership

In short, management has assumed the derogatory 'other' to leadership. The manager has been relegated to an outdated, functionalist and mechanistic mode of operating more suited to the industrial age than the post-industrial workplace. Dubrin points to the need for leadership as well as management

'Without being led as well as managed, organisations face the threat of extinction' (2000: 4). However, there are some notable critics and warnings as to the demise of the manager (Mintzberg, 2004a, 2004b).

Paul du Gay's (2000) *In Praise of Bureaucracy* and Elliot Jaques' article (1990) 'In Praise of Hierarchy' also challenge this general trend, which puts leadership in front of management in contemporary organizational life. Until recently, management existed in its own discourse within business schools and went largely unchallenged. Disputes were about what sort of management worked best rather than questioning management itself. Now management itself, like bureaucracy before it, is being questioned as being the best way to run a business. Failing to ignite the imagination and idealism of the moment and seen as unfit to provide ongoing success in the post-industrial and global 'knowledge society', management has been pushed into a subservient position and become the 'other' which helps define the new popular 'object of desire' leadership. Set within a two-dimensional framework, there is a dualism in which the 'object' and the 'other' help define each other. In this case the leader is defined as a liberating actor bringing meaning to followers, to the 'otherness' of the controlling and bureaucratic manager, who brings alienation. Dubrin (2000) offers the following leader/manager dualisms: visionary as opposed to rational, passionate vs consulting, creative vs persistent, inspiring vs tough-minded, innovative vs analytical, courageous vs structured. Yukl critiques four two-factor leadership examples, Task Versus Relations, Autocratic Versus Participative, Leadership Versus Management, Transformational Versus Transactional Leadership and finds 'These dichotomies provide some insights, but they also oversimplify a, complex phenomenon and encourage stereotyping of individual leaders (Yukl, 1999: 34).

Helping define an object using the 'other' can be helpful, particularly when the object is obtuse and difficult to define, such as leadership. However, duality can also reduce complex phenomena to simplistic forms that lead to misunderstandings. Yukl's (1999) overview of leadership research is that two-factor model research and theorizing are over-simplistic; they stereotype people and are too dyadic and leadership research focuses on the relationships between two people, leader and follower, which does not take enough account of the context.

Leadership is very clearly in vogue and 'sexy', and the claims and hopes are that it will provide answers to the new era rather than manage the present. Managers are presented within the literature as mundane, resonating with a transactional theory of exchange and a more 'rational ideology' as opposed to the contemporary knowledge and learning-based economies of the West which, it is said, are suited to the leader, who focuses more on emotions and meaning rather than control (Barley and Kunda, 1992). The problem is that while 'sexy' attracts attention and gets journal articles and books published and sold, many businesses, practitioners, shareholders and academics are more conservative. The deep-seated ideology of rationality, rigorous empiricism and reliability still holds great power and sway.

In the past century, leadership has often been merged with the management discourse, leadership being seen as one of the attributes of being a good manager. It is only recently, with the popular rise of the leader, they have commonly been discussed as being separate. However, A.K Rice, a Tavistock psychoanalytically informed theorist, writing back in the 1960s points to the difficulty in separating leadership and management:

> Both leaders and managers have to deal with a different number of followers and subordinates, extending all the way from the small intimate face-to-face group of immediate colleagues to extended commands and even crowds … To be successful a manager has to display qualities of leadership and use techniques of management appropriate to the task of the group he is managing. (Rice, 1965: 20)

Rice identifies the blurred boundaries between manager and leader, but acknowledges that some leaders are better at leading and inspiring their followers and institutions than they are at managing them, while some managers are better at managing than they are at leading and inspiring. Other managers are better at developing strategies than at implementing strategy. Rice identifies functions and skills in which a leader or manager may excel. Rice is very clear that a manager also takes up a leadership role because 'any institution whose managers do not give leadership in primary task performance is obviously in difficulty' (ibid.: 20). Mintzberg agrees with this view which is still being debated 41 years later: 'Leadership is supposed to be something bigger, more important. I reject this distinction, simply because managers have to lead and leaders have to manage. Management without leadership is sterile; leadership without management is disconnected and encourages hubris' (2004a: 6).

Rice then takes up an unusual stance from his psychoanalytic perspective and says that a key difference between a manager and a leader lies within the concept of unconscious behaviour. He sees management as essentially rational and conscious (manifest) whereas leadership can also be exercised unconsciously (covertly). This can lead to tensions, as he explains: 'In this sense, whatever the institution, managers need to understand the problems of leadership and particularly to be aware of those kinds of leadership both manifest and covert, which oppose their management,' (Rice, 1965: 20). Rice goes on to identify two tasks of leadership: a conscious (manifest) task and an unconscious task. At a manifest level, the primary task of leadership is to manage relations between an institution and its environment so as to permit optimal performance of the primary task of the institution. At the unconscious level, the leader expresses on behalf of the group the emotions associated with the basic assumption (ibid.: 20). The basic assumption he refers to is Wilfred Bion's (1961) work on the primitive unconscious emotions that groups identify with and which undermine the group and prevent them from working effectively. Rice then says, 'If the manifest leader fails to deal adequately with the repressed emotions and assumptions, other leaders may be thrown up to express emotions that are opposed to the overt task of the group' (Rice, 1965: 22). He is suggesting that leaders need to develop an awareness of their own conscious and unconscious roles. This implies that the conscious manifest role is to manage the explicit environment, and an unconscious role is to manage the emotions and expectations they have placed on them by the group. If leaders are not aware of the unconscious expectations of their followers, which are based on primitive anxieties, then tensions will arise between the explicit, conscious expectations and the unconscious individual and group anxieties which present themselves as powerful fantasies. He suggests, in line with other psychoanalytic theorists, that unless these unconscious fantasies are acknowledged and 'managed', conflict and destructive behaviour will result. A leader can be rendered impotent if the conscious task (e.g. to sell cars) and unconscious task (e.g. to win the approval of the boss) conflict too powerfully within a group. Rice's insights are helpful as they blur the lines between managers and leaders, identifying that they are not dichotomies but that they co-exist: a manager will usually have a leadership role and a leader usually has a management role.

Two key points arise from Rice's work:

1  Managers who do not show some leadership are likely to fail.
2  There are two tasks of leadership: a conscious task and an unconscious task.

The conscious task has many theorists' attention and it is the unconscious task of managing, representing and influencing the emotions and unconscious fantasies of the group, which are often overlooked. The unconscious task relates to understanding and influencing the group culture and the unconscious processes within the organization.

One of the differences between an accomplished leader and manager is that the manager is more likely to be skilled in the conscious task whereas the leader definitely needs both. In practice, mixed messages and confusing expectations exist for those who take up senior roles in organizations, whether they are called managers or leaders.

In this book I will not attempt to separate the manager and leader with surgical precision, as this is not possible. When discussing leadership, I will assume some managers will also have some leadership qualities and responsibilities and vice versa.

## Conclusion

When asking what is leadership, the answer depends on what one is looking for, and from where one is looking. Leadership is many things to many people. Looking awry is vital in this situation to get a multi-perspective view, and to see leadership in new and insightful ways. Leadership has been separated from management in an artificial way, but there are differences, and while the distinctions may not be black and white, they are still important. Management is closely associated with efficiency and control, there is nothing wrong with this, it is very important. Leadership is associated with moving forward, taking authority, creating change through influencing.

Leaders and leadership are very commonly polarized: either idealized or deni-grated. This is a social and psychological process, whereby we project desire and anxiety onto 'saviours' or project our envy and fears onto those 'idiots' leading us. These processes require understanding in context, rather than arguing whether leadership itself is right or wrong. The task is closer to sense-making rather than searching for concrete and definitive answers (Weick, 1995; Pye, 2005). The 'Holy Grail' of leadership is to be found when we stop searching for it, and see that it is all around us, in the processes, behaviours, and the social systems in which we work on a daily basis.

# 3

# Leadership, Power and Authority

Don't follow leaders, watch out for parking meters.

(Bob Dylan, Subterranean Homesick Blues)

## Introduction

Chapter 3 looks at the tension between leadership, power and authority. How can leadership find an ethical and workable fit, using power within the ideals of democracy, equality and fairness? The recent search for changes in leadership styles to lead new organizational forms which focus on flattened hierarchies and participative cultures has revived the interest in working in leaderless autonomous teams, and functioning with a dispersed emergent leadership.

Many egalitarian-inspired individuals and social movements are, and continue to be, distrustful of leadership and point to the many examples of corrupt leaders and abuse of power by leaders with devastating consequences, and they argue for leaderless groups. This distrust of leaders and leadership grew after the Second World War when Hitler epitomized the dangers of leadership and power being abused. This was followed by the socialist left becoming disenchanted following their aspirations being dashed by the communist dictatorships of Mao and Stalin. The impact of the Vietnam War also eroded many students' and young people's attitudes towards democratic leadership in the USA and beyond. The post-war reaction to leadership was highlighted in the 1960s with the anti-authoritarian hippie movement and the liberation-focused social movements which emerged, such as the youth movement, the peace movement, the feminist movement and the Lesbian and Gay movement. The lyric by Dylan in the epigraph, neatly captures the sentiment of the time, which berated leaders, and with it any form of authority. Many activists and critical thinkers who were influenced by these movements remain distrustful of leadership and associate leadership with authoritarianism, manipulation and coercion. This can be seen in the work of some critical theorists writing today. Moves to find more democratic and egalitarian forms of organizing emerged from this distrust. In recent years, the promotion of new forms of leadership, e.g. dispersed leadership, i.e. leadership at all levels in the organization, has become popular beyond egalitarian thinkers and social movement activists. This relates to the changes brought by globalization and post-industrial work whereby it is no longer possible for a leader to control the workforce and new ways of leading successful organizations have been sought. However, the promotion of flattened hierarchies, self-managed teams and dispersed leadership is paradoxically often cited as being best delivered by Transformational leaders. This may simply be the powerful attempting to have their cake and eat it! We will visit the Transformational leader literature later in the book but now will discuss some of the arguments which challenge leadership.

## Distributed leadership: New Social Movements and leaderless groups

The search for egalitarian-inspired organizations is a recurrent theme throughout modern history (Kropotkin, 1902; Woodcock, 1977). In the past century, social movements and social change have impacted on organizational theory as well as economic and technological change. The growing move towards individualism in the West has had a very powerful impact on how organizational structures have developed. The leadership literature has overlooked the influence of new social movements (NSMs), many of which organize in forms that global corporations would be delighted to emulate. For example, many of the anti-capitalist and anti-global movements organize with a committed and loyal 'membership', are extremely flexible, fluid and responsive, are very entrepreneurial and act through autonomous organizing principles. Large corporations and small I.T. companies alike have been attempting to flatten hierarchies, disperse leadership and to create network and matrix structures with self-managed teams that can respond rapidly at local levels with committed and loyal employees.

To get a clearer understanding of some of the issues and themes which impact when leadership itself is challenged, it is useful to go beyond the mainstream management literature and briefly review a selection of egalitarian-inspired organizations and movements whose motivations vary; some are political, others spiritual and others altruistic or utopian. These come in three main groupings:

1   Co-operatives, not-for-profit organizations: charities and self-help organizations, which aspire to democratic structures, sharing profits, often with rotating leadership roles, attempting to limit hierarchy and disperse power wherever possible with various degrees of success.
2   Religious and spiritually inspired communities and organizations with egalitarian leanings from both traditional and 'new age' backgrounds. The Quakers are a living example.
3   New social movements: organizing to contest social and cultural identity (in contrast to old social movements which aimed to gain access to material resources and political power). The environmental movement in all its manifestations is a good example.

The first category has had some attention in the management world and debates on democratic organizations have been around a long time, whereas the second and third categories are a largely untapped resource which has been overlooked. Leadership, particularly, has always been contested in co-operative, democratic and socialist movements who have long debated the issues, as is shown by the publication in Box 3.1, printed in 1912.

---

### Box 3.1 The Miners' Next Step, published by the South Wales Unofficial Reform Committee in 1912

#### GOOD SIDE OF LEADERSHIP

**1. Leadership tends to efficiency**
One decided man, who knows his own mind, is stronger than a hesitating crowd. It takes time for a number of people to agree upon a given policy. One man soon makes up his mind.

**2. He takes all responsibility**
As a responsible leader, he knows that his advice is almost equivalent to a command and this ensures that his advice will have been carefully and gravely considered before being tendered.

**3. He stands for Order and System**
All too frequently, 'What is everybody's business is nobody's business' and if no one stands in a position to ensure order and system, many things are omitted which will cause the men's interest to suffer.

#### THE BAD SIDE OF LEADERSHIP

**1. Leadership implies power**
Leadership implies power held by the leader. Without power the leader is inept. The possession of power inevitably leads to corruption. All leaders become corrupt, in spite of their own good intentions. No man was ever good enough, or strong enough, to have such power at his disposal, as real leadership implies.

**2. Consider what it means**
This power of initiative, this sense of responsibility, the self-respect which comes from expressed manhood, is taken from the men and consolidated in the leader. The sum of their initiative, their responsibility, and their self-respect becomes his.

**3. The order and system**
The order and system he maintains is based upon the suppression of the men, from being independent thinkers into being 'the men' or 'the mob'. Every argument, which could be advanced to justify leadership on this score, would apply equally well to the Czar of all the Russians and his policy of repression. In order to be effective, the leader must keep the men in order, or he forfeits the respect of the employers and 'the public' and thus becomes ineffective as a leader.

*(Continued)*

*(Continued)*

| **4. He affords a standard of goodness and ability** | **4. He corrupts the aspirants to public usefulness** |
|---|---|
| In the sphere of public usefulness there is a great field of emulation. The good wishes of the masses can only be obtained by new aspirants for office showing a higher status of ability than the existing leaders. This tends to his continued efficiency or elimination. | He is compelled, in order to maintain his power, to see to it that only those who are willing to act as his drill sergeants or coercive agents shall enjoy his patronage. In a word, he is compelled to become an autocrat and a foe to democracy. |
| **5. His faithfulness and honesty are guarded** | **5. He prevents solidarity** |
| Hero worship has great attractions for the hero and a leader has great inducements on this side, apart from pecuniary considerations, to remain faithful and honest. | Sheep cannot be said to have solidarity. In obedience to a shepherd they will go up or down, backwards or forwards as they are driven by him and his dogs. But they have no solidarity, for that means unity and loyalty. Unity and loyalty, not to an individual, or the policy of an individual, but to an interest and a policy which is understood and worked for by all. |

I will focus on the third grouping here, the new social movements, as very little attention has been paid to them in the management literature. This is unfortunate as new social movement theorists offer a very rich source of insights which are applicable to new attempts to create collectivist forms of organization elsewhere. New social movements are wide-ranging, from feminist, environmental to anti-capitalist movements and they represent new forms of collective action (Melucci, 1989; Giddens, 1991; Castells, 1997; Della Porta, 1999). Many of the more politicized movements attempt to create non-hierarchical and leaderless organizations. They differ from the traditional workers movements in organizational form, as they do not organize within rigid structures and rather than herald leadership and see organizing as the key aim (i.e. organizing the masses with leaders and vanguard parties, based on Marxist–Leninist ideology) regard this as elitist and counter-productive. Organizing others and winning the control of material resources and power, the focus of old social movements, has been replaced by organizational ideas of fluid networks, without figureheads, or doctrinaire ideologies. The lack of leadership and control, the lack of organization, the lack of hierarchical structure is regarded as their key advantage when challenging the more cumbersome 'modernist' state apparatus (Castells, 1997). Their ability to respond to situations with great speed through networks utilizing modern technology (the ultimate network, the internet and mobile phones, for example) makes them difficult to defeat. These networked movements operate locally but often have global links and are held together ideologically and through shared beliefs, values and identities.

Al Qaeda could be cited as another radical example of a network movement. It differs in that it has a clear leader, Osama bin Laden, but this leadership sets agendas and tone rather than controls the network, which operates through local leadership. John Gray describes Al Qaeda as a very modern phenomenon and draws the comparison between it and new organizational forms in the corporate world:

> It is not only in its use of communication technologies that Al Qaeda is modern. So is its organisation. Al Qaeda resembles less the centralised command struc- tures of the twentieth-century revolutionary parties than the cellular structures of drug cartels and the flattened networks of virtual business corporations. Without fixed abode and with active members from practically every part of the world, Al Qaeda is a 'global multi-national'. (Gray, 2003: 76)

While these social movements are called new, references to early splits between communists and anarchists in the late nineteenth century cite similar differences. The anarchist Mikhail Bakunin (1814–1876) understood the reflexive nature of what he was trying to achieve; that the form a 'revolutionary' organization took, the way it managed power and internal relationships, directly impacted on the society it aimed to create after the revolution. He represented the anarchist view that an authoritarian vanguard party cannot form a libertarian free society. 'New' social movement commentators highlight this reflexivity between the movements and the change they seek to take place. However, as Bakunin demonstrates, this understanding is not new. What may be new is that in the post-industrial form the struggle over material resources has been replaced by a struggle over identity. Even the anarchists hoped a revolution would allow the people to take control of the land and resources; their key debate with the Marxists was who would assume control in a post-revolution situation – the masses or the party elite. Touraine (1981) and Melucci (1989) agree that the aim of new social movements is to achieve self-production for individual and collective identities; it is a struggle for the control of the symbolic realm, not the material, an attempt to negotiate and control at least some of the conditions for collective and individual life. The claim that new social movements contest new ground, which is not economic, is cer- tainly different to the socialist organized labour movements and other twentieth- century 'old' social movements. However, it can be argued that there have always been movements struggling not for power but for identity.

Going back to the mid-seventeenth century during the English Civil War, there were those who fought for civil and economic power and democratic rights of rep- resentation; Cromwell and groups like the Levellers and Diggers who produced a proto-type socialist manifesto (Hill, 1985). However the Quakers, Seekers, Ranters and some other religious groupings and sects struggled for recognition of identity and of libertarian rights to organize, live and worship collectively, as they so chose. These latter groups certainly understood that the communities and relationships they formed and the identities they were creating would be the very basis of the new society or New Jerusalem they were striving for. In this way, they share common ground with new social movements today.

## No God, no master! Anarchists and leaderless movements

Leaderless groups and spontaneous leadership theory have a long history. The anarchist, Mikhail Bakunin wrote in the mid-nineteenth century:

> At the moment of action, in the midst of the struggle, there is a natural division of roles according to the aptitude of each, assessed and judged by the collective whole: some direct and command, others execute orders. But no function must be allowed to petrify or become fixed and it will not remain irrevocably attached to any one person. Hierarchical order and promotion do not exist, so the commander of yesterday can become a subordinate tomorrow. No one rises above others, or if he does rise, it is only to fall back a moment later, like the waves of the sea forever returning to the salutary level of equality. (Joll, 1979: 92)

Bakunin's description of leadership reflects the view of spontaneous leadership arising and then subsiding, but not being fixed or hierarchical. Leaderless action is often characterized as spontaneous (Katz, 1981; McAdam, 1982) but empirical evidence shows organization and negotiations create and sustain leaderless movements. The power of these movements comes paradoxically through not having formal organization or leadership and there have been some considerable successes; for example the anti-capitalist demonstrations, Greenpeace, the environmental movement and the feminist movement (Castell, 1997).

Helen Brown (1989) who researched the women's movement in the UK found that there is little written or researched about the process of 'leaderless' movements with the exception of Gerlach and Hine (1970). In her study of the women's movement in general and the Greenham women's peace camps in particular, Brown suggests that 'Leadership is not absent but it is understood as a set of organizing skills, skilful information search, interpretation and choice. The application of these three is necessary for the successful accomplishment of organisation' (1989: 231). She cites Kerr and Jermier (1978) who suggest that leadership in the traditional hierarchical sense becomes redundant in certain settings: when participants find the task intrinsically motivating and have all the skills and knowledge they need. A difficulty that arises from Brown's work is how leadership is defined, Brown modifies her view of leadership by defining it within a hierarchical context and then differentiating this from leadership acts, leadership skills or organizers:

> Leadership [or organizers] in a hierarchical sense are not necessary for the achievement of social organisation. What is necessary is that participants devise a means of engaging in leadership acts and thus acting as skilled organisers which is legitimate in terms of shared values. (Brown, 1989: 227).

There is a difference between a skilled organizer and a leader. A skilled organizer would fit more easily within the definition of a manager who acts 'with the intention of organizing efficiently'. Participatory leadership may also be a shared value within a hierarchical setting where leaders maximize negotiation, consensus and participation prior to making decisions. Brown goes on to discuss a distributed leadership: 'Leadership is perceived here as acceptable influence, which is legitimated by the agreed values of, distributed leadership [where everybody has a right and responsibility to contribute]. Authority resides in the collective as a whole' (ibid.: 235) Brown's research findings are similar in concept to Starhawk's (1986) description of 'leaderful' instead of leaderless groups, where the leadership is distributed throughout the movement or group. This is very similar to the concept that the egalitarian-inspired religious movement, the Quakers, established; they were accused of wanting to ban the priesthood but they actually wanted abolition of the laity, creating a 'priesthood of all believers' (Quaker Faith and Practice, 1995: 11.01). 'Leaderful' movements have much in common with Distributive leadership. Douglas observes that, 'there is no such thing as a leaderless group, only groups with different degrees of leadership residing in the actions of one person or several' (1983: 43).

Leaderless groups or movements are problematic and often critiqued as being either a fantasy, whereby leadership does exist but is concealed and is more dangerous as oligarchies form. The feminist, Jo Freeman, who wrote *The Tyranny of Structurelessness* (1984), articulates her observations and experiences of leaderless groups in the feminist movement:

1   Thus 'structurelessness' becomes a way of masking power and within the women's movement it is usually most strongly advocated by those who are the most powerful.
2   Awareness of power is curtailed by those who know the rules, as long as the structure of the group is informal.
3   The most insidious elites are usually run by people not known to the larger public at all. Intelligent elitists are usually smart enough not to allow themselves to become well known.
4   Friendship and informal power networks dominate and exclude 'outgroups' within such movements and organisations.

Freeman's main concerns about leaderless groups are regarding the issues of power, transparency and accountability, which occur due to hidden elites wielding unchallenged and unaccountable power. Indecisiveness, group narcissism and impotency could also be added here from my own personal experiences of working in groups which advocate leaderless-ness or simply deny leaders in favour of egalitarian approaches. A typical example is the refusal of a work-team to have a leader, but rather a facilitator. The person who is facilitator often is given a poisoned chalice; the responsibility and accountability without authority.

Freeman argues for rules and formalized structures in non-hierarchical movements, in order to prevent such leaderless tyranny. Another difficulty within leaderless groups and utopian-inspired democratic movements is the denial of difference which occurs when an idealized belief in equality and unity takes hold. Conflict is avoided to prevent the disruption of the ideas of unity, and consensus is attempted through time-consuming negotiations over each contested area and decision. Self-managed organizations or movements can end up as navel-gazing talking shops, in which the internal dynamics of the group or movement take precedence over external tasks. The aims get buried in process and procedures, as power games get played out implicitly rather than explicitly. These organizations often rationalize themselves into rigid and bureaucratic structures. Michels argues that leaderless groups can become the most dangerously authoritarian organizations: 'Organisations that start out with egalitarian or anarchistic political values tend to become as, or perhaps more, authoritarian and alienating than the organisations they were designed to reform or replace (Michels, 1915, in Grint, 1997: 284).

The contemporary anarchist Chaz Bufe similarly argues:

> In the 60's and 70's many leftist, anarchist and feminist groups agonised over how to eliminate leadership, equating all leadership [including temporary, task-based leadership] with authoritarian leadership. Their fruitless efforts confirm what the more astute anarchists have been saying for over a century – that it's a mistake to think that any kind of group or organisation can exist without leadership; the question is, what kind of leadership is it going to be? (Bufe, 1988: 21)

The term leaderless seems as contentious as the term leader or leadership. Much of the debate contests the type of leadership rather than actual leadership itself. Authoritarian leadership and power are the underlying issues. Many new social movements and other egalitarian movements aim to create organizational forms which challenge those that characterize and wield power in modern society. They have shown some success but also demonstrate some of the challenges and problems of idealizing the leaderless group. Experience demonstrates that, except in rare circumstances, some form of leadership exists within all social arenas. The question, as Bufe says, is 'what sort of leadership', and how to create and support leadership which is not oppressive.

## Power and authority

Anton Obholzer, writing in the Tavistock psychoanalytic tradition, discusses authority and its relation to power: 'Authority, without power, leads to a weakened, demoralised management and power without authority leads to an authoritarian regime' (1994: 42). Obholzer says that the role (position) given or not given indicates the power or authority one has and the choice of title often points to the clarity or ambivalence with which an organization regards the person or the role. Therefore, the title of dictator indicates that power is the essential component; manager, chairman or director indicates a mix between power and authority, and the title of co-ordinator, often used in the voluntary sector, indicates very little power and relies on consensus from the group (which Obholzer says is a very unlikely phenomenon). A leader's position does not have to be formalized. However, there lies a danger that the role is going to be constantly in negotiation which may have strengths but also creates tensions and the constant negotiations are time-consuming.

Gastil (1997) states that one of the democratic leader's functions is to sustain the democratic process and to prevent undemocratic structures forming. However, this diverts the attention from external reality, its goals and primary task. The group or organization can become engrossed in its own process and internal dynamics. Envy and rivalry are often rife in such conditions and when this happens, the organization is underpinned by emotional insecurity: 'If collaborative work is to take place in a group, each member is confronted with threats to his sense of "self". This sense of self is their most precious possession. It is bound to be defended stoutly' (Woodhouse and Pengelly, 1991: 29). Many organizations whose ideals are democratic and egalitarian, or whose members aspire to this, are often hybrids, hierarchical in structure but consensual in aspiration, or consensual at some levels but accountable to a hierarchy of leaders, managers at more senior levels or ultimately funding bodies or shareholders. This often leads to role confusion with the inevitable problems and tensions which follow, particularly for the middle manager, or front-line team leader. When democratic approaches are sought, there can often be what Kurt Lewin called a 'pseudo-democracy', which paralyses decision-making, and prevents leaders from taking up their authority. Elliot Jaques' Glacier Investigations found that the need for clarity of role and status for individuals and their colleagues was paramount. Organizations that identified themselves with democratic ideals or consensus decision-making often undermine a leader's ability to take up authority and to lead. The results can be sabotage, confusion and frustration (Jaques, 1955).

Aspiring democratic leaders and organizations are troubled by the concept of power that is often treated as a dirty word and avoided. The mainstream management literature oversimplifies these issues without taking into account the complex sources of power and resistance that are addressed in radical and relational views of management (Kanter, 1979).

An integral part of being a democratic leader in the Human Relations tradition is that a leader should empower employees (Kanter, 1979; Bennis and Nanus, 1985). Hui (1994) believes that ways to share power and the meaning of empowerment have not been systematically articulated and therefore managers are uncertain as to how they can empower employees without diminishing their own power. Power is usually defined in management literature as the ability to make another person do what they would not otherwise do, overcoming some resistance and usually associating it with competition and control (Weber, 1947; Pfeffer, 1978). Power can also be hidden and explains the absence of conflict as much as it does the cause of it. The absence of conflict means that demands are not made, voluntary obedience is the result of totalising power, even if it is not explicit.

McClelland (1975) argues that power is not necessarily competitive and says that this assumption interferes with theorizing and the understanding of both the positive and negative faces of power. Thibaut and Kelley (1959) enlarge on this, saying that power is not just related to coercion power but can be the power to effect outcomes or the power to control valued resources. Power can also be inspirational, people pray for the positive power of an omnipotent God to change them. Likewise, on a daily basis, all of us face an existential choice as to how we use our power; we all have the power to make differences to others' lives. Leaders usually have positional power and/or charismatic power which can place them in a vulnerable position … what choices will they make? How will they use this power? Will their subordinates/followers 'will them' to use their power or resist them? It is often this vulnerability that creates anxiety and a misuse of power. Leaders who are self-confident often demonstrate humility and kindness rather than coercion. Coercion comes from a place of insecurity rather than security.

Power and authority are sought after but often referred to negatively, as if they were always linked to coercion and control. They are also discussed as if they belong in a monolithic hierarchy. This section has highlighted how power and authority reside whether or not there is a hierarchy or leadership. Foucault's insights into power are very helpful as he says that power is not situated in elites, in rulers and ruled, but exists everywhere:

> Where there is power there is resistance, and yet, or rather consequently, this resistance is never in a position of exteriority in relation to power … the existence [of power relationships] depends on a multiplicity of points of resistance; these play a role of the adversary, target, support or handle in power relationships. These points of resistance are everywhere in the power network. Hence there is no locus of great Refusal … or pure law of the revolutionary. Instead there is a plurality or resistances which by definition … can only exist in the strategic field of power relations. (Foucault, 1980: 95–6)

So, for Foucault, power and resistance are one, they are interdependent, and power is not simply repressive, or at the top of a hierarchy it is everywhere and fluid.

Authority also has a negativity about it, the problem is that authority and authoritarian become conflated. Taking up one's authority is different from being authoritarian. The former is to take up one's legitimate agency in role, perhaps on behalf of others as their representative, the latter is to act in a way which implies abusing one's power and position, being repressive and using some form of coercion.

## Co-operation and competition

Tjosvold and Field sharply contrast cooperative and competitive people and goals:

> People with highly cooperative goals discuss their opposing ideas and positions directly, examine each other's perspectives and work for mutual benefit. With open minds, they understand the opposing positions, integrate their ideas and achieve a mutually acceptable, high-quality decision. People with competitive goals are reluctant to discuss their views directly and may belittle and attack another's position. (Tjosvold and Field, 1984: 28 Tjosvold and McNeely, 1988)

This research is limited by its duality and reductionism; the comparison between the competitive and collaborative leader does not address the complexities and the dynamics involved and is reminiscent of McGregor's Theory X and Theory Y theories of management. In new organizational forms, complexity is part of the fabric and there are few organizations with solely competitive goals and even fewer with cooperative goals. Each person, group and organization will have to find resources which, at times, draw upon competitive attributes and at other times cooperative attributes; even within teams, some competition is healthy and can help creativity and task completion. Tjosvold and Hui offer useful suggestions for effective participation:

> To be a democratic manager, both managers and employees must be skilled and able to express their views openly, consider opposing views, work for mutual benefit, show respect though they disagree and incorporate opposing views into the solution. They must also create the conditions under which this open discussion is likely, that is, mutually cooperative goals. (1998: 642)

Competition and cooperation raise psychic challenges and powerful emotions, including envy, rivalry, trust, friendship and security. Working with diversity and across boundaries raises tensions and can create feelings of discomfort and/or omnipotence when we win, in competitive situations, and envy when we lose.

Competition can also provide added dynamic energy, which enthuses, take any major sporting event as an example. However, as any sporting event will demonstrate, leadership has to deal with both competition and collaboration at the same time, collaborating with team members, referees, coaches; collaborating with the opposition at a minimal level to play within the time boundaries and rules. Road cycling is an intriguing sport which lends itself to business as a metaphor for collaboration and competition being intertwined. In the Tour de France, no cyclist can win without their support team, but they also have to collaborate with their opponents. During a breakaway from the main pack, you have riders from different teams totally dependent on each other to keep their speed up in order that one of them will win. At the same time they are trying to gain tactical advantage so it is they who will gain final victory. Leaders in organizations have similar choices to make, similarly, they need to understand how collaboration and competition are closely entwined.

## Democratic leadership and participative styles

Democratic and participative leadership styles are widely accepted as the most relevant styles which can motivate workers and create organizational structures and cultures which are the closest embodiment of the Human Relations Movement's ideas.

Democratic leadership aims to share decision-making and give employees responsibility and a degree of autonomy to bring about double benefits: satisfaction for the employee and increased output. Participative management (Likert, 1961), Servant leadership (Greenleaf, 1977) and now Transformational leadership (Burns, 1978) are all forms of leadership that claim allegiance towards 'Democratic leadership'. Democratic leadership is usually contrasted with autocratic leadership and was an attempt to move away from the rationalistic and controlling manager figure. Kurt Lewin and colleagues produced work on democratic leadership (Lewin and Lippett, 1938), separating it from autocratic and laissez-faire leadership and proposed the argument that democratic leadership was not only morally correct, it was also an improvement on the other styles. John Gastil writes of Lewin: 'He argues that democratic leadership relied upon group decision-making, active member involvement, honest praise and criticism and a degree of comradeship. By contrast, leaders using the other styles were either domineering of uninvolved' (1997: 157). Gastil takes issue with Lewin's work and cites others, making the overall comments that it is at best ambiguous and at worst 'democratic engineering' and manipulative. Barlow (1981) linked Mao's 'mass line leadership' in China with Lewin's work, saying it masks coercion under the guise of partici-pative group process. Lewin's unelaborated label, democratic leadership, is still the basis for research today on democratic leaders and may account for the decreased amount of research on democratic leadership in the past decade (Bass 1990b). Democratic leadership raises many questions; the notion of democracy is in many people's minds contrasted with the notion of leader. The difference between taking up one's legitimate authority as a leader and becoming authori-tarian is one of the key dilemmas within the democratic leadership framework (Obholzer, 1994). Leadership and democracy are always in tension. Kutner writes: 'Leaders need authority … but the delegation of authority in a democratic group is never the mandate for any leader to employ authority without the eventual approval of the group' (1950: 460). This statement is clearly paradoxical; you can-not be given the authority to make decisions and at the same time be dependent on the group to approve those decisions. To give the same authority to the group is to take away the authority from the leader. In democratic bodies, the authority given to a leadership position has to be circumscribed, so that somewhere a line is drawn as to which decisions can be taken by the leader and what needs further approval from the group. Formal and informal structures and rules come with this territory. Bass (1990b) points to the much quoted 'modern view' that leadership is 'behaviour not position'; this is problematic and idealistic, as in practice, surely, it is both. At times a leader can emerge within a flat hierarchy or self-managed team through 'behaviour' but unless this is reinforced by position, sooner or later a power struggle will always occur. What is really meant by this is that a leader who is given a position needs to get followers to follow with 'hearts and minds' and not solely to use their leadership position to coerce people into actions. Followers need to empower a leader in the same way as a leader should empower follow-ers. By being elected, promoted or appointed to a position of leadership (usually because of past behaviour, results, experience, image, charisma, ability to com-municate, technical ability, etc.), that position and role are legitimized and carry with them a certain amount of authority. If a leader acts without legitimacy, either because they do not have the position or because they do not have the behaviours which command respect, then the leader will be ineffectual. To describe leader-ship as behaviour assumes that leadership resides with a solo actor and it is an individual's behaviour which makes them a leader. This does not account for the power of the group dynamic, which may consciously or unconsciously 'elect' a leader. Sometimes this is a leader who is not necessarily displaying the leadership qualities required for the task, but who fits the unconscious defensive needs of the group at the time (Bion, 1961; Rice, 1965). Personal behaviour does not account for group process or organizational dynamics, which is the view taken by relational and psychodynamic theorists (Hirschhorn, 1988; Gabriel, 1999).

## Leadership and followership

Leaders and followers have tended to be seen as dualist opposites, with the main focus being on the leader who is presented as a subject. Through this dualistic lens followers have been presented both individually and collectively as passive objects, to be moulded, coerced and influenced by the leader. However, due to the rise in interest of dispersed leadership and autonomous teams, and with poststructuralists deconstructing leadership, followership has gained importance and the dualistic approach is being challenged. Collinson (2006: Intro) cites a widening literature that insists that followers are integral to the leadership process; 'rejecting the common stereotype of followers as timid, docile sheep, these writers argue that in the contemporary context of greater team working, "empowered, knowledge workers", and "distributed" and "shared" leadership, "good followership skills" have never been more important.'

One reading of this 'raising up' of followership aligns itself with the claims of the transformational leader literature, which maintains that the transformational leader 'transforms' followers. They become empowered great followers and dispersed leaders internalizing the leader's vision and becoming exemplary employees who are committed, autonomous and energized. However, the follower literature attempts to diminish the agency of the leader and assert the agency of the follower, who, if anything, 'raises up the leader' (Meindl, 1995). The literature on followers remains marginal in comparison to that on leadership, and much of its focus places the follower in dualistic opposition to the leader. Much of the follower literature leans towards the idea of follower resistance: 'In sum, post-structuralist studies highlight the importance of resistant selves in the workplace. This focus on followers' opposition suggests that identity construction in organizations may be shaped by differentiation as much as identification' (Collinson, 2006: 185). Paradoxically, while followers are portrayed as resisting the power and domination of 'heroic leaders', they do not always escape the 'heroic' metaphor. Their representation can appear as an undercover 'guerilla resistance' movement fighting against the hegemony of the corporate machine.

In the mainstream leadership literature, a singular leader identity is portrayed which consists of the 'essentialist' or biological self, i.e. a person having leadership traits such as charisma, and also a social self, constructed through consuming leadership experience and development, e.g. personal development, leadership skills, which combine to contribute to the individual's leadership identity. This 'leadership identity' then goes out into the world to influence followers. Haslam and Platow (2001) argue that identity is vital to organizational life, it binds groups together. They see the leader's identity as being both dependent upon followers, and also important to the construction of the group identity. Others also view the construction of the leadership identity as being reflexive between the leader and followers: 'In sum, post-structuralist perspectives argue that the identities of followers and leaders are frequently a condition and consequence of one another' (Collinson, 2006: 182).

Meindl (1995) argues we should concentrate on followers and Grint claims that followership determines leadership:

> In short, the power of leaders is a consequence of the actions of the followers rather than the cause of it. If this were not so then no parents would ever be resisted by their children, no CEO would ever face defeat by the board of directors, no general would ever face a mutiny, and no strikes would ever occur. That they do should lead us to conclude that no leader is omnipotent and that the kind of leadership is a consequence of the kind of followership rather than the cause of it. (Grint, 2005: 38)

Grint's pro-followership stance privileges followers' influence over leader's influence, but the logic here is questionable. We know that leaders are not omnipotent but this doesn't mean that a leader's power is a consequence of follower's actions. Children have always challenged their parents, and workers, soldiers, and employees have always resisted poor leadership particularly when it is perceived as abusing its privilege and power. Even 'good' leadership is resisted, as Foucault states, power and resistance are interdependent.

The relationship between leaders and those they influence is always in dynamic tension. The tension is usually between like and dislike of the leadership, between varying degrees of idealization and denigration. Idealization is often associated with follower's loyalty, high moral, shared values and vision, and also, on the downside, with dependency behaviours. Denigration can cause healthy sceptism or destructive resistance behaviours. Even when the leader is idealized, tensions occur within individuals and teams, between feelings of love, admiration and respect, and envy, desire and jealousy. These feelings are sometimes conscious but often unconscious. When leadership is enacted in a team, organization or a nation, some will respond by idealizing it, others will denigrate it. Psychoanalytic studies of group dynamics (Menzies Lyth, 1960; Bion, 1961; Hirschhorn, 1988; Miller, 1993; Obholzer and Roberts, 1994) show how individual members act out feelings on behalf of the rest of the group, for example, somebody will hold the feeling of envy for the rest of the group. This process is called projective identification, when the person introjects (that is takes into themselves) the feelings of others. This has the effect of freeing the rest of the group from identifying with their own feelings of envy, which they have projected upon another member. They then negatively identify with that feeling which they have projected onto the 'other', and can be outraged by this person feeling envious of their beloved leader! This unconscious process protects them from their own feelings of guilt that are associated with envy. The psychoanalyst Melanie Klein writes extensively on this subject, having studied and researched childhood behaviour (see Klein, 1959; Klein and Riviere, 1974). This happens with groups and departments as well as with individuals. A finance department may hold a 'withholding feeling' on behalf of the organization whereas the research and design department may hold the creative energy of the organization. Different leaders in these departments have to manage these feelings and work across the company boundaries in a collaborative way rather than 'act out' these identities which are projected onto them by their followers and other employees in the organization. Failure to understand these processes can lead to conflict. Follower relations with leaders are by no means singular and straightforward, they are pluralistic and multi-dimensional.

Sometimes a turning point arises when the majority of followers believe the leadership to be corrupt, or abusive of its power and a reaction or mutiny takes place. More often, this happens at a subtle level where others take on leadership informally but in such a case the leader's days are numbered. How a leader responds to these 'projections' from followers and how the followers respond to leadership influence, comprise the reflexive nature of the leadership process.

Therefore, I would argue that leadership is not the consequence of followership. Each of us will probably have personal experience of a new leader taking over the same group of followers, so often having a very different impact. A change in a football team manager is the obvious example. However, the dynamic is not uni-directional in either direction. Leadership and followership are symbiotically interdependent. It is a reflexive relationship, the followers' response to leaders helps define how a leader acts and vice versa. However, I would argue that the influence is not equal and that leaders have more influence. I have a real concern about the contemporary stance in critical approaches which either privileges followers having influence over leaders, or promotes an equal influence over each other. In most situations, leaders have more power, resources, control, authority and therefore more agency than followers and more influence than followers. Denying the potency of leadership, and particularly individual agency, is popular in some critical and post-structuralist accounts. This probably arises as a reaction to the overplaying of individualism and hero and transformational leadership in the mainstream literature. Deconstructing leadership is useful, denying power relations is not, and a critical perspective demands that power and influence are accounted for.

Perhaps the notion of followers should be replaced by a term such as participators. Participators would perhaps describe the reality that leaders do lead and others are influenced and participate in the leadership process, sometimes by following, other times by taking a leadership role. Leadership and followership are dynamic, not static roles.

The question is not whether influence is exerted in both directions, it surely is. The question is how this dynamic can be understood and theory turned into practice that produces the best leadership and the best participation in the leadership process. In this way, ethical leadership which engages and exerts influence to produce healthy and sustainable organizations and which maximizes participation and liberates the human spirit will occur.

## Conclusion

Chapter 3 addresses just a few of the issues raised regarding how leaders exert their influence and the relationship between leadership, power and authority. It explores leaderless and networked movements and identifies some of the problems they face. It questions how democratic and egalitarian leadership functions. Recently dispersed and distributive leadership have become popular concepts, relating to how leadership is manifest not only at the top of a hierarchy but throughout organizations.

While this idea is popular, this chapter identifies some of the problems which occur when attempting to democratize or disperse leadership. Another warning is that organizations often espouse distributive leadership and self-managed teams, particularly when it is the 'latest leadership thing' but in practice this can be no more than a 'rhetorical device' which uses language to hide where the real power and leadership exists. If distributive leadership is to work successfully, it has to arise from the bottom up, as much as from the top down. Critical approaches to leadership ask the question: 'Who is distributing leadership, for what reasons, and with what authority?' There is a huge difference between an open culture, which enables dispersed leadership to emerge and a control-led culture which distributes leadership as a resource in order to strengthen the existing leadership control.

One thing is clear to me, from my personal experience and the research I have undertaken, there is no escape from leadership, like power, it is everywhere, and understanding leadership in relation to power and authority is paramount. How leadership is understood, and how best it is engaged with, are philosophical, political, social and situational questions.

Focusing on followership and process is vitally important, but the trend to deny and downplay the role of the individual leader and of collective leadership agency in an attempt to be critical of misuse of leadership power is often misplaced.

Leaders, particularly when their authority and power emanates from position, i.e. they are senior employees, have more resources (financial, access to knowledge, communications, manpower, etc.) and therefore more power than followers. Informal leaders also get more access to resources via their influencing skills, networking, knowledge, etc. which is why they are able to apply leadership. Although followership studies help explain that this is a reflexive rather than uni-directional process, it doesn't change the reality that some people can influence and lead more than others.

CEOs' increased earnings in relation to employees and an increasingly flexible labour market suggest that leaders at the most senior levels are being given increasing amounts of resource, power and therefore leadership influence. The best safeguard against leadership tyranny and power abuse is to be transparent about the relationship between leadership and followership, influence, power and authority.

# Leadership and Diversity

## Introduction

It is impossible to write coherently about leadership and diversity without addressing the complex issues and multiple and contested theories and views on diversity. To do this effectively would take at least another whole book on each aspect of diversity we were dealing with: gender, race, ethnicity, class, sexuality, disability, religion, etc. So the dilemma is how to address diversity and not to oversimplify the issues, or become reductionist.

I can only attempt to be very modest in my aims, to raise a few of the important questions rather than seek comprehensive coverage or answers. I will write more generally about difference and diversity and focus on common themes which are transferable rather than delve into specifics. I will also aim to be provocative, in order to stimulate further thinking and reading on diversity from a critical perspective.

## Locating ourselves: transgressing boundaries

It is important to acknowledge that we all carry our personal, social and historical baggage with us, and however 'PC' (politically correct) we are, however progressive or liberal, we all belong to social groups, which exclude others, and we all make value judgements on a daily basis, often at unconscious levels. Becoming more conscious of these assumptions is important if we are to become more aware of others' experience, and the structures, which oppress minority and disadvantaged groups, and reproduce the power and privileged status quo.

A gay friend of mine in America told me how he watched the first gay marriage ceremony on television (which he had long supported), and he described how he was shocked by his own homophobic response, 'two men in tuxedos kissing at the town hall … it just didn't seem right'. Even when we are part of an activist group which is discriminated against, even when we are aware and supportive of the issues, social norms instilled in us since childhood, still inhabit our lives, thoughts and our bodies. We carry around our histories, social class, gender, sexuality in our thoughts and bodies and notice these in others.

It is therefore important for anybody in a leadership position to realize that they and their team will be working from a set of assumptions and biases that are based on their personal experience and social location. This includes one's race, nationality, religion, ethnicity, sexuality and class that are imprinted upon us and inscribed with social meanings to ourselves and to others who look at us and relate to us. It is the assumptions from the dominant group that become social 'normative' assumptions:

> If something is normative it is considered the standard pattern of behavior; the term carries with it an expectation that particular behavior ought to occur (Gilbert 2003). But norms are not simply ideas; norms operate through social practices and are difficult to remove from their material context. Norms may or may not be explicit, and when they operate as the normalizing principle in social practice, they usually remain implicit (Butler 2004: 41). Norms are materialized expectations; they are constructions that incorporate both attitudes and action. And they are imbued with power: to define what is considered normal and abnormal, to provoke in individuals who fail to adequately embody them a sense of failure. Within evangelicalism, marriage is the norm, singleness the reverse: it is non-normative. To construct singleness as non-normative is to act as if it were non-standard, even deviant, behavior and to generate within single people a sense of insignificance. (Aune, forthcoming)

In the world of corporate and organizational leadership, the normative expectations, culture and behaviours exclude many marginalized and disenfranchised groups. Kristin Aune points out that in the Evangelic Church, it is non-normative to be single, in the present day company boardroom in the West, it is non-normative to be black, openly gay, disabled, 'working class' or a woman.

## Locating myself

I write as a White, heterosexual, English male. I carry with me the history, social and cultural meanings, stereotypes, power and privileges and disadvantages, associated with this position. I had a 'working-class' school education that offered low expectations and poor quality teaching, the norm was failure. I dropped out of school before gaining A-levels or a first degree. I accessed higher education in my thirties and now have a two Masters and PhD (over-compensation perhaps!) which now adds to my privileged status. This experience gives me a heightened awareness and sensitivity to some issues such as 'class issues', the elitism of education, and less to other issues such as race or disability. In recent years when working as Director of Coaching Programs at a top-ranked University Management School, taking on a role and the title 'Dr Simon Western', I am aware of the powerful unconscious projections[1] I receive that differ so much from other spaces in my 'habitus'. These projections are unconscious feelings that people locate onto me because of what I represent to them. Depending on their personal emotional and developmental histories and their own social location, these projectors will impact on how they respond to me in this role. These projections are unconscious reactions to my presence in a specific role, context and space, i.e. the university lecture theatre. I have observed that these projections I receive are triggered through five key sources, and I name them here as I believe these sources are also applicable to leaders working in other contexts:

1   *The institution and context*: In my case the university, which carries with it the history of academia and elite knowledge, which I represent in the 'here and now' when standing in front of a lecture theatre.
2   *Embodied and cultural self*: My whiteness, my sexuality, being British, my maleness, my age, and my 'able body', etc.
3   *Personality*: Any 'charisma', personality traits, intellectual capability, etc. My personality will trigger some people's feelings in powerful ways, in others they will have a bland reaction to me.
4   *Expertise*: I teach Coaching at Masters Level drawing on my psychoanalytic and systemic background. Coaching and Therapy can carry the mystique of the 'shrink', and with it the fear/curiosity of being able to read the hidden unconscious.
5   *Role power*: As Course Director I have the power and authority to assess students. I also have power and influence in the lecture theatre.

Leaders should reflect on these five areas when in role at work, to begin to understand what they carry with them, how they use it and how others react to them.

People respond to me differently, based on their own social and historical location in relation to mine. In my case, senior executives with little academic experience can be daunted by 'the university'. This can be very unsettling, moving from an important role to a role where you feel like you know very little, and you do not understand the language, the academic writing rules, and the higher educational systems such as the library. They can respond by becoming infantilized very quickly. In a teaching context this is sometimes projected onto me sometimes as anger, when they feel impotent, as I can represent the cause of this impotency, or they can become very dependent and needy towards me, and I can feel like a 'nursing mother' or 'all-knowing Guru'. Other students from China and Korea I supervise often come to me with great deference. Their approach is clearly not about me personally, but about me in a role and their cultural normative response to the student/professor relationship. If I met my Chinese students or executives as an Asian woman, or a 'camp' gay man, what would their response be? My subject expertise impacts on others, and this links my personal attributes and my personal teaching style. I work very differently to many professors, drawing on my experience as a psychotherapist; I deal with emotions and the unconscious in the classroom. I am also aware of the classic 'patient/ analyst' relationship as one of dependency and how easy it is to enjoy these projections of idealization. Having some awareness of my own social location, I have more room to mediate how I deal with different individuals. I am less likely to take their anxiety and projections personally, I am able to distance myself from feelings of omnipotence or being paralysed by negative projections. This comes from my therapist's training. I am able to think with my students about what is happening. I explain these processes to them at the beginning of the coaching course. I teach and ask them to observe their own responses to me; we agree a learning contract, 'This classroom is a learning laboratory, everything that happens, all experience is data for learning … including your feelings … be aware of your responses to each other and to me.' In my experience, this is where the most powerful learning about leadership takes place. For leaders, this ability to understand projections and the idea of social location is very important when dealing with difference. On the first day of class, I also discuss the dependency issue: to learn, one must take up some dependency and let go of knowing in order to create a space for 'not knowing', a space in which new things can be learnt. The university enrolment systems ensure some dependency is created, they ensure the student, however mature, feels like a student! Too much dependency, however, prevents learning, as questions are not asked and students become like sponges, waiting to soak up knowledge rather than think for themselves and learn. I show students Figure 4.1, and tell them that if they all want is infantilized and breastfed knowledge, then I would have to look like this picture, and as I do not, they need to hold onto their adulthood and autonomy. The image sticks and we re-visit the discussion during the course, whenever dependency or compliance emerges in the lecture theatre.

I write this because it translates directly to leadership–follower roles, a parallel process takes place. The students' experience with me as 'Course Director' should tell them something about how they deal with the boss at work, and other leaders and figures of authority. Reflecting on their own leadership roles, to be aware of the projections they personally receive, to ask how their embodied self in role impacts on their relationships at work. What happens when a 'strange body' enters their workplace? A fundamental principle that applies to leaders and to followers is that too much dependency undermines critical and innovative thinking. It may feel good to a leader to have a dependent followership, but it is not a healthy or sustainable dynamic. Without critical thinking, awareness of the role, social location and embodied self, the issues of power, patriarchy and diversity will never be addressed.

In Britain, our colonial past stays with us like a sediment, where 'Black bodies are represented as coming from uncivilised spaces, wildernesses where people are savages and need taming … whites are associated with spirit and mind, representing the flight from the body' (Puwar, 2004: 21). While ground has been made on these issues, unconscious gender, sexual and racial stereotyping is still very much with us. We particularly notice 'otherness' when difference transgresses normal spaces. My own experience alerts me to this as I have transgressed normative gender boundaries; working as a nurse which at the time was a 95 per cent female profession, and as a single parent walking into mother and toddler groups in the early 1980s as the sole male figure. My experience of this was that I was not treated as 'me', the subject, but as an 'object' either to be feared, as I was a threat or contaminating to the homogeneous group (asked to leave some nursing lectures on

**Figure 4.1**    Artemis: Sculpture, Soho, New York

gynaecology, not being allowed to work on female wards) or in the mother and toddler group as an exotic sexualized object to be flirted with, or an object of pity to be 'mothered'. I am therefore interested in gender and race and how spaces and territories become 'normative' for certain groups and exclusionary to others.

Nirmal Puwar's book *Space Invaders: Race Gender and Bodies out of Place* (2004) eloquently describes this process that marks establishment spaces, and excludes those bodies that are not a part of this space. She cites Winston

Churchill's reaction to Nancy Astor, the first woman MP to enter the House of Commons: 'I find a woman's intrusion into the House of Commons as embarrassing as if she burst into my bathroom when I had nothing with which to defend myself, not even a sponge' (Winston Churchill, cited in Vallance, *Women in the House*, 1979 in Puwar, 2004: 13). Frantz Fanon in *Black Skin, White Masks*, writes about arriving in France in 1950, from Martinique, a French colony, and describes his experience of transgressing boundaries, and the effect of the 'gaze' of the other.

> 'The movements, the attitudes, the glances of the other fixed me there, in the sense that a chemical solution is fixed by a dye ... sealed into that crushing objecthood the look imprisoned me ...' He relates this experience to a 'Historic-racial schema ... a racial epidermal schema'. He was assigned ethnic characteristics, through which, he says: 'I was battered down by tom toms, cannibalism, intellectual deficiency, fetishism, racial defects, slave-ships..........I was told to stay within bounds, to go back to where I belonged' ....He cries out 'dissected under white eyes, the only real eyes, I am *fixed*.' (Fanon, 1970: 109–16 in Puwar, 2004: 39)

I would recommend reading Fanon to anybody who is serious about understanding racism and difference in general. His accounts are visceral and insightful from the perspective of how people react to 'otherness' and how this is internalized. One of the most important issues when dealing with leadership and diversity is to look at the spaces in the workplace. Who inhabits which spaces?; who is excluded? and what happens if the space is transgressed? What happens when a woman walks into the boardroom full of men? What happens when a black person enters an all-white establishment? Does the 'other' have to be assimilated? Do they have to learn to be like the majority group, women executives proving their maleness, or black executives their whiteness? Are negotiation and co-existence tacitly agreed? Do they become the 'exotic other' and perform 'otherness' for the majority (see Said, 1973)? Leaders should reflect deeply about what happens in their workplace, what language is used, how they and their teams react to non-normative people and the subtle and the textured responses which determine the normative and exclude others.

## *Whiteness*

Whiteness is a term that aims to make white people visible to themselves as a racialized category (Andermahr et al., 2000). It is argued that white people have viewed themselves as racially neutral, which gives them power. Invisibility is, as noted by Burgin, a general instrument of power:

> Roland Barthes once defined the bourgeoisie as 'the social class which does not want to be named' ... By refusing to be named, the bourgeois class represents itself and its interests as a universal norm, from which anything else is a deviation ... White, however, has the strange property of

directing our attention to color while in the very same moment it exnominates itself as a 'color,' for we know very well that this means 'not white.' ... To speak of the color of skin is to speak of a body. The body denied here is a very particular body. (Burgin, 1996: 130–1, in Puwar, 2004: 58)

This is important for Critical Leadership especially when dealing with a 'Corporate European-American Axis of Maleness and Whiteness'. Power and patriarchy are still intimately linked, and whiteness is still regarded as neutral and normative, especially in corporations, although some progress has taken place. The task for those in leadership is to recognize this state of affairs and address this with urgency. When locating ourselves, the concept of whiteness can help bring 'normative' European-American behaviours and assumptions into focus.

## Working with diversity

The only possible way to take a critical view on diversity is from a perspective that is reflective and recognizes our own individual social location and historical-cultural position. Unless leaders can do this, then they address these difficult issues with huge blind spots triggered by their defence mechanisms. Diversity, as understood in popular culture, is 'white versus the other' or 'the other versus white'. However, when we explore diversity it also happens within 'otherness'. There is no such thing as a homogeneous Black voice, gay people, or women's experience. There are both collective experiences and within these a plurality of diverse experiences. Discussing diversity is problematic, as it inevitably threatens one's identity. When discussed in management and leadership circles dominated by white men, diversity also asks uncomfortable questions about privilege and power. The first thing to say is that marginalized minorities face discrimination in subtle and indirect ways. Treacher discusses the difficulty of addressing difference because it is both 'subtle and yet pervasive', she refers to 'a series of mantras being repeated ... it is not that I think these are inadequate or wrong but that they operate as shutters against thought, feeling and recognition of how we are all implicated in fantasies of self and other' (Treacher, 2000: 12).

My personal experience of workplace diversity and equality workshops is that they too often raise anxieties and often create defensive responses among the participants who are most in need of change, if culture change is to occur. These defences are displayed as either passive-aggressive responses of total compliance and silent resistance. This emerges as vocal resistance in small groups over coffee after the event, or, as one black colleague of mine told me, she was isolated and given silent treatment by colleagues after such an event. Another response is defensive rationalizing behaviours, such as 'we are all individuals here', 'we treat everybody the same' or 'are you calling me a racist?' Building trust in order to free up and have more transparent conversations is the only possible way to make progress. As every good psychoanalyst knows, pushing at resistance only creates more resistance.

When discussing diversity issues it is vitally important not to lose the ability to think or to speak. Diversity policies have made language central to their attempts to change behaviour; however, this has a double edge. It does help to improve negative images of racial and gender stereotypes, for example, but it also has other consequences as Andrew Cooper points out, 'one of the unintended consequences of Political Correctness is that it has bred a generation of stutterers' (1996: 2). People become afraid to speak, for fear of saying the wrong thing, and being accused of being racist or sexist. It is almost impossible to be 'politically correct' because there is no 'correct' and for those outside the academic/diversity discourse, the nuances and changing terms and acronyms used to describe a diverse population is very challenging. For example, what does LGBT mean and who do I apply it to? When should I say Gay, Homosexual, Lesbian or Queer when addressing this issue? How do I use Black, person of colour, brown, mixed-race, African-American, Asian, Indian-British? What is accepted in some countries, regions, and contexts is wrong in others, and finding a common language becomes increasingly difficult. Those outside of the latest agreed terms of reference find themselves stuttering or, worse still, silenced. Engaging people to change from all sides of the diversity spectrum means building trust, openness and understanding.

I am concerned about the alienation that occurs during 'equal opportunity and diversity purges' in the workplace, which can close down rather than open up dialogue. Learning the mantras is easy: 'celebrate difference', 'empower everyone', etc. Yet, if real change is to occur, leadership is required to bring the discussions and debates back to practice, and to tolerate mistakes, slips, misunderstandings in order to bring to the surface what is really happening, the subtle discrimination, and to identify where change is needed and to start a process to achieve this.

Using personal experience to locate 'personal and shared' ideas of normative behaviour and defences is the only starting point when dealing with diversity and difference. This is the place where systemic praxis takes place in leadership; thinking beyond what is the obvious and looking at the systems, structures and normative attitudes and behaviours that exclude and diminish minority and marginalized groups.

This is not something that can be learnt as theory or knowledge from textbooks or diversity workshops; it has to be personally and collectively engaged with. The successful future leaders will be those who are able to cope with diversity and difference.

## Diversity as a business case: beware!

Diversity issues are marginalized in management circles and business schools. When they are dealt with it is too often as an 'add on' to placate the liberal 'politically correct' lobby. Kandola and Fullerton take another approach, which emphasizes the business case for managing diversity:

that there are visible and invisible differences, sex, age, background, race, disability, personality, work-style ... harnessing these differences will create a productive environment in which everybody feels valued, where talents are being fully utilized and in which organizational goals are being met. (1994: 47)

R. Roosevelt Thomas, a US diversity consultant, also makes the business case and argues in more concrete terms that managing diversity is 'not about a moral responsibility to do the right thing', 'it is not a civil rights or humanitarian issue', it is about maximizing employee effectiveness and retaining competitive advantage when working in a global economy with an increasingly diverse workforce (1991: 16–17, in Fulop and Linstead, 1999: 56).

This utilitarian 'business case' for managing diversity in order to improve efficiency strikes me as very naïve and very dangerous when separated from ethical and human concerns. What happens when research shows that the most effective workforce consists of homogeneous groups? Bond and Pyle researched workplace diversity in the USA: 'A predominant research finding shows that while diverse teams can be creative, they also tend to experience less cohesion and greater turnover than more homogeneous work groups' (1998: 591). Using Thomas's rationale, the business case would now argue for diversity in areas that require creativity, such as design teams, and homogeneous teams for production. My guess is that it would have a pretty devastating effect on employee morale if the company divided teams by race, sexuality and gender, citing efficient working teams as the reason. Martin Parker in *Ethics and Organizations* (1998) suggests that utilitarianism is in a sense the logic of organization. While there is an academic debate about how ethics are applied to business, 'Desmond illustrates how marketing allows ethics to always be somebody else's problem' (ibid.: 8), leaders and organizations functioning without ethical concerns or a critical stance opens the doors to huge problems. It is also the case that, presented with an ethical stance, most leaders, in my experience, value it. This is where a critical leadership is called for; to challenge value-free policies that ignore ethics in favour of efficiency, without looking at the whole system ramifications and the human implications. Certainly, the business case will be a partial and important factor when making any decision, but to make it the total single factor opens the door to very serious consequences.

# Do women make good leaders? The essentialist debate

Historically, women have struggled for equality; to not be essentially defined by their biology or the traits that society considers inherently female or feminine, but to be considered as equals in regard to all kinds of tasks alongside men. One of the earliest examples comes from the Quaker movement in the 1650s. Margaret Fell was an important leader in early Quakerism, and later married George Fox, the founder of Quakerism. She wrote a public pamphlet entitled 'Women's Speakers Justified'.

> Those that speak against the power of the Lord speaking in a woman, simply by reason of her sex, or because she is a woman, not regarding the spirit ... such speak against Christ. (Margaret Fell, cited in Trevett, 1995: 57)

> The Spirit must not be quenched where it is poured upon the Daughter (George Fox, 1658, cited in Moore, 2000: 125)

> The role of women in the embryonic Quaker movement in the 1640s and 1650s cannot be understated. Women could access the divine 'inward light' as freely as a man, which put them on equal footing when it came to interpreting their divine inspiration and preaching the gospel. This was a radical revelation and challenged the male only clergy of the state church, but perhaps more threatening it challenged the social status quo, which led to public beatings and persecution. Even more radical was the fact that the Quakers, not only preached this truth but they practised it, in their own community and in the public sphere. Women, at their meetings, were able to speak on equal terms and women ministered to the general public at open meetings, and challenged the authority of clergy by interrupting sermons and they wrote pamphlets in large numbers. (Western, 2005: 355).

Mary Wollstonecraft wrote *Vindication of the Rights of Women* in the late eighteenth century. It has been a long struggle for gender equality, if this awareness was available in the 1650s, our progress has been very slow!

## *Essentialism*

> Essentialism is the view that the body provides the raw materials from which cultures craft their own interpretations and elaborations of gendered identities. Social construction is the view that gendered identities are formed as a result of cultural and psychosocial processes through which men and women are socialized into gender-specific constructions of how males and females are to act, think and feel. (Tolman and Diamond, 2002: 37–8)

Lynne Segal in *Straight Sex: Rethinking the Politics of Pleasure* (1994) finds that the female body is socially equated with passivity, receptivity, penetrability, and the male body with activity, directness, determination, impenetrability, and so forth. Segal says that while these representations may be sexist and seem stupid, we cannot ignore them, as they are inscribed onto us through social discourse, and are internalized. They become part of the lived experience (Sullivan, 2003: 128).

Some contemporary feminist theorists claim that 'essentialism' hinders the progress toward liberation (Rich, 1980; Butler, 1990). This argument is important in this leadership context as most of the management perspectives presented on women in business take an essentialist stance. For example, Professor Lynda Gratton has a new role as head of the Lehman Brothers Centre for Women in Business, the first research centre dedicated to this issue in Europe. When interviewed, she said:

> The sort of things women are good at – innovation, getting work done at the same time as getting on with people – are increasingly valuable as we move into a world in which flexibility and knowledge-sharing are a key ... women are good at networking, they just tend to network with people they like, men tend to network with more powerful people ... if we make organisations more humane guess what? They suit women. (*The Guardian*, 3 November 2006)

The problem with these essentializing statements is that they box women into fixed roles and traits and by implication men also. It is binary and reductionist: 'Men are from Mars, Women are from Venus', creating a polarization between genders and the standpoint that gender is biologically determined and socially fixed. Feminists have been arguing for a long time that their fixed identities based on their reproductive roles, as mother, nurturer and carer, have trapped them in social positions of limited freedom and power. It is very problematic then to claim that in the contemporary world these essentializing characteristics give women leadership advantage. This view that women's natural traits and strengths, listening, caring, relational are going to give them advantage in the post-heroic leadership world of the twenty-first century are supported by Sally Helgeson in her book *The Female Advantage* (1990) and Judy B. Rosener's book *America's Competitive Secret: Women Managers* (1995).

Challenging this essentializing and binary viewpoint, Simone de Beauvoir's classic statement that 'one is not born, but rather becomes a woman' ([1949] 1972: 295) indicates that woman is as much socially constructed as biologically determined. This means that it is the social perception of gender roles that determines how we interpret ourselves as gendered bodies, and how we should act and be in the world. Judith Butler, (1990) claims that there is no natural identity, no essence to gender; gender is something one is always in the process of becoming, through performative acts. It is through performative acts that our gender and identities become normalized (1990). This deconstruction of gender, sexuality and race, fuelled by post-structuralist theory, has created new insights but has also fragmented a notion of the universal. Therefore, when we speak of women, who are we speaking of if there is no essential gender? How can women fight for equality and liberation if the concept of woman itself is in flux?

Arguing that women make better modern leaders because of their specific essentializing traits is reductionist, keeping women in fixed stereotypes they have been struggling to liberate themselves from, and continues to reproduce social norms which are no longer appropriate or fixed. As demonstrated in the following quote, these essentialist norms are also colour-blind, and a hegemonic westernized view.

A woman's fixed identity immediately becomes problematic when location, ethnicity, culture and race are introduced:

> In the Indian context, woman has not been so neatly defined: she is made up of many attributes, some of which may dominate in different contexts and settings, others in other contexts. This is the ambivalent persona of the Indian woman, located in myth and popular culture, as both goddess and dangerous power (shakti), as virtuous wife and dangerous evil, both pure and impure in her embodiment, to be revered and worshipped but also to be controlled through direct regulation of her sexuality. (Thapan, 1997: 4)

Women are making ground, Walby (1997: 64) notes that there are 'massive changes taking place in women's employment and education which are transforming gender relations, for example, increasing their presence in professional and managerial positions in national and local government in the UK by 155%, in Science education and technology by 72% in literary arts and sports by 54%' (quoted in Fulop and Linstead, 1999: 52). On the downside, in the most senior positions women are not yet making significant inroads, only three FTSE 100 Firms have women CEOs, only 12 female executive directors (down from 20 last year) are in the FTSE 100 companies.

When researching this piece, it becomes clear that while gender in management and leadership has a high profile in academia and the media, the other diversity issues are almost absent. Sexuality, class and race, for example, rarely figure in management and leadership literature, and often are marginalized within diversity, alongside the gender issue which dominates. There is also within the diversity context, some marginalized groups that are more privileged than others: 'While the glass ceiling has been cracked quite significantly with gender, for race the concrete ceiling has just been chipped ever so slightly' (Puwar, 2004: 7).

## Conclusion

When I coach senior executives and other leaders, when issues arise regarding empowerment and diversity, for example, when we discuss moving from a command and control hierarchy to a more dispersed leadership, I take the opportunity to ask these questions:

- Who is sitting at the leadership table?
- Whose voices are being heard and whose aren't, and why?
- Whose values are being represented, and on whose behalf?
- Who is absent from the decision-making process?

I ask these leaders to observe their meetings, to observe their organization, to notice what happens in meetings and within themselves, using these questions to stimulate awareness of the structural power issues. They usually come back to the next coaching session with some powerful insights: 'At the board meeting there were ten men and one woman'; 'We had a meeting and the CEO spoke and the meeting went silent, people listened. When the HR director (a female) spoke, people interrupted, went to the restroom, got coffee'; 'We really try hard to be inclusive in this company, but we find at the European–Asian summit it is English and German voices which never shut up. The Asian leaders are much less quick to speak, and they don't often get the opportunity.' These questions open up the normative and strategic and structural issues, they go beyond the content of the meeting and ask the deeper question about power, norms and representation in the organization. As will be addressed towards the end of the book, these questions also go beyond the organization, to the stakeholders, the local community and the ecology and network associated with the organization. To ask questions like these we have to be able ask questions of ourselves. In turn, this creates a more transparent workplace, a more ethical organization. It opens up space for dialogue and for creative solutions to the issues raised by diversity in organizational life. It is an important leadership task to get the support to be able to ask these difficult questions and to work towards addressing the challenges and opportunities raised by the issues of diversity.

# Note

1 By projection(s), I use the term in relation to the object relations school of psychoanalysis. Here it refers to Melanie Klein's (1959) original work on splitting, projection and introjection. Powerful feelings (often unwanted feelings) are split off from the conscious mind, and can be 'projected' and located in another person. These can be feelings of love, idealization, or perhaps hatred or envy. For example, parents often project their unfulfilled ambitions onto their children. An angry boss may project his unwanted feelings of anger onto his personal assistant. Feelings of idealized love may be projected onto a spiritual or powerful leader. In reality, the leader may be full of human frailty but this goes unseen by the adoring follower who only sees through their lens of love. Projection and splitting help to explain how the leaders can at times abuse their power. For example, the child abuse scandal in the Catholic Church was allowed to continue for so long as the priests were held in high esteem; people wanted to believe in their purity and projected their feelings of pure love and idealization onto the priest who represented the church. This meant splitting off and denying the unwanted feelings of distrust, and disgust at the possibility that abuse was taking place.

# Asymmetric Leadership

In an attempt to provide a critical answer to the question 'What is leadership?', I aim to highlight the complexity and nuanced issues that arise when we look in detail at leadership. I have taken a small case study of a single social movement, a few pages of text written about the Communist Revolution. This case study offers an insight into the multiple layers of leadership aims to help identify some of the key issues raised in the book so far, but is not claiming to be a definitive list of leadership themes. It identifies seven leadership themes from this single movement, and makes the case that leadership is asymmetrical rather than a symmetrical, uni-directional, top-down process. However, within 'asymmetric leadership', I acknowledge the important role and agency of the individual leader.

## Lenin and the leadership of the Communist Revolution: A case study

This chapter offers an analysis of a short piece of unpublished writing by Leon Trotsky on Vladimir Lenin's role in the Soviet Revolution. Traditional 'Great Man' theory of leadership would focus solely on the hero leader, Vladimir Lenin. Post-structuralist writing and many critical theorists focus on the process of leadership and minimize the individual's role (Grint, 1997; Collinson, 2006). However, as this short text demonstrates, leadership is not solely situated in a single person, or a small group, but it reveals at least seven faces of leadership, including a 'heroic' individual leader. One of the key tasks of leadership research is to find ways of understanding and explaining how the individual leader and collective process of leadership occur in organizations. Trotsky's description of Vladimir Lenin's leadership provides an excellent account of some of these processes. Leon Trotsky's writing on Lenin's leadership offers a very interesting narrative which gives a valuable account, in its content and sub-text, which I will use to help illuminate the importance of the inter-dependency between solo actors and collective actors when understanding leadership. The relationship between individual leaders and followers, distributed leaders and collective leadership groups, determines the relationship between a leader and the process of leadership. This is not an attempt at using Marxist theory to explain leadership, the case study could have be of any organization or social movement. The text in italics is taken from Trotsky's unfinished work *The Class, The*

*Party and the Leadership* (Trotsky, 1940). I have added the headings in the text. The text is in chronological order and is selected from two pages.

# The setting

*The Bolshevik Party in March 1917 was followed by an insignificant minority of the working class and furthermore there was discord within the party itself. The overwhelming majority of the workers supported the Mensheviks and the 'Socialist-Revolutionists', i.e. conservative social-patriots. The situation was even less favourable with regard to the army and the peasantry.*

## 1 *Intellectual leadership*

*What was the 'active' of Bolshevism? A clear and thoroughly thought out revolutionary conception at the beginning of the revolution was held only by Lenin. The Russian cadres of the party were scattered and to a considerable degree bewildered. But the party had authority among the advanced workers. Lenin had great authority with the party cadres. These elements of the 'active' worked wonders in a revolutionary situation, that is, in conditions of bitter class struggle. The party quickly aligned its policy to correspond with Lenin's conception, to correspond that is with the actual course of the revolution.*

*Thanks to this, it met with firm support among tens of thousands of advanced workers. Within a few months, by basing itself upon the development of the revolution, the party was able to convince the majority of the workers of the correctness of its slogans. This majority organized into Soviets, was able in its turn to attract the soldiers and peasants.*

## 2 *Unconscious leadership: personifying the object*

*A colossal factor in the maturity of the Russian proletariat in February or March 1917 was Lenin. He did not fall from the skies. He personified the revolutionary tradition of the working class.*

## 3 *Corporate leadership: the Party*

*The vital mainspring in this process (the revolution) is the party, just as the vital mainspring in the mechanism of the party is its leadership. The role and the responsibility of the leadership in a revolutionary epoch are colossal.*

## 4 *Dispersed leadership: cadres*

*For Lenin's slogans to find their way to the masses there had to exist cadres, even though numerically small at the beginning; there had to exist the confidence of the cadres in the leadership, a confidence based on the entire experience of the past.*

## 5 *Individual leadership*

*Hence the cheap gibes about the role of individuals, good and bad. History is a process of the class struggle. But classes do not bring their full weight to bear automatically and simultaneously. In the process of struggle the classes create various organs, which play an important and independent role and are subject to deformations. This also provides the basis for the role of personalities in history. There are naturally great objective causes, which created the autocratic rule of Hitler but only dull-witted pedants of 'determinism' could deny today the enormous historic role of Hitler.*

## 6 *Social movement leadership: the masses-proletariat*

*The October victory is a serious testimonial of the 'maturity' of the proletariat. But this maturity is relative. A few years later the very same proletariat permitted the revolution to be strangled by a bureaucracy, which rose from its ranks.*

## 7 *Symbolic leadership*

*The arrival of Lenin in Petrograd, on April 3, 1917, turned the Bolshevik Party in time and enabled the party to lead the revolution to victory. Our sages might say that had Lenin died abroad at the beginning of 1917, the October revolution would have taken place 'just the same'. But that is not so. Lenin represented one of the living elements of the historical process. He personified the experience and the perspicacity of the most active section of the proletariat. His timely appearance on the arena of the revolution was necessary in order to mobilize the vanguard and provide it with an opportunity to rally the working class and the peasant masses. Political leadership in the crucial moments of historical turns can become just as decisive a factor as is the role of the chief command during the critical moments of war. History is not an automatic process. Otherwise, why leaders? Why parties? Why programmes? Why theoretical struggles?*

# Analysis of text

The analysis shows how the Trotsky text offers at least seven differing examples of leadership, which together make up a leadership process:

1  Intellectual leadership
2  Unconscious leadership
3  Corporate leadership
4  Dispersed leadership
5  Individual leadership
6  Social movement leadership
7  Symbolic leadership.

Together, these describe how leadership is asymmetric. It is never static or situated in a single role or place or group. Leadership moves between these positions (and probably others) and this case study demonstrates how leadership is a process. Trotsky describes the leadership process manifesting itself in diverse ways. However, because it is a process, it does not undermine the agency of individual leaders, corporate bodies, collective actors or dispersed leadership, they are all essential parts of the process and the asymmetrical nature of leadership.

## 1 *Intellectual leadership*

Trotsky's first point is that Lenin showed the intellectual leadership that managed to appeal to the masses in a very short period of time. Intellectual leadership is a powerful and vital leadership form and is increasingly being separated from other forms of leadership. Nowadays leaders select specialist experts, strategic consultants, 'thought leaders' or think tanks (collectivized thought leadership) to support them in this role. Intellectual leadership has never been the sole property of an individual. Lenin's thinking was obviously built upon Marx and Engels and was formulated among other leading socialist thinkers of the time. Lenin, however, did manage to do the following:

(a) bring original and creative thinking to this process;
(b) synthesize ideas into a coherent form;
(c) translate these ideas into action and strategies;
(d) communicate these to others.

## 2 *Unconscious leadership*

### *Leadership and projective identification*

Trotsky describes Lenin as 'personifying the revolutionary tradition of the working class'. This means that 'the masses' were able to identify with Lenin, to project onto him the ideals of the revolution, their ideals of freedom. Lenin was able to both stimulate and contain these projections, which made him an extraordinary leader. Earlier, I identified how a leader must work with the unconscious as well as conscious using A.K. Rice's (1965) work and this is a further example of this. One of the key aspects of leadership is to act as a figure that attracts projections from others. In psychoanalytic theory, this refers to transference and counter-transference and projective identification (Klein, 1959). Most of the mainstream leadership texts focus on how a leader projects their image outward, and less on how they attract conscious and unconscious projections. The leader themselves may have differing levels of awareness of this process, and if they are unaware, danger lurks! If they identify with these projections, a powerful energy can be gained between the two parties but a real danger arises if the leader identifies with projections without awareness to such as extent that they lose their sense of self and believe in the fantasy that they are either truly omnipotent and superhuman (commonly referred to as being seduced by power) or, conversely, a demonic bad object when things aren't going so well. Projections take place all the time in small and large groups and at an institutional and even a global level. One of the strengths of the individual leader over group leadership is the capacity to attract projections from large groups, where a 'faceless' collective body, for example, a boardroom or political party can find it much more difficult. This can explain how, even though collective leadership may be taking place, it might appear that an individual is acting as sole leader, as this makes it easier for the wider populace to engage with a process that has a figurehead.

Research has shown how a single leader figure attracts multiple rather than singular projections. Lilley and Platt (1997: 319–37) researched 621 letters written to Martin Luther King and found that followers (activists in the civil rights movement) saw him as one of at least four identifiably different leaders and the division did not map naturally onto the background of the writer, for example, not all Black writers regarded him as first and foremost a black leader.

- Black leader
- Christian leader
- Non-violent leader
- Democratic leader.

King himself acknowledged these projections: 'I am aware of two Martin Luther Kings … the Martin Luther King people talk about seems foreign to me' (Oates, 1982: 283).

Ramor Ryan (2003) describes a living charismatic leader who also attracts multiple projections; the masked 'Zapatistas' leader Sub-Commandante Marcos, who uses writing and intellect as his main leadership tools:

> Marcos' writing is beautiful and expansive enough to fit every revolutionary tradition. His great ruse is to make each tradition think of him as representing them – the indigenous say he is one of them, the guerrillas claim him as one of their own, the intellectuals include him in their pantheon, Mexican nationalists see him as a great Mexican nationalist, NGOs see him as an advocate for NGOs, Marxists see him as one of their sect, anarchists claim him as part of their tradition, even the base church sees him as an advocate of their preferential option of the poor. This potentially complex multiple personality disorder is of course symbolised by the ever-present mask. Would the real Sub Marcos, please stand up?! (Ryan, 2003: 31)

The mask does not cover a multiple personality disorder but is a very astute leadership ploy aimed at attracting the projections of diverse and marginalized groups and their global supporters. The mask makes Marcos mysterious and enhances his enigma, his charisma and therefore influence (he smokes a pipe which comes out of the mask, making him immediately recognizable as an individual), but more importantly it allows others to project onto the mask whatever they wish. Behind the mask is the person they want to believe in and Marcos uses this device as part of his ploy to create solidarity across globally diverse and marginalized groups. This verse comes from a Zapatista international gathering in 1997:

> Behind our black mask
> Behind our armed voice
> Behind our unnameable name
> Behind what you see of us
> Behind this, we are you
> Behind this, we are the same simple and ordinary men and women who are repeated in all races painted in all colours speak in all languages and live in all places.
> Behind this we are the same forgotten men and women,
> The same excluded, the same untolerated, the same persecuted, the same as you.
> (Ruggiero and Sahulka, 1998)

Leaders bear several meanings, projected onto them from their followers. Creating a leadership image, which attracts the desired projections, has become a huge business in its own right. Executive coaching, the make-over, the spin doctor and other 'image creators' all aim to help the leader give out the right image and signals, which in turn determine the type of projections a leader attracts. Contemporary leaders regard this just as important as getting the right message across. A leader is a receptacle of others' projections. Leaders such as Sub-Commandante Marcos can utilize this by establishing themselves as 'screens' to promote and contain specific projections, unifying and gaining support and solidarity around a project.

Lilley and Platt draw an important implication from their work on Martin Luther King: 'That a social movement need not be consensual to achieve successfully an effective solidarity. What King represented was not consensus and yet there did appear to be an effective solidarity within the civil rights movement' (1997: 319). The solidarity described in the civil rights movement under Martin Luther King's leadership is also desired by corporate boards, who want employees to buy into their values and give loyalty to the company. Leadership, which can support this, will be much sought after. Leadership consists, in part, of an individual leader and a personality who, through their persona and image, attracts something with which individuals and collective actors can identify. A leader's ability to stimulate and to psychically contain and make sense of the projections of followers is an exceptional leadership quality.

## 3 Corporate leadership

Trotsky describes the corporate leadership shown by 'the party' as the vanguard of the revolution. Without this corporate and disciplined leadership, there would have been no revolution. The party was the revolutionary movements' inner corporate leadership body which is a hierarchical decision-making body. Within this hierarchy there is a powerful sense of corporate shared responsibility. This corporate sense of leadership can be seen in governments and boardrooms. Any group, whether it is a formal organization or an informal movement, requires organizing activities and some kind of discipline and boundaries, otherwise it would not be a recognizable entity. The collective actors and individual actors within an organization are in dynamic relationship, which is reflexive. The leader needs to be confident in the party leadership and in the cadres (dispersed leadership), who in turn need to be confident in the leader.

## 4 Dispersed leadership

Trotsky realized that without cadres (leading party activists), Lenin's message would not have had any impact. The individual leader (Lenin) and the corporate leadership (the party) needed to have confidence in the dispersed leadership on the ground (the cadres) to make any impact on the masses. It is the dynamic relationship between the individual (Lenin), the group (the party leadership), the network (the cadres) and the masses which makes up the process of leadership. In contemporary organizations it is recognized (as identified by Trotsky) that a dispersed leadership is the vital link between activity on the ground and organizing 'the masses' to take up their followership role.

## 5 Individual Leadership

The interplay and interdependence between the individual leader and the collective actors are paramount in Trotsky's account. Both are absolutely vital; denial of either creates a myth about leadership. In this citation Trotsky states that history is about collective actors struggling (class struggle in Marxist terminology) and he acknowledges clearly that this does not occur automatically but that individual leaders, 'personalities', for good or bad, have an enormous role.

## 6 Social movement leadership

Trotsky also acknowledges the enormous responsibility and role of the collective actors who become more than simply followers (as in most leadership accounts) but a collective leadership actor in their own right. The social movement itself acted as an inspiration and took on a momentum of its own. Recent non-violent revolutions in the ex-Soviet bloc are examples of this social movement leadership, one country inspiring another to change. The 1917 Russian Revolution inspired many in other countries to act: the collective actions empowering others and demonstrating leadership in a global sense. Trotsky also explicitly holds these collective actors 'the masses' to account for the failings after the October Revolution when the proletariat *'permitted the revolution to be strangled by a bureaucracy, which rose from its ranks'*. Collective actors can become more than disparate individuals and passive or active followers, especially given the right conditions. It is not always conscious organized actions in which collective actors take leadership; mass demonstrations, rallies, boycotts are methods in which leadership can be demonstrated. There is another less tangible sense in which 'masses' collectively act without formal organization and find ways to resist tyranny through small multiple acts of defiance or in large outbreaks of resistance. The term 'active followership' doesn't do justice to the role a collective actor can take in the leadership process. The collective actor rarely if ever acts without leaders (sometimes these are informal and temporary) but the energy they act with is not always determined by these leaders, who may be led by the movement itself, causing them to respond in different ways. The collective actor differs from 'the crowd' when it acts to bring about a change. The solidarity and activity of the collective actor are driven by unconscious group processes, which are unpredictable. One of the tasks of individual and corporate leaders is to read and understand these collective processes and then to acknowledge, stimulate and influence them appropriately. This is achieved through reflexivity, feedbacks, loops of communication between complex networks and the leadership, and also through symbolic leadership actions (see below).

## 7 *Symbolic leadership*

Lenin's arrival in Petrograd mobilized the vanguard, which in turn mobilized the masses. Trotsky identifies that an individual leader, who personifies for followers their ideals, can have a huge social impact through symbolic actions, such as Lenin's arrival at Petrograd. These actions are signifiers to followers and can be catalysts providing the inspiration for social movements or organizations to take risks and create change. This symbolic leadership can happen through many mediums, timely appearances, speeches, media messages and images, sometimes many small actions – perhaps a CEO unexpectedly offering support at factory floor levels to show the need for solidarity during lean periods, but sometimes a big 'performative act' creates a dynamic change in a situation. Martin Luther King and his leadership cadre understood the performative act well, and many of his actions were planned and calculated to maximize the symbolic value of his personifying leadership, such as leading demonstrations and getting imprisoned; thus he symbolized the resistance. Mahatma Ghandi was perhaps the master – his famous walk to the sea to produce salt was a typical symbolic action. Britain had a monopoly on salt production in India and Gandhi's decision to produce salt by the sea would have no big real/material impact but symbolically represented two needs: self-reliance and resistance: (1) the need for India to become self-reliant; to produce its own salt which is a fundamental product used by all, and it is a natural product of India; and (2) to resist British rule by not paying the salt tax. Symbolic leadership is in many ways the most potent form of leadership, especially in the contemporary age of media saturation, IT and global communications. But even before this, 'being a leader' and getting the message out has always been about symbolic action, these words are attributed to St. Francis of Assisi: 'Preach the Gospel at all times; if necessary, use words.'

Unfortunately despots and dictators have often excelled in symbolic leadership, Hitler's Nuremburg Ràlly of 1934 was a powerful example of the Nazi leadership turning a political rally into symbolic event which was a living enactment of their future vision of Nazi Germany. Terrorist groups such as Al Qaieda have become media masters of using symbolic leadership to devastating effect.

## Conclusion

This short excerpt from Trotsky highlights key aspects of the relationship between leadership and followership. Trotsky's final sentence of the paragraph brings together some of the key elements of leadership. 'History is not an automatic process. Otherwise, why leaders? Why parties? Why programmes? Why theoretical struggles?'

In this case study, it is the combined impact of individual leaders, corporate leadership and collective actors who co-create and implement leadership actions and organizational strategies. These are underpinned by intellectual theory based on historical analysis and Marxist thinking but which are constantly, contested, revised and developed against experience. The dispersed leadership cadres in touch with the masses are key to creating a reflexive network to bridge the gap between the leadership and the experience on the ground. It is the dispersed leadership which is used to convince large numbers of people, 'the masses', to follow these ideals and support this programme of action. This provides a parallel with the dynamics of leadership operating in the contemporary organizational and business world. Wherever leadership exists within an organization, this dynamic occurs and is particularly relevant when normative control (Etzioni, 1961) is used; when 'hearts and minds' need to be won over rather than coercing a reluctant followership. In the latter case, the followers create a dependent followership acting with little agency, in the former, followership is an active role and encourages dispersed leadership whereby individuals throughout an organization can actively take up their authority and agency. When followers act to make a change, they become a collective leadership actor in their own right.

The leader (and those close to him/her) provides intellectual leadership, personifying leadership and is a symbolic figurehead. The leadership cadres interact with the 'masses' and communicate theoretical ideas, values and strategies/programmes to the followership; also symbolizing revolutionary spirit, commitment and vigour in small actions and engagements. This study shows how all are active ingredients of what we call leadership. Yes Lenin was vital to the Russian Revolution, no, Lenin didn't manifest this on his own!

So leadership is asymmetric in that it has no straightforward logic or symmetry, it is not easily definable and does not easily sit within prescriptive frameworks. Efforts to tame leadership and offer functionalist interpretations at best add to our ever-expanding knowledge of leadership or offer a common language with which to discuss leadership. However, it is important that the common language used for leadership does not demand premature closure on the subject. That it does not seduce us into a sanctuary whereby we feel better because we have a leadership framework or model which acts as a child's safety blanket; symbolically reassuring but no use in an emergency!

This case study and analysis mirror how leadership itself is enacted in the contemporary world. Leadership models, frames and definitions can help us to understand the leadership process if they are presented thoughtfully and acknowledge the asymmetrical and subjective nature of leadership. Equally, they can undermine understanding by presenting reductionist and false symmetrical models which offer misleading solutions.

Leadership as an integrated ideal, whereby individuals and collective actors work together in a seamless leadership process is a desirable aim rather than an achievable one. It is and always will be an ongoing process of adjustment, and theorists and practitioners alike will always contest leadership.

Leadership is not something that innately belongs to, or is situated within, an individual. Nor is it solely a process which happens regardless of individual agency and autonomy. Like it or not, there are exceptional individuals who make great leaders. This is not an either/or choice and presents a false dichotomy. When asking what leadership is, other questions need to be asked, such as, how do a leader and leadership team operate within a system? How do they select, lead and collaborate with others? How does the organization reflexively work with the leader/leadership team? How does the intellectual leadership, the ideas put forward get disseminated and embraced? How do ideas from throughout the organization, from the grassroots, become encouraged? How does dispersed leadership work in practice? How is the organizational culture co-created to sustain or attack the leadership? How does the leadership use power to marginalize or empower, or both? These are just a few of the important questions that require ongoing research.

Asymmetrical leadership acknowledges that leadership is not a mechanistic, rational and functional object. It is multi-faceted and operates at multiple levels simultaneously, as the analysis of the Trostky text demonstrates. The seven different leadership stances found are not comprehensive but do identify how leadership is neither one thing nor the other but all at once. Individuals and collective actors are both independent and interdependent, separate entities and yet paradoxically entwined in a process of organizing and influence. When this process has a direction, is purposeful, and moves towards goals and achievements, this is called leadership.

# 6

# The Discourses of Leadership

## Introduction

The chapter now takes a broad historical overview of management-leadership[1] theory and practice over the past century. Mapping out some of the broad themes of leadership theory provides the necessary heuristic tool through which we can begin to identify leadership discourses. These underpinning discourses originate through wider societal phenomena beyond the world of management and leadership theory. The aim is to identify dominant discourses that determine what the commonly held perceptions, assumptions and norms are when discussing leadership. When these discourses are identified, it becomes clearer to the critical thinker how each discourse impacts on the leadership they are observing or participating in. I have used the term characters of leadership to describe how an individual embodies a discourse of leadership, this draws on Alisdair MacIntyre's work on characters (1985).

## What is a discourse?

> In the social sciences, a discourse is considered to be an institutionalized way of thinking, a social boundary defining what can be said about a specific topic, or, as Judith Butler puts it, 'the limits of acceptable speech' – or possible truth. Discourses are seen to affect our views on all things; in other words, it is not possible to escape discourse. For example, two notably distinct discourses can be used about various guerrilla movements describing them either as 'freedom fighters' or 'terrorists'. In other words, the chosen discourse delivers the vocabulary, expressions and perhaps also the style needed to communicate. (http://en. wikipedia. org/wiki/Discourse, accessed 9 Aug. 2006)

The study of linguistics is complex and the word 'discourse' has various meanings. This Wikipedia definition identifies the generic meaning, and from a critical viewpoint discourses have an immense impact on power and social relations. A discourse defines what can and cannot be said about a subject. 'We embody the discourses that exist in our culture, our very being is constituted by them, they are part of us, and thus we cannot simply throw them off' (Sullivan, 2003: 41). Stakeholders in society or organizations therefore have vested interests in maintaining certain discourses while marginalizing others. It is difficult to grasp how a discourse confines us into a way of thinking as they often represent what seems normal and are therefore out of consciousness (that is the point – they maintain social relations as they are without reference to critique). However, when identified, the 'actor' can step outside of the discourse and begin to analyse its impact. Discourses, which on the surface appear helpful and empowering, can be structurally disempowering. For example, counselling seems unarguably a helpful thing to offer somebody who is distressed, therefore, it is good. However, the therapeutic discourse can have the impact of making people more vulnerable, more self-obsessed and narcissistic, and it has been claimed that it diminishes community at the expense of further individualizing society (Furedi, 2003). So that if you have concerns, you speak to a counsellor which undermines social networks and communal support. The effect of counselling therefore might undermine the individual building long-term support networks, and turning to friends, offering them the opportunity to take up the rewarding role of friend and helper.

But acknowledging the underlying discourse can itself be liberating, for example, understanding the discourses around sexuality and the 'hetero-normative' discourse which marginalizes single people, gay people, etc. can free an individual and group from feeling they are failures, or wrong for not fitting into this pervasive discourse. Finding ways in which to address power elites and discourses which impinge on human liberty can then follow. It is important to mention that discourses are generally hidden because they represent the normative and exist in most cases in an unconsciously unintentional way; both to those they privilege and to those they marginalize. However power élites also use their vested interest in retaining power to control and manage discourses, for example through control of the media. It is not the power itself which is destructive but that the power is hidden and creates truths which become the accepted norm. It is only when the discourses and the tensions they hold are revealed that they can be contested:

> In history as in love, the real harm in power imbalances comes not from the dissymmetry of itself but from the its sentimentalization or institutionalization, from the denial of the reality of unequal power through its normalizing as the truth of gender, class, race, status, beauty, wealth, romance, professional authority, national identity, historical difference. (Halperin, 2002: 21)

## Three main discourses

This book identifies three main discourses within organizational leadership in the past century, and goes on to suggest an emergent fourth discourse in Chapter 13:

Discourse 1   The Controller
Discourse 2   The Therapist
Discourse 3   The Messiah

The following three chapters will describe the historical and social influences on management and leadership in the workplace over the past century. Figure 6.1 sets out each discourse showing the signifying qualities each discourse represents. This should be referred back to as each chapter on the discourse is read.

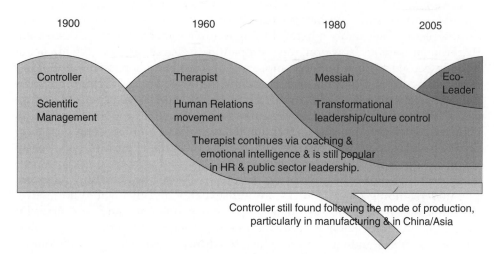

**Figure 6.1**   Approximate timeline of the leadership discourses

Figure 6.1 shows that the *Controller discourse*, while losing dominance, does not disappear but declines. The Controller leader is still to be found in certain industries and sectors in the West, contemporary ideas, such as job re-engineering, demonstrate how scientific management still remains as a discourse. This leadership discourse is very relevant in Asia and China following the same mode of production from which it was derived, the factory, heavy industry and production lines.

Likewise, the *Therapist discourse* emerges in the 1930s, peaks in the 1970s and then declines but still has a strong presence in the leadership discourse, which is epitomized by emotional intelligence and the growth in coaching. The *Messiah discourse* has strong links to the heroic leader of past ages, but was reformulated by the Transformational leader emerging in the 1970s and has been a dominant figure ever since. However, the strong cultures they aim to create and their ability to deliver are now being questioned, hence the decline. The Eco-leader discourse is the new emergent leadership discourse which embraces the ecology of leadership (see Chapter 13).

## The characters of leadership

I will begin by explaining how I use the term 'character', drawing on Alisdair MacIntyre's work (1985). The leadership literature review and the research I carried out for my doctoral thesis (Western, 2005) revealed trends in leadership that require articulating in a new way. MacIntyre's notion of characters offers a structure to explain how an individual leader embodies a discourse. This is different from taking up a role within an organization, it is not taking up a leadership approach or style as such. It is closer to internalizing a specific archetype which embodies a certain discourse. This notion of characters provides a new lens through which to understand what leadership means at any given period in history. It goes beyond the everyday implications of what it is to be a manager or leader. To name somebody a 'leader' signifies a specific meaning within the organization and within society. This empowers but at the same time entraps the 'leader' in a symbolic position in relation to others. This symbolic relationship between a leader character and others has not been static, it emanates from not one, but three distinct discourses in the past century, passing through three main transformations. The three discourses did not follow one another in clean succession. They overlap, merge and blur in different scenarios but at any one time it seems that there is a single dominant leadership character representing a discourse.

Leaders are commonly viewed through a monocular and rationalist lens, from which universal claims are made as to what constitutes a good or excellent leader. Lyotard (1984) describes the 'tyranny of reason' being exposed by post-modern forms of life in an attempt to liberate the modern project from this technocratic rationality. In an attempt to liberate the concept of the leader from this 'tyranny of reason', the book draws upon MacIntyre's (1985) work on characters to explore what social character the leader represents and signifies within their organizations and to society at large.

MacIntyre separates his notion of characters from social roles. He links the character to the dramatic tradition citing Japanese Noh Plays and English Mediaeval Morality plays as examples, as they have a stock set of characters immediately recognizable to the audience. These characters partially define the plots and action and by understanding the characters, the audience has a means of interpreting the behaviours of the actors who play them. A similar understanding informs the intentions of the actors themselves and other actors' responses to them. He suggests that certain social characters hold the same purpose within particular cultures: 'They furnish recognisable characters and the ability to recognise them is socially crucial because a knowledge of the character provides an interpretation of those actions of the individuals who have assumed those characters' (MacIntyre, 1985: 27). MacIntyre views a social character, for example, the English Gentleman in the nineteenth century, as a signifying force within society, who represented elitism, power, honour, etc. but MacIntyre does not provide a full account of this process. Turning to psychoanalytic theory, Jacques Lacan's work illuminates this process. Lacan theorized that the primacy of the signifier entails 'the domination of the subject by the signifier' (Dor, 1997: 49). The signifier is an unconscious process that comes before language. This extends beyond the individual to social manifestations, where signifiers have primacy over the social/ cultural consciousness and our collective sense-making capabilities. Lacan's use of the term signifier in this way complements MacIntyre's description of character and helps explain how they impact on society. It is the unconscious signifying role that gives the character its power. If one can imagine the workplace as a theatre, then a discourse will impose and claim the ground rules, what can and cannot be said and done, it will set the scene for the narrative to unfold. A leadership discourse will frame how relationships take place, how socio-technical systems and work processes unfold, and how the organizational culture is established within the boundaries of any given discourse. A leadership discourse in the modern workplace is embodied by a leader, a leadership team and a dispersed leadership. They all work within a leadership discourse, usually the same one in any given organisation, but sometimes not. When it is different, this can be a sign of creativity, an adaptive culture, or it can be a cause for conflict and dysfunction, or both. All who relate to these embodied leader characters dialogue with and maintain the discourse. The other actors at work, the employees, the leadership colleagues and peers, stakeholders and customers all have roles to play within the familiarity and the confines of the discourse.

MacIntyre's social characters emerge and decline, reflecting cultural and social changes and he cites the manager as one of modernity's characters. MacIntyre sees the manager character as representing the obliteration of the distinction between manipulative and non-manipulative social relations, as the epitome of scientific efficiency: 'The manager treats ends as given, as outside his scope; his concern is with technique, with effectiveness in transforming raw materials into final products, unskilled labour into skilled labour, investment into profits' (MacIntyre, 1985: 30). MacIntyre's view of the manager as a character is insightful and connects the manager with society and culture at large, rather than with the individual actors, confined within the limits of their organizations. MacIntyre continues clarifying his position on what the manager character represents:

> The manager is not ... able to engage in moral debate. They are seen by themselves, and by those who see them with the same eyes as their own, as uncontested figures, who purport to restrict themselves to the realms in which rational agreement is possible ... the realm of fact, the realm of means, the realm of measurable effectiveness. (ibid.: 30)

MacIntyre's view of these characters as being uncontested suggests they are taken for granted in an unquestioned way, even by themselves. The discourse assumes managers are necessary, their role is to ensure efficiency, so it is 'natural' that we have managers. The majority of the mainstream management literature treats them in the same unquestioned manner, attempting to measure or to identify their effectiveness.

Reviewing the management/leadership literature has led me to propose that the manager/leader has not been a single character as suggested by MacIntyre, but has gone through three distinct phases in the past century. Each phase relates to leading organizational change, leading organizational culture, and leading organizational success. The manager character defined by MacIntyre focuses on the Leader as Controller discourse that attempts to influence through command and control, as described in Chapter 7. His description fitting a bureaucratic manager suited Taylorist and Fordist managerial approaches. Business leaders working in this controller discourse identify only with rationality and efficiency. MacIntyre's interpretation of the manager character now seems outdated, a retrospective view, still around but surpassed by the two other leader characters.

## Conclusion

These discourses reflect back to society its own culture and unconscious pre-occupations and concerns. They are not separate from the wider world. The three leadership discourses which have emerged from this research are recognizable when identified, but are unknown to us in everyday transactions. Consciously the leader character is thought of by followers, employees, stakeholders, as simply the organizational CEO, or MD, a business or political leader, an 'uncontested figure'. Unconsciously the character signifies the contemporary tensions within the workplace and the culture surrounding work.

Having established the three leadership discourses, Controller, Therapist and Messiah, I will now describe the historical context and background to each of them in turn. Chapters 7, 8, and 9 will each take a single discourse and highlight critical themes arising in the management-leadership literature and the economic and socio-historical conditions that help explain how these discourses arise and fade. They will also show how the discourses influence the organizational culture and relationships within organizations and wider society. As previously stated, management and leadership are not easily separable. Leadership has only become a popular term within management in the past 30 years, while the activity of managers encompassed leadership prior to this. The Messiah discourse will help to explain the rise of Transformational leader and the contemporary re-awakening and renewed populism for 'heroic' leadership figures and leadership in general.

## Note

1 I use management and leadership interchangeably in this part of the book.

# 7

# The Leader as Controller

The first leadership discourse, the leader as Controller, emerged from the modernist and functionalist movements, which took hold in the early twentieth century. Previous feudal, epic and class models of 'heroic leadership' were eroding, faster in some places than others. Meritocracy as an idea was being led by the USA in the West, and by Lenin and the ideas of Socialism in the Soviet Union. While these societies organized on different political and economic principles, they both share the philosophy of modernity and the privileging of science and rationality as drivers of progress (Gray, 2003). The workplace became a place of economic struggle, the nations who could develop the economy most effectively could also lead in scientific research which further boosted the economy and also weapons development and manufacturing that was hugely important in the first part of the twentieth century (and arguably still is).

In the workplace, 'the efficiency craze' took hold, the mythical, hero-leader of old diminished and the language of 'logos' dominated the language of 'mythos', bringing scientific management, and functionalism to the fore, developed in the USA but it was also embraced by Stalin:

> American efficiency is that indomitable force which neither knows nor recognizes obstacles; which continues on a task once started until it is finished, even if it is a minor task, and without which serious constructive work is impossible ... The combination of the Russian revolutionary sweep with American efficiency is the essence of Leninism. (Hughes, 2004: 251)

## Scientific management, the efficiency craze

In the early part of the twentieth century, industrialization was rapidly developing and with it a rationalistic and technocratic management style emerged. Science, industry and modernity raced forward and with it came Taylor's book *The Principles of Scientific Management* (1911). Taylor's ideas were formulated and disseminated at the turn of the century and became widely acclaimed in 1908 when the Harvard Business School 'declared Taylor's approach the standard for modern management and adopted it as the core around which all courses were to be organised' (Barley and Kunda, 1992: 370). Soon it became the first American business fad which historians call 'the efficiency craze'. Later, Max Weber's (1930, 1947) influential writings advocated that bureaucracy is like a modern machine, while other organizational forms are like non-mechanical methods of production. Weber argued that bureaucratic organization is the most technically efficient form of organization possible, as it is based on 'rationality' but he was also wary of the dehumanizing aspects of this rational and efficient organizational form which he said threatened the freedom of the human spirit and the values of liberal democracy; hence his view that bureaucracy could easily turn into an 'iron cage'. Taylor's scientific management forged ahead within industry, caring little for Weber's concerns and, while Taylor's work was hugely influential, it was immediately challenged as being dehumanizing.

Taylor's aims were to construct self-activating workplaces so that workers could labour without the need of close supervision. Taylor also wanted to remove wage limits for high earning workers, taking away the focus on the division of surplus and creating a collaborative force, not for humanistic reasons but to maximize the actual size of the surplus. Taylor's work was immediately challenged and later the Human Relations movement castigated his work as 'inhuman, reducing workers to the level of efficiently functioning machines' (Pugh and Hickson, 1971: 93). However, as Pugh and Hickson point out, Taylor's principles were often inadequately understood and, while Taylor is demonized, his work was part of a greater context of mechanization and his methods have been widely used in car plants, fast food chains, modernizing the communist USSR and even in athletic and sports training. Taylor may have been misunderstood but the dangers of rationality alone and his assumption that a fair deal could be struck between workers and bosses to maximize profits for both, were also interpreted as naïve in post-war industrialized Europe and the USA. Taylor lacked an understanding of human motivation, the importance of social relationships and emotional needs in the workplace and he used rhetoric about workers not being required to think which supported those who wished to marginalize his methods. Scientific management signified rationality and purely technical solutions and represented the machine metaphor (Morgan, 1986) which, while important and apt for its generation and for the modes of production, it also conflicted with other social metaphors to which workers and social intellectuals aspired at this turbulent time in the early twentieth century. The machine metaphor of rationality and efficiency delivered huge economic success. Henry Ford epitomized this approach by de-skilling work and mechanizing production along the bureaucratic massification of work conditions and experiences. Henry Ford symbolically offered the large wage of $5 a day to his workers to keep them at the production lines. Due to higher income and lower priced goods (the price of Ford cars fell from $780 in 1910 to $360 in 1914) led to a cycle of production and consumption which has been the basis of the expanding economies in the West ever since. The rationalization of the workplace went beyond the factory and into other non-production sites such the education system, and other public sector and service jobs. The management style was, in Etzioni's (1961) terms, 'utilitarian control', where power is based on a system of rewards or punishments, coercive control was also present in some of the more austere factory conditions where the threat of unemployment and hunger were very real in the first third of the twentieth century. Workers were controlled by economic means and complied with alienating conditions to maximize their material rewards. However, this led to workforce alienation and workers, unhappy with being treated like robots, turned to trade unions and labour disputes to improve their working conditions.

# The Leader as Controller discourse

The leadership style and discourse was that of command and control. Managers and foreman were expected by national and industry leaders to control the work-force, through coercion and through offering transactional (financial) rewards. Alerted and worried by the socialist revolutions in the early part of the century, industry and political leaders thought that workers and their organized unions could rise up against the political, economic and elite class leadership. There was also a residue from Victorian days where working-class people were considered, at worst, almost as a sub-human race and, at best, as 'children' who needed a pater-nalistic firm hand. In the UK and the USA, working-class Irish immigrant labour was treated in this subhuman way in the early part of the twentieth century.

The Leader as Controller discourse was produced and maintained by economic, political and social drivers. The factory production lines required a controlling ethos, and offices, banking and the growing public sector were also run on tight bureaucratic, hierarchical and functional lines, which also required leadership characters who embodied the Controller discourse. Particularly in the early part of the twentieth century, social class, deference and hierarchy remained very strong social features, and an elite controlling leadership from the educated classes maintained this.

# Conclusion

Scientific management in the workplace, the machine metaphors abound, mass production and consumption, Fordist production lines and the race towards the promised land of science, efficiency and modernity, all contributed to the Leader as Controller discourse. At work you were given instructions, told what to do. If the managers could coerce, manipulate and cajole their workforce into increased efficiency through controlling their behaviour, then they were excelling at their jobs. In the minds of the workers and in society generally, the  shared idea of a manager was represented by the controlling 'factory foreman' and became a rec-ognizable figure, embedded in the social framework. The leaders of the factory and office were caricatured as the 'tough foreman' or bureaucratic manager, on the side of the company owner, the 'fat cat boss', or the evil and controlling capi-talist by the political left, who used foremen and other managers to oppress the workers in their inhuman factories. When I worked in a factory in the late 1970s, I recall a song which highlights the delineation between workers and first line management; it was sung after a few pints on a Friday night, by the shop floor workers to the tune of 'The Red Flag':

> 'The working class can lick my arse;
> I've got a foreman's job at last.'

The factory, the mode of production at this time, created a workplace in which the Leader as Controller discourse was important and a machine metaphor was in many ways apt. Production lines were machine-operated and could be very dangerous; strict rules had to be enforced to reduce injury and to maximize efficiency. Jobs were designed in line within the context of rationalizing production. Job satisfaction was displaced onto the wage packet at the end of the week. Personal satisfaction came at the end of the shift, where a strong distinction between one's work identity and one's domestic identity was drawn.

The Enlightenment had promised so much, using science and rationalism as its tools, linked to the values of toleration, democracy, personal freedom and human equality. Scientific management was an expression of this movement in the workplace, and played its part in improving production, and the mass production of consumer goods, democracy and personal freedom were however marginalised in favour of efficiency. Economic wealth increased and living standards improved. However, it also created tensions in the workplace and the whole Enlightenment project was questioned after the Second World War:

> Taylorism enacted a view in which managers thought and workers laboured; authority relations were based on obedience and contractual obligation; command and control systems were based on information held by a few; and careers tended to imply a unitary trajectory through a single organization in which one was entirely dependent on one's higher authorities for progress. (Krantz, 1990: 51)

During the Second World War this model of rationalization, efficiency and mass production produced the weapons that changed the face of war. Taylorism and Fordist methods were much admired by Hitler (Gray, 2003) and the concentration camps utilized the factory model and Scientific Rationalism as their organizing means. The Nazis despised the democratic and liberal aspects of the Enlightenment but, like the Soviet Communists, shared the Enlightenment's most hubristic hopes, believing that the power of technology could be used to transform the human condition, including the power to commit genocide on a hitherto unprecedented scale (ibid.: 13). Science, technology and the ideology of modernity had been exposed as a force that could produce efficiency and high production but it did not necessarily deliver the hoped-for industrial utopia. Worse still, a dystopia had occurred in Nazi Germany, followed soon by Stalinist Gulags, and Mao's Cultural Revolution. In the West, the factory and the mass production line also had dehumanizing implications. The machine metaphor of efficiency and rationality at all costs was in desperate need of change. Post-war hopes of a better future in the West meant re-thinking the Leader as Controller discourse, in order to meet new social conditions, cultural expectations and also to improve productivity in a fast-changing workplace. The leadership discourse of the controller was no longer tenable. A better paid and better educated workforce demanded new social relations with its political and workplace leaders.

# 8

# The Leader as Therapist

The second leadership discourse, 'The Leader as Therapist', emerged from the influences of post-Freudian psychology and post-war democratizing movements and they came to a head in the 1960s counter-culture social movements that embraced radical individualism, emotionalism and egalitarianism. This 'therapist discourse' was also a reaction to the cold rhetoric of scientific management and the dehumanizing aspects of modernity.

## The Human Relations movement

Elton Mayo is widely held to be the founder of the Human Relations movement. He was appointed to the faculty at Harvard and brought multidisciplinary perspectives to the problems of industry. Gareth Morgan points to motivation and the relationship between individuals and groups as the important issues arising from Elton Mayo's Hawthorne experiments in the 1920s and 1930s. These experiments raised questions about informal as well as formal organization and placed the importance of Human Relationships in the limelight, which dealt a blow to classic management theory (Morgan, 1986: 41). Mayo argued that group processes amplified an individual's psychopathology and therefore the first line supervisor became the most influential change agent in the workplace.

The Human Relations movement, like much management theory, is discussed in the literature as though it developed in a social vacuum called 'the business world'. A broader perspective is required and the management/leadership literature needs to be placed within its wider context of social conditions in order to understand how leadership trends emerge.

The period between the wars and immediately after the Second World War was extremely turbulent. Workers movements and socialism were gaining momentum and a fear of Bolshevism made leading industrialists to focus on considering that it was in their interests to cooperate with labour (Barley and Kunda, 1992: 372) as they realized that command and control, 'the Controller discourse', wasn't working. Those returning from the Second World War demanded a 'land fit for heroes' and returned with a new confidence and raised expectations, no longer willing to put up with pre-war class and social divisions and dire working conditions: 'The new rhetoric focused on entitlements and improved working conditions ... the upshot of which was the birth of the personnel administration' (Barley and Kunda, 1992: 372).

Leadership at this time was regarded as hugely important but was also problematic. The key focus was on classical leadership and trait theories that produce 'great men' and hero leaders such as Winston Churchill and Ghandi, but they also produced Hitler and Stalin. After the Second World War and, fearful of another rise in fascism or the rise of communism, social scientists and organizational psychologists, as well as political figures, worked on building democratic social structures, institutions and on democratizing the workplace. This was aimed at preventing a return to autocratic leadership styles, to promote democracy and also to appease a workforce who wanted more than to be treated like production line machines and live in urban slums. The challenge for leadership was to find ways to move from 'Great man' and trait theories towards more democratic models, which could counterbalance power abuse by individuals and elites. Democratic leaders would attempt to empower passive followers in the hope of undermining their tendency to behave like compliant actors blindly following dictators. The other aim was to avoid class war, and prevent social revolution which was fuelled by poverty and anger at poor working and living conditions and mistreatment at the hands of controlling leaders and exploitative capitalists. For example, in post-war Britain, the Tavistock Institute was formed to work on these democratizing organizational issues. This signified a change from the pre-war Tavistock clinic which worked on a much more paternalistic model. The link between the Human Relations movement and previous attempts at industrial betterment are important, as there was an important change in the values that underpinned the efforts to improve working life. The industrial betterment movement came from a tradition linked to the Protestant notion of duty, where philanthropic and paternalistic wealthy owners had a moral duty to their workforce to educate them and to improve the workers rather than improve working conditions. The Human Relations movement shifted the focus from paternalist duty to an ideal based on a win–win situation. Production would improve as 'happier workers work more productively' and to get happier workers meant improving democratic structures. More production also meant more consumption, improving living conditions and the national economy. Motivation linked to productivity was the key, set within greater democratic structures, and more worker autonomy and greater satisfaction at the workplace. The Human Relations movement was led by Mayo and influenced by Kurt Lewin. An example of the Human Relations early success came through the Tavistock Institute's researchers Trist and Bamford (1951) who pioneered new 'open socio-technical' systems after researching the coal mining industry. They applied the biologist, Von Bertalanffy's open systems theories to organizational theory, linking the interdependent relationship between technological changes and the human-social system. They found that new technology could bring work improvements but only if the social and psychological effects were accounted for.

A paradigm shift took place in organizational leadership thinking. The leadership/manager role was no longer to coerce and control the workforce but to motivate the workforce. Good industrial leadership meant privileging employee social and psychological welfare over controlling their behaviour. New technology in the coal industry had brought in new work practices, initially inspired by scientific management, which were causing many difficulties. Trist and Bamford designed and restructured working relationships, creating autonomous self-regulating teams, which they called 'composite work-groups'. Moving away from individual piece-work rates and working on monotonous partial tasks, with individuals competing with each other, workers gained satisfaction from completing whole tasks together in teams and were paid bonuses on what the team achieved. This proved very successful and a model that was widely copied. There was a general ideology at this time in the USA and Western Europe, which wanted democratic workplaces for the betterment of the human race, matched with an economic striving for socio-technical systems, which took Human Relations into account. This was to have the effect of both motivating and stimulating the workers and maximizing production and output.

We will now look at some examples of leadership and management theory, arising from the Human Relations movement.

## Therapeutic culture and the rise of emotional management

The Human Relations movement began as an optimistic movement to provide an antidote to scientific management, rationalism and the failings of the Leader as Controller discourse. Another cultural shift took place in the 1960s, beginning in the USA, and it was a move away from liberation collectivist ideologies (e.g. socialism), which sought a change of power relations with greater material equality. The 1950s and 1960s had delivered rises in living standards for many, and a grow-ing middle class with new mass-produced appliances and consumer goods focused their attention on other things. A counter-culture flourished and the personal growth movement (Rogers, 1961; Maslow, 1968) epitomized the new focus on the self. This counter-culture soon became mainstream and it promised salvation no longer through organized religion but through personal therapy techniques, eastern philosophy and spirituality in its widest sense. The 'self' became an icon, which required nurturing. Collective activity became a struggle for identity and equal opportunity. New social movements such as feminism, the environmental movement and the peace movement grew and while they were collective actors and they had a social agenda, their influence was to shift from the politics of the social, to the politics of identity; the slogan 'the personal is political' highlighted this move (Giddens, 1982; McCarthy and Zald, 1987; Melucci, 1989; Diana and Eyerman, 1992; Castells, 1997). As these trends became mainstream and the workplace became an increasingly important site of community and identity formation, so personal growth became aligned to workplace ideology through the Human Relations movement. Abraham Maslow was a key influence as manage-ment theorists took on board his work on self-actualization:

> Early research into the psychology of work undertaken in the 1950s stressed communication processes and individual adjustment needs and worker motiva-tion. Following Maslow's hierarchy of needs schema (1954, 1956) researchers tried to find ways in which workers' higher needs, for self-esteem and self-actualization, could be met at work. (Casey, 1995: 79)

Maslow's work was formative and led to research methods in an attempt to test the ideas as to how participative or democratic leadership improved workers' motivation. It became widely accepted that healthy relations between individuals and groups are vital to create democratic and personally fulfilling workplaces, promising to put people before machines and taking a developmental model of human potential. Harnessing social and psychological theories, the Human Relations movement reflected the personal growth explosion, privileging the emotions and personal identity. The Human Relations movement merged with the wider and pervasive 'therapeutic culture', harnessing this to the leadership discourse. This new leadership 'Therapist' discourse underpinned leadership thinking in the mid to late twentieth century.

## *The triumph of the therapeutic*

The American pychologist Philip Rieff announced in 1966 'The Triumph of the Therapeutic' predicting later events which have led to an 'ever widening definition of psychological distress' which require some form of therapeutic intervention (Furedi, 2003: 111). Furedi calls this an age of traumas, syndromes, disorders and addictions which give rise to a culture of fear and vulnerability and the pathologization of emotions, applied to an ever-widening section of the population. This in turn has led to a huge increase in counsellors, therapists and self-help books to offer professional help with these burgeoning problems. Therapeutic culture has gone beyond the realm of treating the suffering; Dineen (1999) argues, 'Therapy is too good to be left to the ill.' Therapy has gone beyond treating the ill in four ways:

1   The definition of 'illness' became much broader with new 'illnesses' being recognised such as post-traumatic stress disorder, attention deficit disorder, multiple personality disorder, all syndromes rather than illnesses and with them huge rises in diagnostic rates took place.
2   Other areas of 'ordinary' life, one's self-esteem, relationships, bringing up children, all became potential areas of concern and therefore areas accessible to therapeutic intervention.
3   Recognised 'illnesses' such as depression found a much wider constituency. What in the past was understood to be misery or melancholy became a treatable illness called depression, encouraged by the pharmaceutical industry. It found a mass market for treatments such as Prozac encouraging this trend. In Britain, depression accounted for 1% of the population born in the First World War, 5% in the Second World War and jumped to 10-15% in the 1960s.
4   Therapy culture entered healthy social arenas and became 'a way of thinking rather than a way of curing psychic disorder'. (Bellah et al., 1996 in Furedi, 2003)

Fitzpatrick (2006) writes:

> A therapeutic culture has become pervasive. It is apparent in the emotionally charged speeches of the Prime Minister, in the conduct of royal funerals, in the

numerous confessional TV shows, in the shelves full of self-help manuals in every bookshop. It seems that everybody now speaks the language of 'self-esteem' and 'support'; displays of emotional incontinence and claims of victim-hood are guaranteed social approval.

So what led to the shift from an optimistic movement focusing on liberation and human potential to the adoption of an 'emotional illness' mindset, which highlights vulnerability and requires professional intervention? Some claim the erosion of traditional community and intensifying feelings of uncertainty and alienation have led to this response (Rieff, 1966; Giddens, 1991). The 1960s, which led to the explosive growth of the Human Potential movement, helped create a culture, which Lasch (1979) describes as individualistic and narcissistic.

The focus on identity and self-realization aimed at and has been successful in, liberating individuals and their particular collective movements from the baggage of traditional, religious and social constraints, which now seem to belong to a past era. However, as Moskowitz (2001) points out, the progressive forces, which focused on identity and aimed at personal liberation, freedom and acceptance of diversity led to something quite different: 'The identity politics of the 1960s laid the ground for America's obsession with feelings in the 1970s.'

Frank Furedi (2003) argues that the optimistic 1960s became less radical and less optimistic, creating today's therapeutic culture of vulnerability. Melucci (1989: 134) discusses the continual diffusion and penetration of therapy into daily life; he also sees this as a symptom of the growth, in complex societies, of need for identity and self-realization. However, Melucci does acknowledge the real psychological tensions thrown up by what he calls our complex society:

'The vast differentiation of modern life, the multiplication of roles and social masks each person is called to assume and the burdens of making choices quickly create enormous psychological tensions' (1989: 141).

With the loss of traditional sites of community, the extended family, lifelong neighbours, of the church, the workplace has become an ever-important communal site where these tensions are played out. Therapeutic culture has had a huge influence on how leadership is enacted in the workplace, and how emotions and subjectivity are managed and organized.

## The workplace and therapeutic culture

The reaction to scientific rationalization and wider social changes led to the Human Relations movement, which adapted psychological theory and helped ease therapeutic culture into the workplace. Initially a positive movement, aiming to motivate and help employees self-actualize, it began to reflect the tensions and culture of wider society. This changed the mood from focusing on motivation and happy workers towards a growing concern as to how the emotions are being used and manipulated in the workplace. The use of emotional labour and emotional management (Hochschild, 1983) are seen as worrying developments for some, and there is growing evidence of workplace survival techniques alongside motivational theories. The Human Relations movement opened the way for the manager/leader to become an active agent in the management (and manipulation) of the emotions:

> Managers all the way down to first line supervisors were said to require commu-
> nication skills, sensitivity in interpersonal relationship, methods for instilling if
> not inspiring motivation and knowledge of how to mould the dynamics of a group.
> (Barley and Kunda, 1992: 375)

Zaleznik (1997: 56) likens the role of the leader to that of a medic or therapist running a clinic:

> Nevertheless, the Human Relations school was right in that organisations are
> indeed social systems and are arenas for inducing cooperative behaviour. As
> such, they are quintessentially human and fraught with all the frailties and
> imperfections associated with the human condition. So much so, in fact, that one
> especially wise chief executive officer once commented, 'Anyone in charge of an
> organisation with more than two people is running a clinic.'

The quote from Barley and Kunda suggests a positive developmental attitude from the Human Relations movement, while Zaleznik promotes the distortion of this, as therapeutic culture takes ascendancy. The idea that CEO is running a 'clinic' in an attempt to 'induce cooperative behaviour' is an example of the change in mindset from the optimistic idea of liberation and human potential to likening the workplace to a psychiatric clinic and the implication that the leader's role, therefore, is that of a senior clinician or therapist.

MacIntyre (1985) points out that the manager is very much a modern character, a product of the Enlightenment. His 'manager character' epitomizes the positivistic principles that scientific knowledge enables us to master our environment and ourselves, which Gray (2003: 2) calls the Enlightenment faith. The manager's role, due to the influence of the Humans Relations movement had now changed, as Nikolas Rose (1990) points out: 'The management of subjectivity has become a central task for the modern organization'.

A contemporary leadership/management role has shifted from leading an organization to managing the internal life of the employees. To be a successful manager or leader, one now has to expertly manage emotions:

- their own emotions;
- the emotions of their reportees;
- the emotions and psychodynamics of the group/team;
- the cultural/emotional expectations from above (not always explicit).

## Emotional intelligence

Therapeutic culture within the leadership discourse has blossomed. Emotional intelligence (EI), popularized by Goleman (1995), has become an everyday expression and within the leadership discourse a 'good' leader is expected to have a high emotional intelligence. EI focuses on change through the conscious process of the individual self-improving through self-awareness and a new form of personal growth. Mayer and Salovey, who first used the concept and term Emotional Intelligence, describe EI as 'A type of social intelligence that involves the ability to monitor one's own and others' emotions, to discriminate among them and to use the information to guide one's thinking and actions' (1993: 433). EI has been used and changed in many directions but these five headings are common to its essence:

1   *Self-awareness*: Observing yourself and recognizing a feeling as it happens.
2   *Managing emotions*: Handling feelings so that they are appropriate; realizing what is behind a feeling; finding ways to handle fears and anxieties, anger and sadness.
3   *Motivating oneself*: Channelling emotions in the service of a goal; emotional self-control; delaying gratification and stifling impulses.
4   *Empathy*: Sensitivity to others' feelings and concerns and taking their perspective; appreciating the differences in how people feel about things.
5   *Handling relationships*: Managing emotions in others; social competence and social skills.

Essentially EI has been developed by Daniel Goleman and others to fit the business mindset and highlights the use of the management of emotions as the primary tool of the manager/leader. Many assessment and training techniques are available to support this type of leadership work. Mayer and Salovey have criticized Goleman for his expansion and distortion of the term and theory they founded:

> What makes you smarter is understanding your own feelings better argues John Mayer. Goleman has broadened the definition of emotional intelligence to such an extent that it no longer has any scientific meaning or utility and is no longer a clear predictor of outcome. (cited in Schwartz, 2000: 296)

The contemporary popularity of EI reflects trends in American human psychology as it offers a positivistic, empirically measurable and developmental model (even if, as Mayer points out, the science is unscientific). The subject can measure their personal levels of EI and attend training to improve their intelligence. This is seductive and naturally creates a market place in assessment and training tools and offers HR leaders valid measurable outcomes, for which it is easier to justify their budget expenditure than if they entertain more complex phenomenon with less measurable outputs. It cleverly links the competing trends of leadership discourse; the rational and the emotional rhetoric (Barley and Kunda, 1992), which make those on both sides of the debate happy. There is, however, a growing scepticism about measuring EI and its unsubstantiated claims (Mayer et al., 2000).

## Emotional management and emotional labour

Emotional management is the attempt to manage employees' emotions to improve productivity. In Huy's paper, 'Emotional balancing', he advocates that 'to maintain operational continuity in a radical change context, recipients' emotions also have to be carefully managed' (2002: 33). Huy, in a three-year research study, praises middle managers' ability to manage competing emotional demands as they experienced a severe downsizing of the workforce. He praises them for working 80-100 hours a week, over a three-year period: 'to implement change whilst simultaneously attending to their work-group's operational continuity and their subordinates' emotional stability' (Huy, 2001: 49). Huy calls this 'emotional balancing' but his work ignores questions about the emotional balance between work and home life, and the state of these managers' mental and physical health after this long slog. The middle managers, he claims, balanced the emotional pressures coming from above, senior management and below, their reportees. At one point a memo was received from senior management to middle management, articulating 'expressions of cynicism will not be tolerated. We are in positions of leadership and must display enthusiasm at all times to everyone' (ibid.: 49).

Huy goes on to describe a manager leading an 'emotion-attending' training session which followed a morning's communication briefing regarding turbulent changes where job losses were raised. Huy writes that, despite his scepticism of 'touchy feely' approaches, these subsided when he interviewed workers following this session. In the 'emotional attending' session employees were asked to draw their collective experiences of the work situation: 'Anxious people in lifeboats, caravans lost in deserts and big thunderstorms began to appear and were displayed around the room and individuals started to realize how similar they were and they started to laugh and joke about them' (ibid.: 52). The consultant running the session then showed them a model of transition and explained how it was 'normal and common to have these feelings' (ibid.). Huy goes on to draw on psychological literature to support the notion that expressing one's feelings is healthy. In Huy's study, he says the outcome of these sessions produced more work from the employees and less absenteeism. However, the evidence linking these types of 'emotions sharing' sessions with increased productivity is very weak. The whole psychotherapeutic project from which these emotion-sharing workshops are derived is contested, and the empirical evidence for the success of therapy or that expressing one's feelings improves mental health is also contested (Eysenck and Hans, 1953; Masson, 1990). The superficiality of an afternoon's 'emotional session' is unlikely to have any deep personal impact and, worse, can create cynicism. It is a weakness throughout the management literature that the successful claims regarding emotional intelligence and emotional management are accepted with limited research and with little critical attention. Writing as an experienced psychotherapist, it is difficult to hear management trainers and coaches who make outlandish claims about their 'life-changing' programmes. Human change is hard, personal change is a struggle, behaviour and emotional patterns go deep. When counselling individuals, change occurs but it is often slow, arduous and not guaranteed.

Emotional labour is 'to create a publicly observable facial and bodily display' (Hochschild, 1983: 7) or 'to mask all emotions and intention behind bland smiling and agreeable public faces' (Jackall, 1988: 128). The aim is an attempt to create the correct company persona, whatever that might be. R. Janie Constance writes about best leadership practice and cites the Chief Executive of Yum Brands (Taco Bell, KFC, Pizza Hut, etc.) as an example: 'Each person is trained to be a customer maniac. Yums' goal is to train all 750,000 [a global workforce] to have a customer maniac mindset' (Constance, 2003: 47). There is nothing in her article to suggest the probable coercion involved in this process of getting low paid employees to go through basic training to learn how to perform the emotional labour required to demonstrate the expected company persona of being a 'customer maniac'. The Yum employees are rewarded through patronizing tokens of recognition that are described as best practice, e.g. prizes and email congratulations. This is reminiscent of the discredited treatment of mentally ill patients in total institutions (Goffman, 1961) using a form of behavioural treatment known as 'token economy', whereby tokens were given as rewards for good behaviour, e.g. cigarettes were given for 'good' behaviour and were withdrawn for 'bad' behaviour. This example offers an interesting mix of theory, taking the ideology of motivation from the Human Relations movement and distorting it to produce emotional labour. Taylorism is then recalled where diversity is eliminated and production takes place precisely and homogeneously across the globe to produce exactly the same burgers and pizzas in each outlet. The employees are expected to mirror the Tayloristic production approach, with the added pressure of also mass-producing conformist emotions to create a mono-cultural workforce of 'customer maniacs', aiming to eliminate global difference and give the customer a uniform burger with a uniform smile, and a uniform 'Have a nice day'.

## Coaching

The newest kid on the therapeutic-managerial block is Executive Coaching. Coaching has become a big industry and is growing in popularity, and is particularly focused on leadership:

> It is speculated that there will be 70,000 coaches in the US in 2007, with a similar proportion in the UK, with membership of the International Coaching Federation having soared from 1500 in 1999 to 8200 in 2005'. (Joo, 2005, cited in Swan and Cwerner, 2006: 17)

> What is clear is that the market has spoken. Many of the world's most admired corporations, from GE to Goldman Sachs, invest in coaching. Annual spending on coaching in the United States is estimated at roughly $1 billion. (Sherman and Freas, 2004: 83)

Coaching is clearly a manifestation of counselling and therapeutic culture in spite of some denial from parts of the coaching community, which likes to differentiate itself from counselling and therapy, however, the similarities are indisputable:

> Two people sat in a room talking. One charges the other for their time and skills. The 'expert' listens to the 'client' and is expected to help her/him, hence the financial exchange. This scenario describes a number of activities, for example, executive coaching, life coaching, counselling, psychotherapy or individual consultancy. While these activities have different emphasis, what they have in common is a direct lineage to what became known through the work of Sigmund Freud as the 'talking cure' i.e. psychoanalysis. (Western, 2006: 31–4)

Despite the attempts at differentiation, the link to psychotherapy is clear, the couch is replaced by office chairs, but the activity remains grounded in the therapeutic principle: talking about oneself to an expert listener with psychological or 'people skills' as a way of improving oneself.

Coaching has other lineages and influences such as sports coaching and consultancy, but, in essence, coaching is the 'talking cure' for leaders and managers. The reason why the coaching community tries to make a sharp distinction between itself and therapy has two key underlying factors; marketing and pricing. First, selling counselling and therapy relates to selling a deficit model, i.e. 'you have a problem' which is a difficult sell in the commercial world! Work-focused coaching followed the explosion of counselling. Psychoanalysis and psychotherapy had been for the rich or the very disturbed, whereas the growth of counselling had become mainstream. It was cheaper as counselling training was less arduous and the client contact time was shorter than classical psychotherapy. Counselling became widely available through tele-counselling support lines, and many institutions including workplaces offered counselling in their support systems.

Coaching at work emerged through the growing use of one-to-one consulting, career counselling and through 'employment assistant counselling programmes' offering support to workers as part of their health and benefits package. Initially coaching was slow to become popular as it was offered as either 'remedial coaching' following the deficit/problem counselling model, or focused performance coaching which echoed sports coaching techniques and worked on specific issues such as giving a presentation.

In the early days of coaching, the perception was that if you were recommended, or instructed, to see a coach, you were in trouble, your performance was not up to scratch, you needed 'fixing'. There was also a stigma to coaching reflecting the fascination and an underlying fear of therapy. The power of the shrink to see your shadow side, the fear of being exposed, the fear of showing emotions, remained associated with the coaching process, although as therapy culture became more pervasive socially this diminished. Senior leaders in male-dominated workplace cultures (Collinson and Hearn, 1996) were initially particularly resistant to these perceptions. Warren Bennis agrees that coaching and counselling overlap; he argues that coaches go beyond corporate matters and ask personal questions such as what makes you happy, and that it is easier to say I am going to see my coach (for counselling) than it is to say I am going to see my therapist (Salerno, 2005).

Another underlying factor that separated coaching and counselling was cost, therapy and counselling were available at up to 20 times less than coaching costs. As a business proposition, it was wise to differentiate the products; making coaching expensive also helped it become a prized possession.

While coaching clearly grew out of counselling, there is a different emphasis. Coaching, like counselling, has many manifestations, but in the workplace coaches on the whole focus on work-based performance and often very short-term interventions. The aim is to change behaviour and enhance workplace performance. When directing the Coaching Masters level programme at Lancaster, I differentiate coaching and counselling by suggesting that counselling focuses on self-actualization, while coaching focuses on role-actualization.

When working with leaders as a coach, one can work deeply on personal issues but the anchor point for the coach is always performance. If you work on the self, how does this impact on role and performance? This helps keep the coaching from drifting into pure therapy. Coaching draws upon many therapy traditions, for example, from the cognitive behavioural approach, the non-directive approach, solution-focused approaches from the family therapy tradition, and neuro-linguistic programming which is a magpie approach drawing on multi-therapeutic sources, with questionable credentials.

To market coaching and entice business leaders to engage and purchase it, the image had to change from reparative work to dynamic performance-focused work, and change it did. Coaching took a positivistic turn and re-branded itself as the new leadership panacea. A typical website for coaches demonstrates how coaching embraces positivist psychology, promising quick and easy solutions, to increase both your performance and your happiness. A secular version of the 'Prosperity Gospel', see Box 8.1.

---

## Box 8.1    Example of a coaching website

From the San Francisco East Bay Coaches International Coaching Federation website http://www.eastbaycoaches.org/faq.htm

**What is the basic philosophy of coaching?**
Simply put, that we humans are great, that we're all discovering what we really want, and that we can get what we want faster and easier by having a coach who can help us remove the obstacles that get in our way.

**Who hires a coach and why?**
People hire a coach because:
They want more.
They want to grow.
They want it easier.
It's as simple as that. Coaches help a client get all three. Quickly.

**What happens when you hire a coach?**
Many things, but the most important are:
You take yourself more seriously.
You take more effective and focused actions immediately.
You stop putting up with what is dragging you down.
You create momentum so it's easier to get results.
You set better goals that you might not have without the coach.

---

Within the workplace, coaching has become a badge of honour, a privilege, you are given a coach if you are being fast-tracked to success. Coaching became cool, rather than a stigma.

In reality, coaching can be an effective developmental tool, its main strengths are its one-to-one focus and the creation of a reflective thinking space (Western, 2006). Individual coachings strength is that it really does tailor development to an individual; the disadvantage is high cost of one-to-one coaching, and the individual focus of many coaches can drift in to personal growth and therapy, buying into narcissism and individualism at the expense of a systemic approach. The coaching relationship is a confidential one-on-one relationship but who knows what goes on behind the closed doors of coaching? How does a coachee (the client) or the HR director judge what is good coaching unless they have a lot of previous experience?

The positive feedback reported from coaching is skewed in the favour of coaches, as any one-to-one attention, a person paid to listen to you, is attractive to one's personal ego and is usually welcome. An experienced skilled coach will create a reflective space, a space to think, a space to be creative, amidst the noise and busy-ness of business life and will offer valuable feedback and interpretations leading to improved self-understanding and behaviour change. For leaders, improved self-awareness, communication skills and an understanding of the psychodynamics and the projections one receives in role are valuable indeed. This is the main task of coaching (ibid.) which is difficult to achieve in a contemporary workplace that embraces a culture of manic activity. Swan cites Anthony Giddens who believes that therapeutic culture (including coaching) is useful in this way:

> Anthony Giddens (1991; 1992) argues that traditional sources of guidance on how we should lead our lives, such as religious authorities, local communities and our families have become much less influential. Referring to this process as 'de-traditionalisation', he suggests that how we understand who we are, how we should live, and who should help us, is being reconfigured in contemporary society. In essence, for Giddens, this means that the self is no longer given to us, but has to be made. This is where therapeutic cultures can be helpful, according to Giddens, since they provide both solace and resources for self-formation. Solace is needed in his view, because the modern self is much more insecure … Therapeutic cultures, in his view, do not destroy the self, and its relationships, but make them. (Swan, 2006: 4)

However, from a critical perspective, one must look beyond an individual's solace and to the wider structural and systemic issues. Swan and Cwerner go on to assert that the view of coaching cannot be seen as ideologically benign:

> The irony is of course that coaching and other apparently content-free pedagogies do carry and reproduce ideas and ideologies. As Foucault shows us, techniques are not neutral … therefore, what we have in coaching is a *covert content, an invisible curriculum* that is determined by the very techniques of coaching, the modes of questioning, the language used, etc. (Swan and Cwerner, 2006: 16)

The pedagogies which coaching inhabit in the workplace re-affirm and reproduce the therapeutic culture in the workplace. For some, like Giddens, there are many positives, for others (Rieff, 1966; Rose, 1990; Furedi, 2003; Western, 2005; Swan and Cwerner, 2006), there are dangers that therapeutic discourse helps to reproduce dissatisfied narcissistic individuals whose lives becomes obsessively inwardly focused and risk-averse. This in turn reinforces a fragmented alienated society, undermining solidarity, community and agency.

Coaching is both a therapeutic intervention to support leaders, but coaching skills are also becoming essential for today's managers and leaders. Company cultures are now being told that they should embrace 'coaching cultures'. These websites are indicative of the mood:

> Coaching is becoming a new model for leadership.
>
> A leader-coach actively works with their staff to help them be more productive and satisfied. Coaching improves the quality of managerial ability, which subsequently improves employee and customer satisfaction.
>
> Organizations who have employees being coached experience higher retention rates and higher performance standards. Individuals have better odds of reaching success with a coach. Leader-coaches often develop themselves as a result of the experience of coaching others. Coaching really is a win/win. (www.odysseycoaching.com, accessed 12 Sept. 2006)
>
> Our vision is:
>
> In a COACHING CULTURE, all members of the culture courageously engage in candid, respectful coaching conversations, unrestricted by reporting relationships, about how they can improve their working relationships and individual and collective work performance. (http://www.wabccoaches.com/bcw/2005_v1_i1/feature.html, accessed 12 Sept. 2006)

The 'Leader-coach' is perhaps the final confirmation, if needed, that the Leader as Therapist character is truly here. Rieff's 1966 book announcing the *Triumph of the Therapeutic* seems to be an accurate description in which the therapeutic age has entered one of the last bastions of patriarchy, the competitive, male-orientated world of leaders within corporate America.

## A cradle to grave therapeutic work experience

The Leader as Therapist, discourse has been the dominant discourse from the 1960s until it was challenged in the 1980s. However, it still remains a powerful force as demonstrated by the rise in coaching. Emotional management and emotional labour are examples of the expectations laid upon management to influence the emotions of employees. Emotional intelligence, psychometric testing, coaching and examples such as 'emotion attending sessions', which are essentially brief therapeutic interventions in the workplace, led by managers-leaders or consultants are common. Within the management training and development industry, 'therapeutic culture' is found everywhere. There are outrageous claims of success from some of these interventions with claims of life-changing experiences and personal mastery that would shock even the most experienced and optimistic psychotherapists who know how desperately hard it is for people to change their behaviour. Even Freud, the architect of modern psychology, believed that intensive psychoanalysis at best, could not provide a cure but could only help people live better with their misery!

The therapeutic tools available to the manager begin at recruitment with the various psychometric testing and interview techniques, continue through the employee's life, with the huge array of 'pop' psychological approaches to management, training and personal and team development, including personal profiles, reviews, assessments. Many workplaces offer 'employee assistance programmes' of free counselling. Then there are the coaching sessions, emotional attending sessions, consultancy training events and the more subtle and tacit implications of leaders as therapist characters creating 'therapeutic or coaching culture'. Finally, comes the outplacement counselling-coaching interview providing the final touches to the complete cradle to grave emotional management service!

## Conclusion

Human Relations managerial approaches used very different methods to the preceding scientific management but had the same overall aim of raising production and efficiency. Scientific management relied on controlling workers, using transaction and coercion as a means. Human Relations management aimed to raise morale, promote motivation and enhance co-operative working. The focus of the manager/leader shifted towards managing the emotions rather than controlling the workforce.

> Management can get things done through others by traditional activities of planning, organising, monitoring and controlling – without worrying too much what goes on inside people heads. Leadership, by contrast, is vitally concerned with what people are thinking and feeling and how they are to be to linked to the environment to the entity and to the job/task. (Nicholls, 1987: 2)

Nicholls' quote is a clear example of change between the *Leader as Controller* discourse and the *Leader as Therapist* discourse. It is not so much about the difference between managers and leaders but the difference between discourses. Two senior executives, operating in different times, and different contexts, with different values and normative assumptions.

Democratic and other emotional forms of leadership were attempts to give employees responsibility and instil willingness, pride and interest in their work, offering them personal growth, strong identities and satisfaction as rewards rather than material benefits alone.

The Human Relations movement brought an eclectic mix of human sciences, including sociology, psychology and anthropology, to bear on the problem of getting the most from the workforce. It began with Mayo's theories that group processes amplified individual psychopathologies and that the role of first line supervisors was vital to the enhancement of or hindrance to a firm's objectives (Barley and Kunda, 1992). Restructuring work, to increase satisfaction, became linked to a form of emotional management and human engineering, attempting to change behaviour, belief systems and to link workers' self-actualizing tendencies to work output. The social changes during the 1960s accentuated the human potential movement and with it the manager took on new responsibilities: to change people emotionally and to help them to change themselves. What began as a counter-culture and progressive movement became mainstream and, as it did, 'therapy culture' took hold and the liberating ideology shifted to a reliance on professional help to manage emotional vulnerability. The 'Leader as Therapist' character became a key player as the workplace assumed a greater importance as a site of community, while traditional sites of community fell away. From a rational controlling figure, leaders and managers took on the therapeutic discourse and the ideal leader became an individual with highly developed people/coaching skills, emotional intelligence, and self-awareness The leader's task is to use these skills to support individuals and teams in order to improve working relationships, communication and get the best out of people. Motivation is a by-product of feeling valued, and personal growth in the workplace.

The Human Relations movement proved very successful but ran into problems in the 1970s. Despite the Western assumption of America's cultural and economic dominance, which placed them as leaders in the field of management thinking and practice, the USA's economic performance was falling behind and facing a severe challenge. Motivating workers to self-actualize was no longer producing the answers to a stagnating economy and the Human Relations project was running into trouble. The Leader as Therapist character had delivered much early success but new answers were needed to stimulate growth in an increasingly competitive and turbulent knowledge-based global economy. What was missing was the bigger picture, how to influence those beyond the reach of personal and emotionally based interventions? In this new world of the global market it was whole cultures that required changing. The therapeutic milieu continued to be embraced but more was needed to produce economic success. The surge of new technology and the focus on knowledge meant that new organizational forms emerged and a new leadership was required to influence these fast-changing environments. The American economy was falling behind rising Asian Tiger economies and the Human Relations movement and the Leader as Therapist character was no longer able to deliver on its own. A new leader with the power to inspire culture change and transformation in large numbers of dispersed employees was required.

# 9

# The Leader as Messiah

## Introduction

The Leader as Controller discourse was successful in terms of improving production but faded as it alienated workers. The need for a more engaged workforce, changing modes of production and social advances led to the Leader as Therapist discourse. The Therapist discourse set a leadership culture which focused on emotionally and psychologically engaged workers, linking motivation to production. However, the late twentieth century brought new challenges of the global market place, technological and communication advances and changing social conditions which meant that a new leadership discourse was required to lift Western economies which were being overtaken by Japanese and Asian Tiger economies. The Therapist character was unable to find the power to meet these challenges and a new 'hero leader' arose like a phoenix from the ashes.

It is only since the late 1970s that the new Leader as Messiah discourse has come to prominence and a hero leader had been 'resurrected', epitomized by the Transformational leader. Those suspicious of leadership often mistake the hype and assume that the Transformational leader is a repeat of past 'Great Man' hero leaders, and it is true there are significant similarities. But there was also a new edge to the Transformational leader entering the twenty-first century, they would attempt to find ways to create strong collectivist cultures which enabled dispersed leadership to occur within the bounds of a leadership vision and normative control. This chapter will critically review Transformational leadership and the messiah discourse, tracing its rise, its power and impact and challenging its proponents' more extravagant claims.

## The arrival of the Messiah: The Transformational leader

> The most careful ask today: 'How is man to be maintained?' Zarathustra however asketh, as the first and only one: 'How is man to be surpassed?' (Nietzsche, [1899] 1996)

It seems that the question asked by Nietzsche 'How is man to be surpassed?' is one which engages Transformational leaders. Transformational, new-hero style

rship has remained headline news in the management literature since its
ception in the late 1970s and its big impact in the early 1980s. Transformational
eadership has become a very desirable capability closely linked to the new organizational cultures. Transformational leaders have been heralded by some as the
answer to contemporary organizational dilemmas, who criticize hierarchical and
bureaucratic forms of traditional organization (Ouchi, 1981; Naisbett, 1982; Peters
and Waterman, 1982; Kanter, 1983). They have also been critiqued by others, as
promoting totalizing cultures, mono-cultures through a process of culture control
(Axtel Ray, 1986; Kunda, 1992; Casey, 1995). Either way, the Messiah leadership
discourse ignites passions and exerts potency.

When viewed as a coherent whole, rather than viewed only through its component parts, i.e. the leader's behaviour or style, Transformational leadership is
focused on leading organizational cultural change and managing the culture,
more than being a transformer of individuals. The Transformational leader's popularity arose mainly from the research of leadership practitioners who, it was
found, excelled specifically in cultural change (Deal and Kennedy, 1982; Peters
and Waterman, 1982).

Barley and Kunda (1992: 383) point to three tenets of this new cultural leadership:

1   The company as community; the company being the main site for many
    employees to experience community would mean that ultimately the company
    would become fully-fledged communitas – bringing pride and a feeling of
    belonging.
2   Strong cultures could be consciously designed and manipulated.
3   To value conformity and emotional commitment would foster financial gain.

Barley and Kunda also identify how emotional management continues to be used
but, unlike the emotional management of individuals and teams as seen in the
Human Relations Therapist discourse, this is clearly linked to cultural change
using religious overtones to help 'convert' the organizational members to the
new vision:

> Management was advised to exorcise unwanted thoughts and feelings from the
> workforce to replace them with beliefs and emotions that benefited the organiza-
> tion. To make the point proponents employed an imagery of cults, clans and reli-
> gious conversions, [see Ouchi and Price 1978, Deal and Kennedy, 1982]. Authors
> exhorted managers to become 'highpriests' of their organization's values to
> appoint mythic heroes and fabricate sagas. (Barley and Kunda, 1992: 383)

Ulrich uses religious imagery to encourage the manager attempting cultural change:
'to take the role of missionary … converting key personnel … institutionalising
new rituals, symbols languages and heroes' (1984: 126). Peters and Waterman
(1982), with other proponents of this new culture, argued that autonomy was
increased within the confines of value conformity; organizations with strong
cultures could trust employees to act in the company's best interest and therefore
afford them more autonomy and individualism. However, there were dangers.
Peters and Waterman (1982: 15–16) describe excellent companies with strong
cultures as: 'Fanatic centralists around core value … yet as one analyst argues

"the brainwashed members of an extreme political sect are no more conformist in their central beliefs".

Collins and Porras (2000), in their book *Built to Last* (first published 1994), claim that what made 'the most difference in having an enduringly great company was the greatness of the leader'. They cite vision and charisma as the characteristics of greatness and agree with Peters and Waterman in their chapter entitled 'Cult-like Cultures' saying: 'In short, understanding that cult-like tightness around an ideology actually enables a company to turn people loose to experimental change, adapt and – above all – act' (ibid.: 123). This view shows the continuing ideology of visionary leadership which influences through the creation of strong cult-like cultures. There is a general lack of critique in the mainstream Transformational leadership literature as to how cult-like collectivist organizations have dangerous totalizing tendencies. Peters and Waterman and Collins and Porras take a utilitarian approach to leadership, judging it to be great if it creates successful organizations. Success has seduced their reasoning to 'approve of cult-like' cultures if they deliver 'organizational success'. The Transformational leader clearly is problematic, and, as the above quotes show, the claims of this leadership are very potent, linked to religious language and focused on trying to create a passionate followership and thereby total culture control. This chapter will critique these grandiose claims and identify key themes arising from the Transformational leadership literature.

## The social context: lessons from Japan, anthropology and practitioners

Management theory usually points to three areas to identify the influences whereby Transformational leadership emerged: the Asian influence, the influence from anthropology, and from practioners in the field. During the 1970s and 1980s, the Japanese had the world's fastest economic growth and their phenomenal success, particularly in areas previously dominated by the US economy, e.g. car production, challenged the American management theorists and practitioners to review what they were doing and to find out what was making the Japanese economy so successful. Ouchi's Theory Z (Ouchi, 1981) is the best-known work that attempted to learn and translate the Japanese model of management and integrate this to the American way of managing and companies. Ouchi found that the Japanese success was attributed to their collaborative working methods, based on cultural differences. The American/Western axis of individualism was put under scrutiny and with it the prominent management discourse of the Leader as Therapist was seen to be under-performing. The Japanese model emphasized strong cultures focusing on family teams, flexibility, quality and service. Loyalty and commitment underpinned company cultures, which opened up a new way of thinking about organizations. Previously culture was thought of as something a company had, but in the late 1970s (at the same time as the rise of the Transformational leader) theorists were viewing 'organizations as cultures'. A debate over how much of the Japanese success was cultural and how much structural followed. Whitley (1992) claims social, political and economic institutions were more important. Wilkinson (1996) believes that both culture and institutional theorists overplayed their hands and that groups of actors embedded in certain cultural, political, economic and institutional contexts impact most on the formation of strategy. Interest was also shown in Scandinavia, where, among others, Volvo's car plants had a long tradition of collaborative working, establishing work-group autonomy and a holistic approach (Berggren et al., 1994). The Japanese economy has struggled more recently and the reversion of Volvo's plants back to less radical practice, meant that practitioners' interest in these practices has waned. Like many other management fads, the quality circles, the move towards the 'Japanese social groupism' and Swedish style job-designs, faded. What has survived and grown from the Japanese and Scandinavian experiences is the premise that strong corporate cultures are vital to success.

The second influence came through anthropology. Theorists argued that organizations should be viewed as socially constructed systems of meaning. They focused on meaning being socially rather than individually constructed. This changed the 'social field' where a leader should aim to influence and act. This shifted the emphasis away from leaders working on the psychology and dynamics of influencing individuals and teams, towards how to influence culture-as-a-whole because that is what impacted on how individuals, teams and organizations could be influenced.

The third influence was via the leadership study of practitioners, coming via consultants and applied researchers, whose arguments were more pragmatic (these practitioners were also influenced by the Japanese success). One of the consequences of the new organizational forms was the inability of leaders/managers to control or to motivate and influence teams, whose expert and technical knowledge within their increasingly specialist fields made them more autonomous and empowered. Flattened hierarchies were being introduced which removed a middle and lower order of managers who were becoming obsolete. The question arose, how to lead and influence these newly de-centralized and self-managing teams? Peters and Waterman (1982) identified, however, that this de-centralization was not a one-way process as they had imagined. They found that both a centralization and de-centralization occurred in the 'excellent companies' they studied. At the heart of the centralizing tendency was a powerful leadership figure forming a culture of excellence (Peters and Waterman claim they came to this finding unexpectedly and reluctantly). They found that the normative (emotional) culture control the leader established helped enable a de-centralized workforce to self-regulate its own activity.

Deal and Kennedy's *Corporate Cultures* (1982) and Peters and Waterman's *In Search of Excellence* (1982) became best sellers, promoting their ideas drawn from practitioners' research. The strong culture ideology took hold in the early 1980s; team-family caring atmospheres, shared beliefs and values, leadership and a focus on success were the ingredients to create the new cultures that would be winners. Passion from employees became a key success factor. Companies would aim to create cultures of commitment, cooperation, mutual trust and recognition that the contribution of each individual is important to success (Wickens, 1987: 38). These strong cultures needed a new visionary and potent leadership character to transform tired American business cultures, and to find ways to instil the passion needed to succeed.

# Transformational leadership: a critique

The recent ascendancy of the Transformational leader began as a legitimate search for a new framework to manage the task of successfully leading and motivating the workforce for the socio-economic conditions of the twenty-first century. Transformational leadership was initially contrasted with Transactional leadership (Burns, 1978; Bass, 1985). Transactional leadership is based on an exchange relationship between the leader and follower, i.e. the leader offers incentives and in return the job is done efficiently. The Transformational leader was said to possess new behaviours and qualities and worked on different assumptions that are more suited to the high-tech, global and new forms of knowledge-based organizations, than manufacturing and old style working.

The term 'Transformational leadership' took on a more specific meaning within management circles when introduced as a particular leadership style by Burns (1978). Burns' ideas were expanded by Bass and others and since the 1980s growth in the interest in Transformational leadership and leadership itself has been explosive (Bass, 1985; Conger and Kanungo, 1987; House, 1977; Shamir et al., 1993; Tourish and Pinnington, 2002). The terms 'charismatic' and 'visionary' leaders are often used to cover similar territory and are seen as integral aspects of Transformational leaders. The Transformational leader now has particular meanings and this leadership style has gone through much reductionism. Studies have attempted to codify the behaviours of the Transformational leader to fit the 'trait and competency' approach to theory and training. However, the definition of Transformational leadership in this book will go beyond the competency definitions and will cover all leadership which has been promoted since the 1980s to create and lead strong cultures by offering vision and charisma and which seeks a higher purpose than managing performance. That is a leadership which aims to transform organizations and employees; a leadership who has perceived qualities of transformation and salvation, hence the Messiah Leadership discourse.

# Hail the Messiah!

> During the 1980s, charismatic leadership returned with a vengeance, complete with all the accoutrements of biblical charismatics including visions, missions and zealot-like disciples. (Grint, 1997: 13–14)

The claims made about the Transformational leader are quite literally astonishing. Bernard Bass, who is a seminal and highly respected voice in the field of Transformational leadership theory and research, writes:

> The immature, self-aggrandizing charismatic leader is pseudo transformational. He or she may seem uplifting and responsible but on closer examination is found to be a false Messiah. Much more needs to be learned about the ethical and moral factors that distinguish the truly Transformational leader from the pseudo Transformational leader. (Bass and Steidlmeier 1999: 185)

This comment identifies one of the unspoken assumptions and unconscious desires behind Transformational leaders. If the pseudo-Transformational leader is the false Messiah, then the truly Transformational leader will, by inference, be the true Messiah. Psychoanalytic and other critical theorists often position the Transformational leader as creating an unconscious fantasy of a saviour who will provide refuge and safety in a world full of turbulence, upheaval and uncertainty. This critique of the leader stems from the notion that individuals become regressively infantilized when faced with a charismatic leader who creates a psychological dependency in their followers (Hirschhorn, 1988; Masson, 1990; Kets de Vries, 1991).

Bion (1961) clearly articulated this unconscious phenomenon and how it played out in groups by describing Basic-assumption Dependency (BaD):

> In BaD the group acts 'as if' the leader will protect and sustain the members and will make them feel good. The group members avoid the responsibility of developmental activity and individual responsibility due to a pathological dependency. This group seeks an omnipotent and omniscient leader. (Western, 2005: 286)

This can certainly be one of the effects of this strong leadership style but this critique underestimates corporate America's and multinational businesses' wisdom and drive for success. If they were simply returning to an old-style charismatic leader who created paralysed, dependency cultures, they were sure to fail.

Current journals, articles and books continue to peddle omnipotent and exceptional claims about Transformational leadership, buying into this regressive tendency. Here are two examples, found in two of the best-known mainstream management journals, the *Harvard Business Review* and the *Academy Management Journal*:

> Transformational leaders exhibit charismatic behaviours, arouse inspirational motivation, provide intellectual stimulation and treat followers with individual consideration. These behaviours transform their followers helping them to reach their full potential and generate the highest levels in performance. (Dvir et al., 2002: 736)

Changing people, an individual and collective actor, is a tough business and meets huge resistance; transforming large numbers of people in a working situation is a grand claim. Bennis and Thomas, in a *Harvard Business Review* article, the 'Crucibles of leadership' (2002), write about leaders as though they are magical, with Peter Pan characteristics and support their theory by using the language of scientific rationalism to add legitimacy to their claims. They discuss four essential skills they believe great leaders possess:

1   the ability to engage others in shared meaning;
2   a distinctive and compelling voice;
3   a sense of integrity (including a strong set of values);
4   'adaptive capacity', an almost magical ability to transcend adversity, with all its attendant stresses and to emerge stronger than before.

They continue, 'But by far the most critical skill of the four is what we call adaptive capacity' (Bennis and Thomas, 2002). The idea that heroes transcend adversity to become stronger is recycled theory and rhetoric, but rhetoric which meets the demand of a popular audience. From a philosophical perspective, the existentialist view of Nietzsche clearly sums up the idea of their 'crucible' as 'that which does not destroy me makes me stronger' (Nietzsche, [1899] 1996: 297). Nietzsche wrote of this in context of the 'superman' (Overman or Ubermensch) who, having rid himself of God, overcomes the limitations of man:

> There are no higher men, we are all equal, man is but man, before God – we are all equal.
>    Before God! But now this God has died. And let us not be equal before the mob. You Higher Men, depart from the market place! (ibid.: 297)

Bennis and Thomas's contemporary Transformational leader is similar to Nietzsche's superman: one that must rise above the mob and leave the public place for a higher calling. But Bennis and Thomas's article outlines a leader who not only is a tough cookie but also has values, integrity and is a great communicator. However, even this is not enough. What makes this leader really different is another quality and this article certainly buys into the contemporary cultural ambitions of staying youthful and gaining immortality; like Peter Pan, these leaders just refuse to age:

> To understand why this quality [youthfulness] is so powerful in a leader, it might help to take a quick look at the scientific principle behind it – neoteny as an evolutionary engine. It is the winning, puppyish quality of certain ancient wolves that allowed them to evolve into dogs. (Bennis and Thomas, 2002: 43)

They offer examples of these leaders with Peter Pan characteristics:

> Robert Galvin, former Motorola chairman now in his late 70's, spends his weekends windsurfing. Arthur Levitt, Jr., former SEC chairman who turned 71 this year, is an avid Outward Bound trekker. And architect Frank Gehry is now a 72-year-old ice hockey player. But it's not only an affinity for physical activity that characterizes neoteny – it's an appetite for learning and self-development, a curiosity and passion for life. (ibid.)

What you have is a new mythical leader, a new 'superman' who has overcome ageing, and able to transform the worst situations into the best. Interestingly the title of their article exposes the reality. They call the paper the 'Crucibles of Leadership' because the leaders go through an epic struggle, 'the crucible' and are transformed into these youthful and dynamic leaders: 'We came to call the experiences that shape leaders "crucibles," after the vessels medieval alchemists used in their attempts to turn base metals into gold' (ibid.). However, as is well known, the alchemist's crucible base metals never did turn to gold; youthfulness does not last forever, despite cosmetic surgery, medication, fitness regimes, or specific leadership qualities and the super-hero leader described is no more real than the alchemist's gold. This example demonstrates how the discourse of the Leader as Messiah has taken hold.

This description of an individual heroic leader does sell leadership books and courses, as it appeals to the narcissism of those in leadership roles, and to the dependency instincts of followers who would like to be saved/led by messiah leadership characters (and shareholders who would like their money to be in safe hands). But why, after the discourse of the Leader as Therapist, has the Transformational leader become so popular at this moment in history, after a period of attempting to democratize the leadership process? Is there something more than the heroic veneer about this leadership style? To find answers we need to first of all examine the Transformational leader in more depth.

## The components parts of a Transformational leader

Taking a closer look at Transformational leaders, we are offered a breakdown of the component parts, the 'behaviours and actions' that represent Transformational leadership which are commonly known as the four Is:

1  *Idealized influence or charisma*: Measured by the followers' reactions to the leader, leaders are thoroughly respected, trusted, have much referent power, high standards and set challenging goals for their followers, i.e. 'the leader has my trust to overcome any obstacle'.
2  *Inspirational motivation*: The leader uses symbols and images and simplified emotional appeals to increase awareness and understanding of mutually desired goals and to focus followers' efforts. He/she elevates followers' expectations.
3  *Intellectual stimulation*: Followers are encouraged to break with the past and to question the old way of doing things. They are supported in questioning their own values, beliefs and expectations as well as those of the leader and the organization.
4  *Individualized consideration*: Followers are treated differently but equitably on a one-to-one basis. Needs are recognized, perspectives raised and their means of more effectively addressing goals and challenges are dealt with.

The four Is provide the best-known criteria with which Transformational leaders are researched and this is known as the Multi-factor Leadership Questionnaire (Bass and Avolio, 1994). These four Is representing the behaviours of the Transformational leader seem designed to cover a variety of eventualities that a leader may face and address foreseen criticisms at the same time. However, as they look towards the attributes of Transformational qualities in individual leaders, they omit important aspects:

• promoting a common culture;
• the alignment of moral values;
• a compelling vision.

These and other wider goals are difficult to encapsulate when reductionism to behaviours and actions takes hold of a research and development agenda, as identified earlier (Yukl, 1998).

# A 'hero' leader for all occasions

An overview of the Transformational leader literature suggests a larger-than-life, one-size-fits-all, hero leader who seems to excel in all four behaviours identified. This charismatic, visionary would, however, overwhelm many individuals who may respond to a more sensitive personality, working quietly behind the scenes to make things happen. Essentially, a leader cannot be 'all things to all people' or all things to all organizational contexts and situations. Transformational leadership is critiqued for ignoring the contingency theorists who argue that different situations determine appropriate leadership approaches (Fulop and Linstead, 1999). Schein (1988) and Alvesson (2002) place leadership in a cultural context, which is largely ignored in much of the popular Transformational leadership literature that focuses on the traits of the leader. This is strange since changing culture is the overall focus of such leaders.

Alvesson says that contemporary leaders are said to work *on* rather than *in* culture, however, he claims that leaders who work in cultures can, with exceptions, transcend existing cultural patterns or even contribute to the creation of a culture (Alvesson, 2002: 108). What Alvesson is challenging is the ability of Transformational leadership to be common.

Using Etzioni's (1961) basic types of organization – coercive, utilitarian and normative, Schein says that different organizations require different leaders. Organizations which do not require tasks or missions with high levels of involvement would not respond to a charismatic leadership (even if such a leader could be found). He gives the examples of a company manufacturing textiles or a government bureaucracy and says a charismatic leader could not transform these into normative organizations because they are fundamentally utilitarian organizations requiring a different leadership style. To sum up his position, Schein writes: 'Leadership is partly a cultural phenomenon and must be analysed within a given cultural, political and socio-economic context' (1988: 110).

# Learning charisma: is mass ability possible?

Charisma is regarded as a key attribute of Transformational leadership. Bass (1999) chose to substitute the term *idealized influence* (meaning being influential about ideals) for charisma in an attempt to diffuse some of the criticisms that surround charismatic leadership and to link charisma to ideals and morality. Bass felt that charisma can be used to manipulate and even indoctrinate followers when lacking a moral stance (the issue of morality is vital and will be discussed later). However, a simple name change does not change the qualities (commonly known as charisma) required by a leader to transform others. Charismatic leaders have been defined as exceptional leaders who, by force of their personal abilities, are capable of having profound extraordinary effects on their followers (Steyrer, 1998). Weber links the idea of mission to the charismatic leader, 'the bearer of charisma enjoys loyalty and authority by virtue of a mission believed to be embodied in him' (cited in Bryman, 1993: 292).

A Transformational leader has to be a special type of person to fit all the four Is criteria, including being visionary and charismatic. One of the claims for

Transformational leadership which separates it from the hero-leader of old, is that Transformational leadership should be a dispersed leadership. Transformational leaders are required throughout an organization and not just at the top of the tree. To achieve this, it is proposed that Transformational leaders can be trained but Bass (1999) acknowledges that, to date, scant research attention has been devoted to the issue of training and whether Transformational leaders can be trained. This sets up a paradox for the theorists, which has not been resolved, that Transformational leaders should be both common and at the same time, exceptional.

## Follower compliance

Using the Multi-factor Leadership Questionnaire, Bass and Avolio (1994) claim that Transformational leaders diagnose and evaluate follower needs to promote development, succeed in developing higher levels of potential and align followers to a sense of purpose and future orientation. However, this research is based on follower perceptions of leaders. Coopey (1995) points to research showing that leaders crave power. Linking this to their need for positive affirmation from their followers, he claims, distorts the research. A leader with power, who needs affirmation, creates a leader/follower dependency which constrains creative or critical thinking and is likely to produce a highly cohesive group. However, this group will be in danger of 'Groupthink' (Janis, 1972), as it will be reluctant to allow individuals to express alternative solutions to an emerging group consensus.

## The effectiveness of Transformational leaders

Dvir et al. (2002) put forward four hypotheses (1a, b, c, and 2) to research the effectiveness of Transformational leaders:

1a  Transformational leadership has a positive impact on the development of followers' motivation in terms of their self-actualization needs and extra effort.
1b  Transformational leadership has a positive impact on the development of followers' morality in terms of their internalization of their organization's moral values and a collectivistic orientation.
1c  Transformational leadership has a positive impact on the development of followers' empowerment in terms of their critical-independent approach, active engagement in the task and specific self-efficacy.
2.  Transformational leadership has a positive impact on followers' performance.

If these hypotheses are analysed, the impacts of a Transformational leader on their followers are:

• that they will work harder and more efficiently for the company (1a and 2);
• that they will be more motivated to self-actualize and think critically and independently (1a and 1c);
• that they will 'internalize the organization's moral values' so that they are aligned and working for the same vision (1b).

There are inherent contradictions in the last two points. Thinking critically and independently is often contrasted with internalizing values and becoming a 'company man or woman'. At one level, companies clearly desire autonomy, innovation and entrepreneurship; at another, they demand conformity of culture and homogeneity and desire a certain amount of 'groupthink' which has been positively 'spun' and marketed as the alignment of followers' values with organizational values and morals and promoting a 'common culture'. The dangers presented by charismatic leaders are the creation of an 'idealized transference' (Coopey, 1995: 207) where followers will do all they can to please the leader.

## Empowerment

In contrast to early charismatic theories, Transformational leadership theory has emphasized followers' development towards autonomy and empowerment over automatic followership. The Transformational leader's aim is to 'elevate followers' expectations' to go beyond what they expect of themselves. This type of empowerment is key to the Transformational leadership discourse. However well meaning, this act of empowerment is very problematic. To empower is 'too give power or authority' (*Collins Dictionary*, 1992) but as Eric Miller explains:

> It is a term I avoid because of its ambiguity: between becoming more powerful and making more powerful. The notion of giving power is inherently patronising – it implies dependency – and hence is itself dis-empowering. Power cannot be given, only taken. That having been said power and dependency are central issues for a consultant working with organisations. (1993: xvi)

Empowerment is particularly disempowering if it is being used with the aim of increasing productivity or to enhance the career or goals of the powerful leader. Greiner's 1973 research into what managers think of participative leadership concluded with these findings:

> Managers aren't authoritarians who manipulate their puppet sub-ordinates, neither do they accept participation as a blind ideology. Participative leadership is a sound general model if individual leaders can choose to be directive at will and if they can choose a variety of actions which fits their personal and career needs.

This demonstrates the ambiguities and the managers' fickle understanding of real participation and empowerment. Choosing to be 'directive at will' fitting with their own careers, makes participation sound like tokenism, and exposes the managers' shallow and naïve understanding of what participative leadership really means.

In a similar vein, work trips to Kosovo and Sudan, to train senior leaders in the United Nations and the International Federations of the Red Crescent and Red Cross, have forced me to consider 'capacity building', a currently popular empowerment term, used in the not-for-profit sector, as of limited value when set in contexts that are systemically and structurally disempowering. The empowering helpers can too easily become part of the problem they are there to resolve. Observing leaders working in similar contexts (Western and Gosling, 2003) also revealed that those individuals who are committed and align their personal values and beliefs to the organizational goals and values of empowerment, can be blind to their own and their organization's behaviours on the ground, which often produce the disempowering outcomes. They are simply too invested in their causes to take a critical stance. Argyris' (1964) Model 1 and Model 2 research supports this finding; he suggests that most people, when asked, will *espouse* Model 2 learning which is more reflective and open, but will actually practise Model 1 learning which is more defensive and closed.

The ideology of empowerment of followers within Transformational leadership literature promotes the desire for follower autonomy and yet at the same time promotes a leader who 'sees beyond what the followers can see for themselves'. The Transformational leader takes the follower beyond his or her own visions and goals to a higher level of emotional, moralistic (and perhaps spiritual) maturity. This sets new standards; the Promised Land is now beyond Maslow's 'self-actualization' and is somewhere in the stratosphere, decided by the leader rather than the follower. Paradoxically this sounds rather disempowering, and leader knows best. The Transformational leader also asks the followers not just to work for their own benefit but for the greater good of the many, the collective. Fortunately in this case the many are the company or organization, with the leader gaining huge benefits for greater success.

The concept of empowerment is troubling with its rather grandiose claims to give power to another. For a leader to know what is best for the follower has a patronizing tone. The suggestion that a leader brings intelligent, adult employees to a new moral maturity is reminiscent of the Victorian paternalistic ideology which attempted to bring a new morality to the working class.

Yukl critiques the aims of Transformational leadership research which shows that leaders use power and influence to overcome resistance rather than using resistance to be a source of energy that enables people to collectively make better decisions about what type of change is needed:

> Inspirational motivation includes encouraging subordinates to embrace, disseminate and implement the vision, but not encouraging subordinates to challenge the vision or develop a better one. Intellectual stimulation includes communicating novel ideas to a subordinate, but not providing opportunities for subordinates to learn from experience and helping them interpret experience in a meaningful way. (Yukl, 1999: 38–9)

The empowerment ideology which is central to Transformational leadership conveys a uni-directional process and does not offer the intellectual space for real exchange of ideas or for the leader to learn from the followers. This produces the impact Yukl describes and leads to a state of collusive harmony, which denies learning through creativity and the healthy conflict that is necessary for deeper learning and growth.

# Morality: the raising up of leadership

To be transformational one must be morally uplifting. (Burns, 1978)

For Transformational leaders to be authentic, they must incorporate moral values as a central core. (Bass and Steidlmeier, 1999: 210)

When Burns (1978) cited morality as a quality Transformational leaders must
possess and later, when Bass cited morality as a differentiating feature between
Transactional and Transformational leadership, they identified a vital yet very
problematic area. The philosophy surrounding morality is a huge subject, too big
for this book, but it is important to go beyond the meaning conveyed by Burns,
Bass and other leading writers on Transformational leaders, who discuss morality
as an uncomplicated 'mother and apple pie' generic sense of goodness:

> Leaders are authentically transformational when they increase awareness of
> what is right, good, important and beautiful, when they help to elevate followers
> needs for achievement and self-actualisation, when they foster in followers
> higher moral maturity and when they move followers to go beyond their self
> interests for the good of their group, organisation or society. (Bass, 1998: 171)

One could easily replace the words 'leaders' and 'followers' with 'parents' and
'children', exposing the infantilizing dynamic set up here between leader and
follower. It dangerously locates a great deal of power with an omnipotent leader.
The charismatic leader who is elevating followers to what is 'right, good, important
and beautiful' is returning to the industrial betterment model used in Victorian
philanthropy, whereby well-meaning bosses acted in this way towards a subservient and a totally dependent workforce. The linking of morality to charismatic personalities as the means to transform a followership is dangerous
territory.

The idea that a Transformational leader offers 'individual consideration' seems
an attempt to address diversity issues, but the literature doesn't clearly account
for how 'individual consideration' takes place throughout a large organization,
nor does it account for how all individuals freely think and express themselves in
all their diversity and at the same time sign up to a unified vision and culture.
Transformational leaders with charisma represent a full range of personality
types. Cuilla discussed 'The Hitler problem' (Cuilla, 1995) which asked, can Hitler
be viewed as a Transformational leader and if not, who sets the standards as to
what constitutes morality, using what criteria and validated by whom?

This important distinction goes beyond Transformational and Transactional
Leadership or beyond managers and leaders. Macintyre's statement referring to
managers relates to a subset of managers/leaders who are situated in the
*Discourse of the Controller*: 'Managers themselves and most writers about management conceive of themselves as morally neutral *characters* whose skills enable
them to devise the most efficient means of achieving whatever end is proposed'
(MacIntyre, 1985: 74).

Enteman reasons that if managers/leaders are too moral, then they cannot engage their expertise fully in the transactional process and also points out that management (or leadership) can take place in immoral organizations:

> Managerialism recognises the potential importance of all organisations. Their importance is not a function of historical precedent or romantic wishing. It is a function of their power, which is in large measure a function of their management. There is no interest, which cannot be represented including illegal and immoral ones. There is only the question of the ability of the organisation, through its management, to engage in the transaction process. (Enteman, 1993: 186)

Enteman identifies that if managers/leaders are too moral, they cannot use their expertise because it reduces their ability to make the organization more effective and therefore they lose their source of authority: 'If one side has deep moral convictions its bargaining ability may be weakened, if both sides have deep moral convictions, unless they share the same ones, managers may be unable to find common ground' (ibid.: 163). Enteman, however, ends up taking a middle position saying that 'managerialism makes room for the moral dimension but it finds the rigid pursuit of the moral dimension dysfunctional' (ibid.: 165). This statement has increasingly important implications for many leaders in corporate life, who are charged with making complex and difficult ethical and moral choices. These usually involve a tension between profit and success and the social well-being of others (employees, outsourced workers, communities affected by the industry, and the environment). CSR or Corporate Social Responsibility is now a huge concern for multinationals who can lose business very quickly through social-activists identifying poor social practice. Whether their concern is mostly a marketing veneer, what environmentalists refer to as 'greenwash' or whether the concern is a pragmatic business self-interest which makes a real difference is debateable, and I believe in transition. The link between social and environmental concerns and business success is being made stronger each month (see Chapter 12).

However, for Transformational leaders, the emphasis is on taking a moral stance to imbue their 'followers' with values and new personal goals; this stretches the dilemma beyond the ethics of Corporate Social Responsibility, and encourages leadership interventions into the personal lives of the employees; their values and their beliefs.

The real distinction when introducing morality into the leadership debate is between the first two discourses, the *Controller* and the *Therapist*, and the third, the discourse of the *Messiah*. The morality of the *Messiah Character*, sits in opposition to the morally-neutral *Controller Character*, whose ultimate aim is efficiency through control, and the *Therapist Character* whose aim is efficiency through well-being, but neither of whom take a moral stance. They both work to be efficient in their fields of expertise and both characters are technocrats (MacIntyre, 1985). The leadership discourse of the *Messiah Character* goes beyond that of the technocrat. As we have seen, the discourse is underpinned by quasi-spiritual qualities: passion, beauty, inspiration, the greater good of all, underpinned by values and morals. The Transformational leader, it is claimed, reaches to a higher calling.

Despite claims of moral authority through developing individuals, Transformational leaders are constrained by the same goals as the manager: 'efficiency and effectiveness' to maximize profit or output at minimum cost, i.e. to be competitive (this is also increasingly the case for public and voluntary sector organizations). Inevitable contradictions need to be faced in this situation, particularly when CEOs are under increasing pressure to ensure short-term, shareholder success. As long as effectiveness is the goal of the organization, the manager/leader will always be compromised and associated with, as Macintyre puts it, the 'manipulation of human beings into compliant patterns of behaviour' (1985: 74). Transformational leaders have been created/discovered because, apparently, they are more effective than other leadership styles. This puts the morality claims into further dispute; how moral is it to use morality as a tool to maximize output and profit? Other critics express similar concerns: 'It is not always in the best interests of employees to maximise benefits for other stakeholders [such as owners or customers]' (Stephens et al., 1995). Tourish and Pinnington (2002: 149) ask: 'Downsizing, delayering, multi-skilling, re-engineering and job enhancement are venerated by some and reviled by others, what is good or moral?' Milton Friedman takes a polemic view, claiming that within a corporation it is moral to maximize profit and immoral to consider anything else: 'The executive is an agent serving the interests of his principle to serve the stockholders and thus there is only one social responsibility of business – to use its resources and engage in activities designed to increase its profits' (1962: 132–5). He goes on to say that trends such as social responsibility, 'undermine the very foundations of our free society' (ibid.: 132–5).

Drucker takes the opposite view and has criticized the assumption of profit maximization, believing the concept is meaningless because it has been 'qualified out of existence': 'The rhetoric of profit maximisation and profit motive are not only anti-social. They are immoral' (Drucker, 1973: 810). Drucker's view is the opposite of Friedman's whose claim to morality is that for a company not to focus on profit undermines a free society. John Ladd suggests that the machine metaphor supports this drive for profit and any 'inefficiency' on behalf of a leader or manager is dealt with, simply because, despite changes, 'managers are still cogs in a wheel' and are like any other commodity:

> One of the givens in organisations is that managers are easily substitutable: Individual office holders are in principle replaceable by other individuals without affecting the continuity or identity of the organisation … any individual is dispensable and replaceable by another. (Ladd, 1970: 488–9)

A Transformational leader may act with moral certitude in a society in which there is a moral social consensus (if one exists); however, many believe that in the past three decades important cultural changes have occurred 'which undermine the assumption of a consensus on what constitutes moral integrity in society' (Furedi, 2003: 96). Lasch believes that 'therapeutic morality encourages the permanent suspension of the moral sense' (1979: 389) which supports the view that the *Therapist Discourse* in leadership is that of the technocrat, aiming to create efficiency through skilfully manipulating the workforce through their emotions and relations. The Human Relations theorists helped the passage of individualism and the pervasive therapeutic culture into the management discourse, which brought with it liberal permissiveness, and the rise of individualism, which undermined socially consensual morality. This left a moral vacuum, or at least a confused and unclear view of what constitutes morality. The Transformational leader theorists attempt to recover this lost moral certitude or perhaps create a new one. However, the ground on which their ethics and morality stands is very unstable. If leadership is to engage in imposing and/or influencing employees with morality, then it is vital to account for the power relationships and competing and ulterior motives (their own gains, the company profits/bonuses). How leaders impart their morality, and know what's best for a hugely diverse workforce seems an outrageously omnipotent and dangerous claim.

## Engineering culture

While mainstream commentators (and in my experience, many practitioners) relished the new leadership discourse uncritically, others found the new ideologies of Transformational leaders attempting to 'engineer culture' (Kunda, 1992) and to create 'designer employees' (Casey, 1995) very troubling. Carol Axtell Ray (1986) describes contemporary corporate culture, in which employees are controlled, as using the ultimate form of manipulation. Her argument is that the type of culture espoused by Transformational leaders is one that seeks devotion from employees at all levels with the aim of getting them to love the firm and its goals. By so doing, Axtell Ray argues that individuals have an additional form of control put upon them (she maintains that bureaucratic and social control remain). This ultimate form of control, 'normative control', comes from within the individual themselves through the internalization of the leader's organizational culture. This makes constant surveillance unnecessary, requiring no external policing. Howard Zinn books in his *Declarations of Independence*, (1991) writes 'If those in charge of our society – politicians, corporate executives and owners of press and television – can dominate our ideas, they will be secure in their power. They will not need soldiers patrolling the streets. We will control ourselves' (Zinn, cited in Snow, 2002). In return for the employees' devotion and loyalty to the company, they receive the benefits of sharing collective values but, Axtell Ray warns, they may become ensnared in a hegemonic system. Despite talk of alignment of follower and company values, the two will often struggle to comfortably align and the question of the coercion to achieve effectiveness remains.
   Edwards writes:

> Under normative control the workers owe not only a hard day's work to the corporation but also their demeanor and affections. Control tends to be a more totalitarian system – totalitarian in the sense of involving the total behaviour of the worker. Hard work and deference are no longer enough; now the 'soulful' corporation demands the workers' soul, or at least the workers' identity. (1979: 148)

Kunda describes life in a high tech company, exposing the subtlety of the new approach:

> Tech culture is not a prison and its managers are not jailers or tyrants in the simple sense of the word, but it does, nevertheless, represent a subtle form of

domination, a 'culture trap' combining normative power with a delicate balance of seductiveness and coercion. (1992: 224)

Common cultures, aligned cultures or mono-cultures, depending on your viewpoint, are inherently dangerous and at one extreme they clearly indicate a trend towards total cultures and a subtle form of totalitarianism as Marcuse explains: 'In the realm of culture, the new totalitarianism manifests itself precisely in a harmonising pluralism, where the most contradictory works and truths, peacefully co-exist in indifference' (1964: 61). These total cultures are not run by dictatorial regimes, but subtly eliminate difference and critical thinking. Foucault makes an important contribution to this debate, he points to Bentham's Panoptican to describe how surveillance and control can become internalized:

Bentham's Panopticon is, for Foucault, an ideal architectural model of modern disciplinary power. It is a design for a prison, built so that each inmate is separated from and invisible to all the others (in separate 'cells') and each inmate is always visible to a monitor situated in a central tower. Monitors will not in fact always see each inmate; the point is that they could at any time. Since inmates never know whether they are being observed, they must act as if they are always objects of observation. As a result, control is achieved more by the internal monitoring of those controlled than by heavy physical constraints.

The principle of the Panopticon can be applied not only to prisons but to any system of disciplinary power (a factory, a hospital, a school). And, in fact, although Bentham himself was never able to build it, its principle has come to pervade every aspect of modern society. It is the instrument through which modern discipline has replaced pre-modern sovereignty (kings, judges) as the fundamental power relation. (http://plato.stanford.edu/entries/foucault/, accessed 18 Sept. 2006)

Foucault writes: 'the subject who is subjected to a field of visibility, and knows it, assumes responsibility for the constraints of power ... becoming the principle of his own subjection' ([1977] 1991: 202–3). Foucault's theorizing in *Discipline and Punishment* ([1977] 1991) and his ideas suggesting the Panopticon make uncomfortable reading in contemporary culture which is imbued with surveillance cameras and technology. The modern office, for example, lends itself to Bentham's Panopticon, and enables the Transformational leader to exert culture control through the structure of the new organizational form: the open plan office. This office is open, but often with individual dividers. Thereby anybody can walk by at any time, observation by the boss or peer is constant and unpredictable. Your diary is likely to be communally open to all, thereby your hourly activity is known, and anything that might cause a breach of company policy would mean your computer hard drive and e-mails can be historically searched. The new organizational form, under the Transformational leader, is a remarkable replica of the Panoptican and Foucault's ideas. Individuals internalize and, conform to the norms established, and self-control their behaviours and, more importantly from Foucault's perspective, their thoughts.

Organizational culture is too often described as a total system, disconnected and de-contextualized from wider social and cultural implications. The external socio-economic reality has a huge impact on employees, i.e. the fear of damaging future career progression and of unemployment, need to be taken into account when discussing cultures of compliance. If one is seen to challenge, or not to fit into the company culture, the threat of job loss can have a devastating impact (on healthcare plans, children's education and one's home, social status and security). Nancy Snow, a teacher and author in the USA, describes her dilemmas on questioning cultural norms, when teaching students:

> I'd like to tell them that the body politic is more public square than Wal-Mart and that democracy is more an uproar than an unquestioning nod. But they pay good money for their educations and I wonder: what kind of career track decision would it be to think – or worse to speak – outside the all-American comfort zone? Two seconds later I hear a voice in my head. 'Look at all you have. Then look at the alternative. A or B freedom or terror' (Snow, 2002)

Snow is an example of employees who resist these cultures but keeps quiet in order to keep her livelihood. Casey (1995) describes this resistance within organizations and Melucci (1989) describes how resistant communities form and attempt to reclaim identity outside of organizational life. Some critics question the validity of these strong cultures established by Transformational leaders, believing 'normative control' to be largely rhetoric and a disguise for more traditional practices (House and Aditya, 1997; Yukl, 2002). Others argue that charismatic leaders exist but damage company performance because these cultures lead to 'organisational man' (Whyte, 1956) and monocultures, which create conformity and limit creativity.

## Visionary leaders and cult leaders

Calas and Smircich describe the contemporary leader as 'a priest/saint whose concerns for morality bring him close to God' (1995: 366), clearly the *messiah leader*! The parallels with religious conversion and the use of religious language, imagery, symbols and rituals abound in organizational life. Tourish and Pinnington describe the similarities between Transformational leadership and leadership traits within spiritual cults (See Box 9.1).

---

### Box 9.1   Transformational leadership and cults

*Transformational leader trait:* **Charismatic leadership**

**Similar Cult traits**
Leader viewed in semi-divine light by followers.
Leader sole source of ideas.
Power increasingly concentrated in leader's hands.
Leader has privileges far in excess of other group members.

*Transformational leader trait:* **A Compelling vision**

---

*(Continued)*

**Similar Cult traits**
Vision 'Totalistic' in its implications.
Agreement with vision for group membership.
Vision communicated uni-directionally from top to bottom.
Dissent from vision penalized.

*Transformational leader trait:* **Intellectual Stimulation**

**Similar Cult traits**
The vision presented as an intellectual key; unlocking secrets that others cannot comprehend.
The vision monopolizes the time, thoughts and physical energies of members.

*Transformational leader trait:* **Individual consideration**

**Similar Cult traits**
Members rewarded for compliance and penalized for dissent.
Leaders maintain that the vision is tailor-made to meet the deepest needs of the member.
Members encouraged to believe that the leader has a personal vested interest in their welfare.

*Transformational leader trait:* **Promotion of a common culture**

**Similar Cult traits**
Members begin to copy some of each other's speech mannerisms, dress codes and non-verbal gestures.
Dissent from common culture punished by withdrawal of valued social rewards.
Common culture seen as essential precondition for the group's ultimate success.

(*Source*: Adapted from Tourish and Pinnington, 2002: 162)

The associations between Transformational leadership and cult leadership do have much in common. The link between the Transformational leader and culture control is key to this claim. The Transformational leader aims to engineer and influence culture and win the loyalty and commitment of members to the organization, an area in which cult leaders have demonstrated a perverse excellence.

Transformational leaders paralleling cult leaders is more likely in a scenario whereby the leader draws their moral legitimacy explicitly from the spiritual realm. While Tourish and Pinnington do identify very similar traits between Transformational and cult leadership, they omit key differences between the two.

The definition of cults varies, but in the West they are generally thought of as dangerous because of their zealous and unquestioning commitment to a common purpose, which is at odds with orthodox religious belief (Wallis, 1975). They are also regarded as deviant and usually led by authoritarian and controlling leaders, who, to the outside world, demonstrate little of the subtleness of managing a culture within a major organization. Despite the proximity of the leadership styles, cults do not easily translate to larger, secular, organizational forms, which rarely are seen as deviant and more likely to be regarded as mainstream and an essential part of the establishment.

Transformational leaders of these organizations, while they may be powerful and charismatic, clearly do not see it in their interests or that of the company to be explicitly authoritarian and controlling through a personality cult. This is recognized by Tourish and Pinnington in their conclusion. The aims of the Transformational leadership may be to manipulate an organizational culture and followers to improve productivity and profit but this is a very different aim from that of a cult leader whose totalistic vision enters all spheres of the follower's life. The reality is that a continuum exists; the dangers of Transformational leaders turning organizations into cults are at the extreme end of this continuum, but the traits are similar enough to raise concerns. This book finds similarities not between religious cults and corporate cultures but with another religious movement, far more powerful and far more mainstream, Chapter 10 will explore this in-depth.

# Conclusion

Chapter 9 has identified why the new Messiah Leader discourse emerged. Key critical themes which emerge are the Transformational leader being a recycled and remarketed 'hero leader'. This places individualism, trait leadership and charisma back at the fore with the inherent dangers this presents. There is a particular danger of concentrated power flowing in a uni-direction from leaders to followers, which does not account for the reflexive learning loop between followers and leadership. The other main danger is a dependency and conformist culture.

The chapter finds that while the Transformational leader may have some heroic traits, this alone does not account for their popularity. The question of whether Transformational leaders really exist is posed by Yukl who asks a pertinent question and partly answers it himself through descriptive research:

> How many managers do you know that are really transformational, much less charismatic? In contrast to the survey research, descriptive research using observation and interviews to study Transformational leadership in managers found that they were not charismatic in the usual sense of the word. (2002: 38)

House and Aditya sum up this critical viewpoint:

> There is little evidence that charismatic, transformational, or visionary leadership does indeed transform individuals, groups, large divisions of organisations, or

total organisations, despite claims that they do so ... There is no evidence demonstrating stable and long-term effects of leaders on follower self-esteem, motives, desires, preferences, or values. (1997: 443)

However, the evidence is not conclusive and the huge growth in the literature and training resources provided to support this leadership style suggest that, whether leaders can be transformational or not, the discourse in which the transformational leader is situated the Leader as Messiah remains a hugely powerful influence on leadership thinking and practice.

## *Organizational culture*

Strong new cultures were required to transform the economic slump in the early 1970s and, to achieve this, a new leadership to lead and 'engineer' these cultures was sought. Peters and Waterman (1982) believed they had found the recipe, although subsequently many of the 'excellent companies' they identified fell by the wayside. They claimed the leaders needed to be charismatic and have vision without being overtly authoritarian. They needed to win people over to their beliefs and values instilling common purpose, which could encourage participative dynamics and encourage entrepreneurship and innovation to keep their organizations ahead of competitors. Employees needed to feel emotionally committed and loyal while also feeling that they retained their individuality and could align the company values to their own personal needs and growth. The *Leader as Controller* acting with a coercive and utilitarian control was no longer effective. The *Leader as Therapist* focusing on individual and team welfare helped but did not answer the paradigmatic nature of the changes the companies faced. Leaders and theorists turned to the use of normative control, to using a signifying leadership as the change agent with the aim of engineering the desired corporate culture.

## *Dependency*

Leading from a position of Messiah character is dangerous because a prophetic figure creates disciples rather than active followers and follower dependency is often the legacy of such a stance. The individual and collective unconscious social fantasy or desire is that an extraordinary leader or leadership can offer salvation from anxiety and despair, bringing new hope. By offering a vision of success, a new dawn, the new Messiah character also provides the enticing possibility to followers that if they follow the leader, they may become like the messiah. Theorists have suggested that Transformational leadership may be a retreat or flight from reality rather than an answer to it:

As despair and helplessness deepen, the search and wish for a Messiah [leader] or magical rescue [leadership] also begins to accelerate. (Gemmil and Oakley, 1992: 115)

Instead of looking for saviours, we should be calling for leadership that will challenge us to face problems for which there are no simple painless solutions – problems that require us to learn in new ways. (Heifetz, 1994: 2)

> The leader has been likened to a saviour-like essence in a world that
> constantly needs saving. (Rost, cited in Barker, 1997: 348)

The messianic idea representing leadership is popular because the messiah represents hope, fulfilling the fantasy of being saved from anxiety, fear and the unknown. Bion identifies an age-old problem for messianic leaders: 'The messianic hope must never be fulfilled, only by remaining a hope does hope exist' (1961: 151). If the hope is fulfilled and a Messiah is found, they are prone to underachieve and fail. Envy, fear, blame, disappointment and anger are attached to the failure due to the high expectations of followers and the claims of these leaders. The messianic idea is therefore very prone to being crucified as many CEOs find out.

However, the Transformational leader and Messiah character is more than a solitary charismatic hero leadership figure. This reductionist view does not account for the wider narratives which are played out in this discourse.

The Messiah leadership discourse holds the tensions that arise from the social anxiety that is produced during turbulent times. The Messiah character (the Transformational leader) is a container for these tensions. Individual and collective actors use the workplace as a theatre in order to 'enact' these anxieties in an epic living drama. The Messiah character reflects back to society its own vulnerabilities, anxieties and desires. The collective anxieties at the turn of the millennium demanded a reassuring leadership figure, to offer hope and reassurance, salvation from economic insecurity and existential alienation, the desire for community and belonging, the instillation of hope and vision.

# 10

# Religious Fundamentalism:
# Looking Awry at the Messiah Leadership Discourse

## Introduction

Chapter 10 'Looks Awry' at the Messiah discourse and seeks alternative explanations as to how and why the Transformational leader specifically, and the rise of leadership generically, rose so rapidly to the fore in the 1980s.

Jung et al. (1995) argue that while Transformational leadership can be applied to any society, it is more easily accepted in collectivistic than in individualistic societies. This is because in a collectivistic society the followers are more open and culturally aligned to being led by Transformational leaders and their methods of normative control using strong cultures.

As has been stated, Japanese economic success was one of the main catalysts for the re-thinking of leadership and organizational culture during this period. The Japanese success at managing culture rather than focusing on individual performance (Ouchi, 1981) stimulated management theorists to find ways of transferring this practice to the North American way of managing organizational culture. However, the Japanese culture and context were very different from the USA. In Japan, a pre-existing Asian collectivist culture existed and could be adapted to business success. In Japanese corporations, morning exercises and songs of loyalty were sung to the company, and the company–individual relationship was one of absolute loyalty and dependence, it was a life-long relationship. This kind of collectivism was alien to the USA with its focus on free choice and individuality.

While lessons could be learnt, the wholesale transfer of a communal Asian culture with specific Japanese attributes could not be taken and implanted in a USA individualist culture. The challenge was to find a distinctively American path to create dynamic and collectivist cultures that delivered as competitively as the Japanese economy. An indigenous, culturally relevant example of Transformational leadership was required that could act as a template for such a radical change to occur in the United States. But where could an American leadership style be found which could lead the desired radical cultural change?

What has been overlooked and omitted from the management and leadership literature is that, within the USA itself, there existed brilliant examples of Transformational leaders of collectivist cultures: Christian fundamentalist organizations.

These leaders had managed to successfully transform extreme conservative organizations into dynamic organizations with exceptional success and growth that any business leader would envy.

From a critical leadership perspective it is important to draw upon religious fundamentalism for two reasons. First, religious fundamentalism provides the leadership literature with a new resource to explore leadership of collectivist cultures, which utilizes strong culture and normative control as a method to influence followers. Second, because religious fundamentalism in the USA provides a comparative case example of the Messiah leadership discourse and the collectivist, dynamic and ultimately totalizing cultures they create. Chapter 11 argues that corporate cultures directly learnt from and mimicked Christian fundamentalist leadership styles (albeit unconsciously), replicating their visionary evangelical language and the collectivist, conformist and dynamic cultures they created.

To fully understand these links, it is important first of all to gain a greater insight into religious fundamentalism itself. This chapter now looks beyond the populist rhetoric about religious fundamentalism to find that it contains postmodern forms of leadership and organizing, which help to explain its international rise and its success in the past 30 years, and also the rise of the messiah discourse.

## An overview of religious fundamentalism

Religious fundamentalist leaders in the twentieth century achieved huge success. They demonstrated powerful charismatic and inspirational leadership, set new visions, re-invented religious practice. They successfully challenged tradition and orthodoxy, re-structured their organizations and movements, creating dynamic new organizational forms, often with a highly active and effective dispersed leadership. This will be familiar if you have read anything on Transformational Leadership in the management literature or Chapter 9 in this book on the Messiah leadership discourse.

For this reason, it is worth taking these religious fundamentalist leadership styles seriously. Not only did they create successful growth and output in their own spheres within a very short time frame, they also created grass-roots political social movements that were so successful that in the USA they reached into the heart of the USA political establishment, and on the world stage religious fundamentalism managed to influence world affairs. The following analysis of fundamentalism will challenge orthodox critical accounts that dismiss fundamentalism as a return to the past, and a dangerous non-thinking approach to religion. It is my belief that fundamentalism offers real insights into the Messiah leadership discourse. For this reason it is necessary to approach fundamentalism with a curious rather than a dismissive mind. Having established and explained the underpinning strengths of fundamentalist leadership and the cultures, I will suggest that this form of leadership is not sustainable and that the cultures it produces in the long term are 'totalizing and conformist', losing their dynamism.

# What is fundamentalism?

Fundamentalism is a disparate phenomenon – a confused category. (Hardt and Negri, 2001: 146)

Religious fundamentalist leadership, and the cultures formed within their movements and churches, provide a new resource for understanding the Messiah leadership discourse. The contemporary literature on leadership is vast; this is also true of the literature on religious fundamentalism, currently a very hot topic. Both, however, stay firmly within their separate spheres of interest and the management and leadership literature does not recognize any influence from fundamentalism on its own practice. Religious fundamentalism is, however, far more complex than it initially seems; it is a challenging contemporary phenomenon, which raises high emotions when discussed. From a secular-liberal position, the arch-enemy of fundamentalism, one often gets a negative knee-jerk response. Huff (2000: 96) sites six of his early responses, which he now sees as being reactive, but he provides a good description of a commonly perceived view of fundamentalism:

> To my way of thinking, fundamentalism, at least in its U.S. Christian form, had six dimensions. Sociologically it was related to the outdated values and repressive code of small-town America. Culturally it manifested an inclination toward the lowbrow and the vulgar. Psychologically it was marked by authoritarianism, arrogance and addiction to conspiracy theories. Intellectually it was characterised by a lack of historical consciousness and the inability to engage in critical thinking. Theologically it was identified by literalism, primitivism, legalism and tribalism. Politically it was linked to reactionary populism and the 'paranoid style'.

Barr says of Christian fundamentalism that it carries the suggestion of 'narrowness, bigotry, obscurantism and sectarianism, though this may be unpleasant it may also be true and just' (1981: 2).

Fundamentalism arouses such strong emotions that Christians who once proudly called themselves fundamentalists now use different terms to avoid the links with 'bigotry and narrowness'. One person's fundamentalism, however, is another person's defending of the true faith. It is important that fundamentalism is thought about within a critical and thoughtful context in order to make sense of it, without overlaying it and dismissing it within the hegemony of Western liberal ideology where it becomes simply a 'bad object'. Those who claim to support and represent plurality and liberal democracy so often take up an 'unthinking' and reactionary response to religious fundamentalism, mirroring the intolerance and rigidity they claim to reject.

Fundamentalism has returned religion to the main political stage when it was in serious decline. Its impact on the world's great religions, national and international politics, as well as on the personal lives of millions of people, is a testimony to its power and influence. Fundamentalism has shown itself to be a global phenomenon and is not restricted to 'less developed' nations, the USA being a clear example.

Fundamentalism is a term applied to religious reforming movements, there are Buddhist, Hindu and even Confucian fundamentalists (Armstrong, 2000). The term fundamentalism has also been applied to the secular 'movement' the neo-liberals and 'corporatism' (Ali, 2002) reducing the term fundamentalism to its most populist meaning; a movement which is rigid, radically conservative, totalitarian in its aspirations, convinced of its righteousness and acting with evangelical and religious zeal. There are, however, multiple understandings of what defines religious fundamentalism. Castells writes: 'that religious fundamentalism has existed throughout the whole of human history, but it appears to be surprisingly strong at the end of this millennium' (1997: 13), whereas Armstrong stresses that 'fundamentalism is an essentially twentieth century movement' (2000: xi). Both, however, agree that religious fundamentalism is a reaction against modernism and secularism and that its contemporary rise has been remarkable and very successful. It is widely accepted that the term fundamentalism was first used in the early twentieth century to describe a movement within the Protestant tradition in America:

> The word fundamentalism appears to have been derived from a series of booklets entitled 'The Fundamentals', which were published in America during 1910–15. In them the term was used for elements of traditional doctrine – the inspiration and authority of scripture, the deity of Jesus Christ, the virgin birth and others – which are dear also to the fundamentalist of today. (Barr, 1981: 2)

Cole (1931) writes of 'The Fundamentals': 'They [a group of earnest believers] delivered their orthodox manifesto as a test of Christian loyalty and as a corrective to the position of the liberals. In this action the historian finds the clear emergence of fundamentalism.'

Some religious scholars see fundamentalism wholly in this Christian context and believe it cannot easily be used in relation to Islam, Judaism, or Hinduism or secular movements. Barr (1981) takes this traditional view and pronounces the following three general characteristics of Christian fundamentalism:

- a very strong emphasis on the inerrancy of the Bible;
- a strong hostility to modern theology and to the methods, results and implications of modern critical Bible study;
- an assurance that those who do not share their religious viewpoint are not really Christians at all.

By this definition, most contemporary evangelicals would also be fundamentalists. Interestingly, he challenges the general belief that Christian fundamentalists' core belief resides in the authority of the Bible. Barr maintains that fundamentalism is a particular kind of religious tradition that controls the interpretation of the Bible, rather than actually treating it as inerrant as they claim (1981: 11). Frosh (1997: 422) agrees, expanding this to all fundamentalisms, saying that all sacred texts require an interpretation and he says it is the ownership of the texts and the authority to interpret them that is important, not the literalist adherence. Armstrong and others point out that religious fundamentalists usually begin with a spiritual war within their own religious group.

The term fundamentalism is now used beyond its Christian Protestant origins and has a much broader meaning, which is pluralistic rather than singular. The term 'fundamentalisms' is more adequate than the singular 'fundamentalism' as it takes account of different forms in different religions (Vuola, 2002). Armstrong believes 'Each fundamentalism is a law unto itself and has its own dynamic' (2000: Intro). She does acknowledge its wide common usage and says that, despite their differences, these fundamentalist movements bear a strong family resemblance. I will briefly address Islamic fundamentalism before focusing on Christian fundamentalism in the USA and the link to Transformational leadership.

## Islamic fundamentalism

Islamic fundamentalism has a variety of roots and expressions. Most commentators agree that Islamic fundamentalism is not a traditionalist movement but a modern movement, which reconstructs a cultural identity. Islamic fundamentalism is itself plural but John Gray claims that Islamic fundamentalism is mistakenly thought of as a return to mediaeval society, which was founded on a belief in authority. He refers to the movements as 'radical Islam' which he claims draws heavily on early modern millenarian movements, such as anarchists like the Russian Mikhail Bakunin who rejected established authority (Gray, 2003: 20). Gray also links it to radical liberation movements saying that modern writers such as Frantz Fanon and the existentialist Jean-Paul Sartre have inspired Islamic fundamentalists. Islamic fundamentalism's radical movements such as Al Qaeda have gone beyond the usual boundaries of fighting within one's own religious tradition and nation–state and are examples of how, far from being mediaeval, they have embraced contemporary globalization. They have taken their fight beyond national borders to challenge the global hegemony of Westernization and have created new networked organizing forms to create an 'asymmetric warfare where the weak seek out to exploit the vulnerabilities of the strong' (ibid.: 82). It seems that the more fundamentalists face oppression, the more likely a violent reaction will be the response. Armstrong explains why American Christian fundamentalism has not been so violent as other forms of fundamentalism:

> Americans have not resorted to the same degree of violence as Islamic fundamentalists because the attacks on them have been far less extreme. But they inveigh against the 'secular humanism' of the federal government in language that often seems as paranoid as that used by their Muslim counterparts against America or Israel. In small-town America, people feel almost as 'colonised' by the alien ethos of Yale, Harvard and Washington as do some of the inhabitants of Muslim countries. (Armstrong, 2001)

Violence is not restricted to fundamentalists from other religions and countries. In the USA, the State versus Christian fundamentalists have had battles, with lives lost on both sides. Eighty men women and children died at Waco, Texas, when the FBI besieged David Koresh's Branch Davidian sect. Timothy Mcveigh's bomb attack on the federal building in Oklahoma City on 19 April, 1995 was said to be inspired by the ultra-right, extreme fundamentalists such as 'Christian Identity'. Their aim was to get rid of the federal government which they call ZOG the 'Zionist Occupation Government', believing it to be dominated by Satan and Jews, and they are preparing for Armageddon (Armstrong, 2000: 363).

Box 10.1 shows the common themes from different religious fundamentalist movements.

---

## Box 10.1    The fundamentalist mindset

### Authority and truth
The movement's leaders have the divine authority to interpret sacred texts and formulate the truth from these texts. Within fundamentalism is the acceptance of absolute authority, interpreted by leaders. Hostility to modern theological methods and new insights into the original reading of text.

### Militancy
Evangelical militancy often begins within the movement's own faith community, e.g. Christian fundamentalists condemn liberal Christians over issues such as biblical inerrancy, homosexuality or women priests before taking their concerns to other faiths.

### Leadership
Fundamentalist leadership is transformational, innovative and charismatic, rather than an institutional hierarchy in traditional religious leadership. It usually has a male bias.

### Anti-modern
Fundamentalists look to an idyllic past and claim to be against modernity culture. They revere mythos and distrust rationality and reason. However, while anti-modern, they can also be seen as post-modern social movements, dynamic and re-inventing their faith communities to meet contemporary needs. They are conservative radicals rather than emancipatory radicals.

### The chosen community
A chosen people to enact 'God's' will for a purpose in the world.

### Social change
Wishing to change society, social codes, structures and constructs in line with their beliefs either through changing legal governance or through creating a new social order within their community and colonizing other social spaces to achieve this.

*(Continued)*

*(Continued)*

**Denial of difference**
Gender and sexual issues often feature highly. Childbirth and the role of women in society are prominent. Women are often both idealized by fundamentalists as mothers and 'bearers of culture' and also denigrated as 'other', i.e. as sexual objects (Frosh, 1997: 422). Also diversity is feared, fundamentalists usually appeal to single ethnic/religious groups and fear other religious practice.

**Martyrs and persecution**
Very often fundamentalists attract persecution and also idealize it as part of the sacrifice which binds them as a group, fits with a mindset of paranoia about the world and also convinces them that they are on track with their mission (usually supported by sacred texts).

**Millenarianism and perfection**
Fundamentalists have an 'edenic ideology' a belief in perfection from sin, and the immanent arrival of the 'kingdom'. This is enacted in diverse ways in different fundamentalist movements.

## Fundamentalism: pre-modern or post-modern?

The populist idea that religious fundamentalism is a pre-modern regressive force is one of the commonest themes refuted by critical scholars: 'The term also gives the impression that fundamentalists are inherently conservative and wedded to the past, whereas their ideas are essentially modern and highly innovative' (Armstrong, 2000: x). According to Castells (1997: 25), fundamentalism is a reactive movement, idealizing a past, looking to a utopian future in order to overcome an unbearable present. Others argue that while fundamentalists often have millenarian perspectives, they are also very effective and innovative in the present. Fundamentalism is very much a modern movement and some suggest a hyper-modern movement (Gole, 1997), others a post-modern movement (Frosh, 1997; Hardt and Negri, 2001). Fundamentalists in various traditions teach that there was a 'perfect moment', an idealized past and they endeavour to recover that moment. Hardt and Negri state '[the] return to the traditional family as not backward-looking at all, but rather a new invention that is part of a political project against the contemporary social order' (2001: 148). Frosh discusses religious fundamentalism generically and suggests it is a specific anti-modern movement: 'A response to the crisis of rationality which draws on the same emotional forces as do feminism and post-modernism but to different ends' (1997: 417). He characterizes it by:

> [the] acceptance of absolute authority, militancy and anti-humanism. It casts women as both 'ideal' as [mothers and bearers of the culture] and 'other'

[as sexual objects]. It embodies the failure of the imaginative capacity to tolerate difference and otherness, linking it with other narcissistic responses to the tensions of modernity. (ibid.: 417)

Frosh describes modernity inflicting a fragmentation of social life, which produces uncertainty, 'the sense of tragedy, degradation and annihilation being just around the corner' (ibid.: 417). He then makes the unlikely link to postmodernism: 'Fundamentalism is like postmodernism in that it is a response to the crisis of rationality to the despair of modernity. Fundamentalism responds in a time honoured way; it refused them absolutely' (ibid.: 417).

Hardt and Negri agree, saying fundamentalism 'is not a re-creation of a pre-modern world but rather a powerful refusal of the contemporary historical passage in course' (2001: 146–7). This is an odd coupling, according to Hardt and Negri, who claim that the difference between those social movements who claim to be post-modern and those who become fundamentalist is that 'Post-modern discourses appeal to the winners of the process of globalisation and fundamentalist to the losers' (ibid.: 148). Armstrong uses Ayatollah Khomeini of Iran to further the point that fundamentalism is much more than it appears on the surface and has a revolutionary and innovative side as well as a reactionary one:

> The Ayatollah Khomeini was essentially a man of the 20th century. Instead of harking back to the Dark Ages, he was really introducing a revolutionary form of Shi'ism that was, in fact, as innovative as if the Pope had abolished the Mass. But most of us didn't understand enough about Shi'ism to appreciate that. (Armstrong, 2002)

Taking into account the diversity within the term fundamentalism, one must look beyond initial appearances of conservative, reactionary and anti-modern, movements. Fundamentalism needs to be understood within a wider historical, global and social-political context. Religious fundamentalism today usually takes on the paradoxical position of being innovative in their anti-modern stance and radical in their conservatism. They are far from antiquities and the descriptions of them as post-modern movements seem apt. The fundamentalists are radical religious conservatives, often with charismatic leadership and dynamic organizational cultures. Re-inventing their religious beliefs, they confront the pervasive forces of secularism and modernity, aiming to protect their communities from atomizing and alienating forces which undermine their morality, their community and their deity.

## Communities: a fundamentalist challenge to individualism

An explicit feature of fundamentalism is the way it manages to re-invent new forms and at the same time defends existing forms of 'traditional' community. Modernity's success limits traditional sites for community and the increasingly individualized social fabric means that the idea of community itself has become counter-cultural. A fundamentalist church community, sharing a collective identity and strongly held values and beliefs, stands as a symbolic witness to the power of the group and to a reliance on relationships. While part of the Christian fundamentalist discourse celebrates individualism, which is deeply embedded in both Protestantism and American culture, individualism can also be an attribute of collective identity (Lasch, 1979; Castells, 1997). The Christian fundamentalists have created a very strong collective identity, with individual salvation, to be 'born again' as one of its bedrocks. One of the fundamentalist's primary tasks is to evangelize individuals. Addison Leitch (1956) writes: 'There is no salvation by way of the social gospel, but only in the individual's call to Christ. But there is no such thing as an asocial Christian'. Leitch, like Billy Graham, believes that community comes as a by-product of individuals being born again:

> The government may try to legislate Christian behaviour, but it soon finds that man remains unchanged. The changing of men's hearts is the primary mission of the church. The only way to change men is to get them converted to Jesus Christ. Then they will have the capacity to live up to the Christian command to 'love thy neighbour'. (Graham, 1968)

However, while the fundamentalist language fits with the culturally dominant view of individual freedom being sacrosanct, the practice is very much one of building a community, with the individualist rhetoric as part of the cement which binds the collective together. As a community, they are 'the chosen people', fulfilling God's will on earth. There is a spiritual reliance on a deity and, practically and psychologically, a reliance on each other, the community.

Their shared beliefs, shared worship and commitment to the collective church community, become a symbolic challenge to the hegemony of atomization. Despite their emphasis on individual salvation, they present a serious unconscious challenge to the view that individual freedom is the highest aspiration. Etzioni (1993, 2002) has long called for communitarianism and praises religious communities:

> Compare social conduct in strong communities like Mormon Utah, the Hasidic neighborhoods of New York City and Israeli kibbutzim to behavior in our prisons, where the state oversees individuals in the most direct way. When communal bonds are tight and belief [religious or secular] is fervent, we find that abortion, drug and alcohol abuse and violence are rare and that voluntarism and social responsibility flourish; the state plays a small role in sustaining the social order. (Etzioni, 1993: 56)

The Christian fundamentalists' communitarian side is powerfully present and active. Putnam's (2000) book *Bowling Alone*, powerfully depicts the atomization in the USA and he shows a decline in civic engagement in the USA. Membership of clubs, voting in elections, going to meetings and also socializing with friends, have all decreased. Putnam says these activities grew in the first part of the twentieth century but have been in decline since the 1960s. However, one reversal of this trend is the evangelical Christians, which, he points out, were traditionally a Protestant Quietist movement:

> Religious conservatives have created the largest, best-organised grassroots social movement of the last quarter century. It is, in short, among evangelical Christians, rather than among the ideological heirs of the sixties, that we find the strongest evidence of an upwelling of civic engagement. (ibid.: 162)

Roger Scruton points out the contemporary dilemma that takes place around individual freedom and the community:

> The question that I raised in 'Communitarian Dreams' is precisely the one that Etzioni has not answered: namely, to borrow his own terms, how do we fashion a viable 'we' in modern conditions, while retaining the sovereignty to which the 'I' has become accustomed? (in Etzioni, 1997: 72)

This question is fundamental to the corporate leader who wishes to create strong aligned cultures and also encourage individual creativity.

It is my observation that the Christian fundamentalists have attempted to address this, by harnessing the 'I' as the essence of their discourse – the only way to salvation is for each individual to be born again – and have created a shared reality and experience of personal salvation in which the 'I' becomes the bedrock for a very powerful 'we'.

The atomization, loss of community and alienation within westernized society, are the reasons given for people turning to fundamentalist religious beliefs. This quote is given as an example of why some British Muslims join fundamentalist Islamic groups in the Middle East:

> Many British Muslims go to Damascus seeking a spiritual experience: One local student studying there said, 'They are known as "spiritual refugees", escaping from the soul-less wastelands of modernity. Some of them go native – they don't come back.' (Bright and Alam, 2003)

The fundamentalist communities often go beyond identification and shared meanings and develop highly effective social structures that provide grass-roots social welfare and education facilities. Christian fundamentalists in the USA (and their immensely effective missionaries in South America and Africa), Hezbollah in Lebanon, Hamas in Palestine, the Muslim Brothers in Egypt and Jewish funda-mentalists, for example, all excel in creating and nurturing communities of spirit and of action. Fundamentalists often gain widespread support through social activities which they provide in areas where the state provision fails; whether it is to feed the poor in Egypt, provide education and social care in Palestine, or help the aged, urban homeless or to create a gym at the local church for the youth group in the USA. Another form of fundamentalist solidarity taken to an extreme comes from Al Qaeda, which successfully fuses modern Western influences with Islamic themes. Gray writes about their organizing, using pre-modern social forms such as extended families:

> Its clannish structure makes it extremely difficult to penetrate ... Al Qaeda has the strength that comes with its rejection of individualism. The relationships of

trust on which its organisation can rely and the willingness of its operatives to go to certain death, give it a powerful advantage. Liberal societies cannot replicate this suicidal solidarity. Values of personal choice and self-realisation are too deeply encrypted within them. (Gray, 2003: 83)

While leaders of corporate businesses don't actively wish for this extreme level of solidarity from employees, the Transformational leader does pursue ever-increasing commitment and attempts to replicate the solidarity, clannish culture and strong emotional bonds between employees exhibited by the fundamentalist communities. The atomization and alienation experienced in secular modernity may attract individuals to this type of corporate collectivized culture. One of the stated aims of Transformational leadership is to give the follower something to believe in beyond themselves, i.e. the leader's vision and morality, as Bass (1990a) states: 'These leaders will generate awareness and acceptance of the purposes and missions of the organisation and stir the employees to look beyond their own self-interests for the good of the overall entity.'

The Christian fundamentalist movement managed to produce a style of Transformational leadership that offered a vision and a clear set of beliefs from which emerges a dynamic and collective actor. Individuals, however, retain an identity of personal special-ness, a personal relationship with Jesus (and their pastor). This individual and collective sense of belonging and meaning is converted into commitment and action. This is precisely what the Transformational leaders are attempting to replicate in their organizations within the business world.

## Families, teams and clans

New organizational forms have emerged in an attempt to find ways of being more responsive to the speed of change required in organizations and commercial life. The team and the family as metaphors are promoted (as advocated by Peters and Waterman 1982; Ouchi, 1981) as one of the basic structural forms of social organization which, it is hoped, will achieve these company goals. Kunda's (1992) research into a high tech company he renamed 'Tech', found employees using the family as an oft cited metaphor about their teams and their relationship to their company. Casey (1995) found that the family metaphor was not optional, but essential for these progressive companies and is now part of the architectural design of organizations. Casey went on to describe how strong team mindsets broadened participation in management, leading to employee empowerment. The Japanese culture was cited as one of the sources of this cultural approach using family teams; however, another closer to home model was the successful Church house group movement, which became popular in the 1960s and 1970s as a counter-culture Christian movement. This became very important as a bedrock of the fundamentalist movement, acting subversively sometimes within and often in opposition to, the institutional church.

The fundamentalists, acting against a failing and staid institutional church, innovated a new movement and organizational structure which cut through the old denominational divisions. This structure places its members in a flattened hierarchy, at the centre of worship, rather than watching a performance like an audience. Some of these house groups form what are now called cell churches and worship without any formal leadership or ministers, others are essential parts of the new super-churches, led by fundamentalist pastors but are not part of the 'old' institutional order. The dynamic house church movement precedes what Casey calls the new architectural design of organizations (which uses this same formula): small family-sized groups, a flattened hierarchy, and committed to and sharing in vision and values of the larger 'parent' organization.

The family metaphor seems purposively chosen by business Transformational leaders to create associations with the idealized family, which would help create the solidarity that comes from feeling part of a clan or family:

> The family metaphor actively evokes pre-industrial romantic images of human bonding and shared struggles against adversity ... employees assume family-like roles with each other and are managed by family rules and processes. The family is also hierarchical paternalistic and deferential to higher external authorities (Casey, 1995: 113).

Casey's ethnographic research found that small teams were set within the whole company, which extended the metaphor and was referred to as the 'great team'. Ouchi called these processes 'clan control', as they produce deep loyalty and dedication to the team. Kanter claims that work in these new company cultures, 'may be the closest to an experience of "community" or total commitment for many workers, a dramatic, exciting and almost communal process brought to the corporation' (1983: 203). The use of the family as a metaphor and organizing into house groups and family-teams had similar and powerful cultural impacts in their respective environments.

## Corporate fundamentalism

The term 'corporate fundamentalism' is sometimes used to describe corporations as the main collective actors of the neo-liberal agenda, which itself has a totalizing tendency within global politics. Corporate commercial advertising through the TV, the internet and billboards is accused of colonizing and 'polluting' public spaces. Out-of-town shopping malls make car ownership essential, leaving behind empty shops in local streets and a diminished sense of community:

> I picture the reality in which we live of military occupation. We are occupied the way the French and Norwegians were occupied by the Nazis during World War II, but this time by an army of marketeers. We have to reclaim our country from those who occupy it on behalf of their global masters. (Ursula Franklin, Professor Emeritus, University of Toronto 1998, cited in Klein, 2000: 311)

Klein argues in *No Logo* (2000) that the commercial pressures put upon artists, advertisers and filmmakers leads to an increasing level of censorship by retailers and the end result is a colonization of everyday life. The expanding power of the corporates, set within a neo-liberal framework, is a powerful socio-political as well as economic force. The intellectual 'left', anti-capitalist movement and diverse political and religious movements critique this trend, which they call free market or neo-liberal fundamentalism. Naomi Klein used the term 'McGovernment' to describe the free-marketeers' rampant march:

> This happy meal of cutting taxes, privatising services, liberalising regulations, busting unions, what is this diet in aid of? To remove anything standing in the way of the market. Let the free market roll and every other problem will apparently be solved by trickle down. This isn't about trade. It's about using trade to enforce the McGovernment recipe. (Klein, 2001: 87)

The opponents of neo-liberalism argue that an Orwellian doublethink takes place, whereby freedom, democracy and individualism are espoused, while at the same time thought, dissent and action are repressed, through the colonizing of public and private space. The anti-capitalist movement claims that the economic-political system produces a fundamentalism as the corporate wealthy own the media, fund election campaigns and politicians and undermine dissent. Madeline Bunting calls it a Westernized fundamentalism:

> A westernised fundamentalism believes that historical progress is most advanced in the west and the neo-liberal agenda attempts to bring underdeveloped nations up to higher [more civilised and economically developed level]. The west is toler-ant towards other cultures only to the extent that they reflect its own values – so it is frequently fiercely intolerant of religious belief and has no qualms about expressing its contempt and prejudice. (Bunting, 2001)

Corporations and multinational companies led by Transformational leaders are identified as the main collective actors within this neo-liberal agenda. It is argued that they create interdependent, dominating power elites, which are global and largely unaccountable. Some view them as a hugely successful economic force set within democratic structures and a means of providing wealth and economic growth throughout the world. Others see them as 'fanatical preachers of neo-liberalism' (Ali, 2002: 312), a hegemony with totalitarian tendencies. It is not only anti-capitalists and other 'leftist' critics' who use this language; the influential and Nobel Prize-winning economist, Joseph Stiglitz, writes:

> The scandals over conflicts of interest in accounting and banking were predictable fruits of 'market fundamentalism'. The image is Adam Smith the reality is Enron ... We live in a world driven by economics. Liberal democracies use it as a theology to justify taxation policies, the ownership of the media, immigration policy and an unelected official's ability to overrule the manifesto of an elected president. (Stiglitz, 2003)

And President Chirac of France warned in a speech on cultural policy that:

> 'The champions of unlimited trade liberalisation are once again lining up against those who believe that the creations of the mind cannot be reduced to the rank of

ordinary merchandise' and went on to accuse these 'free traders' of seeking to
foist cultural 'products pre-formatted for the masses' on an unsuspecting world.
(cited in Hrab, 2004)

The neo-liberal project is in the ascendancy and operates from a position of ideology which its supporters believe to be righteous. It leads them to protect their
existing free market economies and to export their economic and political system
in order to protect and export democracy, freedom itself. Habermas (1987) calls
this process the 'colonisation of the lifeworld'; others agree, using a different language, as their book titles demonstrate; Hertz (2001) *The Silent Takeover*, Hardt and
Negri (2001) *Empire* and Monbiot (2000) *Captive State: The Corporate Takeover of
Britain*. The claim has been made that, at a meta-political level, the neo-liberal
agenda has fundamentalist overtones.

# New social movement theory

New social movement (NSM) theory is under-utilized to understand the leadership and organizing process in both religious fundamentalist movements, and
corporate organizations. It brings another resource to the leadership table and
helps look awry at leadership. There are sharp differences between new social
movements and organizations such as corporations, but also growing areas of
cross-over. The move away from hierarchy and towards dispersed leadership,
self-managed teams, normative control, matrix structures and the focus on networking suggest much can be learnt from the NSM research carried out by sociologists, anthropologists and ethnologists. Utilizing this theoretical resource helps
clarify some theoretical issues as to how we can understand fundamentalism and
it also has applications to how we understand leading new organizational forms
from a critical leadership studies.

Casey argues that fundamentalists may be post-modern, but what separates them
from other social movements is that they are reactionary, rather than emancipatory.
Referring to fundamentalism, she writes: 'These manifestations of the struggle
over the symbolic realm and over identity may be interpreted as reactionary post-
modern events in that they defy the completion of modernity's rationalising project
and the emancipatory endeavours of new social movements' (Casey, 1995: 18).

New social movements arise as communities of resistance to what they perceive to
be a threat (Melucci, 1989; Etzioni, 1993; Castells, 1997), which is also true of fundamentalist movements. The sociologist Alberto Melucci's work is important in that it
reveals a social dynamic that is valuable to the understanding of religious fundamentalism and can be applied to leadership of organizations. He says that moving beyond
grand narrative and single order systems of explanation opens up possibilities to
move from reductionist theories to those that attempt to account for complexity:

Social movements are cast as figures in an epic tragedy, as heroes and villains
who are moving towards some grand ideal or dramatic destiny, with the public
having to side with one or other of the play's main characters – the hero or the
villain – since this choice determines the destiny of the society, its progress into
civilisation or its descent into barbarism. (Melucci, 1989: 25)

He claims it is the imagery of social movements as a heroic single personage that needs challenging, Melucci states: 'Only then can we begin to understand the plurality of perspectives, meanings and relationships, which make up any given collective action' (1989: 25). This is also true when attempting to understand the Transformational/heroic leader: it is only when we get past the heroic single personage and address complexity that a more complete understanding will emerge.

## *The movement is the message*

In 1967, Marshall McLuhan and Fiore famously claimed the 'medium is the message' and that 'all media work us over completely'. He was indicating the power of communication and that meaning was no longer communicated simply through what is said, but more importantly through how (the medium) it is communicated. Melucci claims that new social movements operate in this way, as a 'message' or a 'sign' to society: 'From their particular context, movements send signals, which illuminate hidden controversies about the appropriate form of fundamental social relations within complex societies' (1989: 206). Likewise, religious fundamentalists offer symbolic messages through their 'movements', contesting social domination which they perceive as pervasively infiltrating and 'colonising their lifeworlds'.

Melucci (1989) proposes that new social movements have three forms of symbolic challenge:

1  *Prophecy*: the act of announcing, based on personal experiences, that alternative frameworks of meaning are possible.
2  *Paradox*: reversal of dominant codes by their exaggeration.
3  *Representation*: the movement plays back to society itself, revealing contradictions and irrationality.

Clearly, this could have been written specifically for religious fundamentalist movements, some of which have highly developed these ways of symbolic challenge. How the fundamentalists organize and live within their communities, i.e. the form they take which signifies a message to society, is often lost, missed or purposely ignored.

These signifying messages are the driving forces within the fundamentalist movements. Depending on how these messages and signs are prioritized internally within movements and which particular social context they face which societal responses they receive will determine the tensions and social dynamics that occur.

Religious fundamentalism should be viewed through two dimensions in order to understand why it has such an impact on individuals and society:

1  *Explicit aims*: the stated religious, political and social goals of the movement.
2  *The signifying message*: fundamentalist movements acting as signs and messages for society at large. The forms they take represent the message: how they organize their communities and their collective actions, specifically, the conflicts they choose to contest, reveal the tensions and hidden power structures within society.

The first dimension is often the only lens through which fundamentalists are viewed, often with incredulity, as they seem so out of place with modernity and particularly with liberal democracy.

The second dimension is often misinterpreted, for example, the Old Order Amish, who dress plainly, have become a tourist industry for the thousands who take a bus and watch them in Lancaster County, 'stuck in their quaint time warp'. But their plain dress and lifestyle are much more than a people stuck in a frozen historical moment, and an opportunity to idealize the past for the visiting tourists. This is not a movement stuck in the seventeenth century but one that considers innovations and changes very carefully. The community discerns whether a technological innovation, tractors, mobile phones, for example, will or will not benefit the community and its way of life, and its calling to follow God. In continuing to live 'plainly', the Old Amish Order both act for themselves and their own beliefs but also as a signifier for wider society (Western, 2000). The plain dress and plain simple lifestyle are a sign, a message, witnessing that all are equal under God, that one shouldn't be vain and attached to fashions, that consumerism isn't the only way of life, that technology and materialism do not necessarily bring happiness, and that continuity is as important as change. The Amish have been doing what Melucci describes as the 'new' social movements for more than 350 years: 'Participation within movements is considered a goal in itself. Actors practice in the present the future social changes they seek' (Melucci, 1989: 5–6). The Amish attempt to live in the present, how the future should be; a divine focused simple life. In 2006, a gunman walked into an Amish school room, and shot and killed a number of Amish children. Their community response was immediate forgiveness of the gunman and they visited his wife and family to pray with and for them. This contrast to how most of the Western world responds to aggression, whether it is personal or at national levels, demonstrates the power of cultural norms. In the Amish community, the deeply embedded cultural norms of nonviolence and forgiveness, overcame other possible and likely responses even under this extraordinary and extreme pressure.

In the case of the Amish, this power of community and the cultural norms present an extreme and fundamentalist form of religion which does little harm to others, and holds to an ethical position on violence which is widely admired (except at times of national war, when their refusal to fight has caused problems). In other cases the power of cultural norms and culture control act in the opposite way, as we have seen with suicide bombers in the Middle East, for example.

Melucci describes how 'the message' operates for new social movements:

> The very forms of the movements, their patterns of interpersonal relationships and decision-making mechanisms operate as a 'sign' or 'message' for the rest of society. E.g. the women's movement for instance, not only raises important questions about equality and rights. They also, at the same time, deliberately signal to the rest of society the importance of recognizing differences within complex societies. (Melucci, 1989: 5–6)

Religious fundamentalists operate on this same symbolic realm as new social movements. The conflicts they choose are on symbolic grounds; they are not just operating on an explicit level as characters to gain political power, but as signs translating their actions to symbolic codes, that overturn dominant cultural codes. The effect of this is '[to] render power visible ... The power in complex societies is often concealed – submerged diffuse, hidden behind bureaucracy administration or show business politics' (Melucci, 1989: 76). Once a hidden power is made visible and explicit, it can be challenged.

# Conclusion

Religious fundamentalist leaders created dynamic collectivist cultures which have been internationally successful. Karen Armstrong claims that, 'Religion has once again become a force that no government can ignore' (2000: x). This is quite a feat in a world dominated by science and rationalism. Chapter 10 aimed to highlight the successes of fundamentalist leaders, demonstrating how they formed collectivist cultures with dispersed leadership, and the power which strong cultures could have. I have not focused on the dangers of these movements and their powerfully conformist cultures as these are well rehearsed elsewhere. I will, however, turn to these issues and be more specific about the dangers of conformist and totalizing cultures in Chapter 11, when I deal with Transformational leaders following the lead from fundamentalist leaders and the impact on corporate and organizational culture.

New social movement theories add to our knowledge of how these collectivized cultures act at two levels, the Messiah leadership discourse in the world of organizations also acts at these two levels. *The explicit level* is conscious and the known, i.e. the need for a leadership style that can succeed economically. In this case, the competencies of the transformational leader with the ability to create strong cultures.

*The signifying message* is unconscious and hidden. The workplace as a contemporary site of community reflects the broader social issues, the crisis of confidence in secular, atomized society. A growing sense of alienation and insecurity linked to huge global and technological changes. The atomized subject seems bewildered amidst an overload of information and change, with very little job security and  inundated with news/media flashes relating to a culture of fear, regarding health, terrorism and environmental catastrophe. This produces an unconscious desire for a leader to offer hope, vision, community, solidarity, and security. A *Messiah character* embodies this discourse, signifying our contemporary age of anxiety.

Chapter 11 will now explore the links and connections between the Messiah discourse in the business world and religious fundamentalism.

# 11

# Christian Fundamentalism and Corporate America

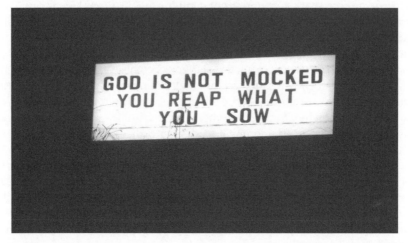

**Figure 11.1**   A neon sign outside a fundamentalist church in California, USA, 2006

Religious fundamentalism must be regarded as one of, if not the most, successful forms of social movement of contemporary times. In the USA, the charismatic leadership of American Christian fundamentalists achieved what many corporate leaders sought: a homogenized collectivist culture based on the leader's vision; shared values and beliefs, high levels of cohesion, loyalty and commitment. Most importantly, these leaders had transformed southern conservative churches into highly motivated, dynamic cultures with an entrepreneurial spirit, leading to huge growth in numbers and in prosperity. These Transformational leaders also translated this new social movement into a political power base that shook the USA. Making connections between corporate leadership and religious fundamentalist leadership and culture was and is heterodoxy in the management literature. The negative connotations that fundamentalism raises help explain why these links are missing from the management literature.

I will now address the links between Christian fundamentalist leadership and corporate culture in the USA. I will begin by outlining the differences and similarities between the two in Box 11.1.

---

## Box 11.1    Christian fundamentalism and corporate culture

### *Differences* between Christian fundamentalism and corporate culture

**God/Deity**
The ultimate goals differ: fundamentalists follow their prophet; corporations make a profit.

Despite the similar usage of evangelical language, of mission statements and visions, there are real differences, which affect how they organize and how the membership identifies with the leader. The belief in a transcendent God creates a particularly powerful *messianic character* in the church.

**Outputs**
The outputs from diverse secular organizations and the outputs from a Christian community differ. The product/output affects organizational cultures, both through modes of production, the division of labour and psychically how members identify and associate with the output/product. An arms manufacturer differs in culture from a hospital and the output of saving souls is different to that of maximizing profit.

**Voluntary membership and paid employee**
To be a paid employee rather than a voluntary member of a church also creates a different dynamic, although these boundaries are being broken down as the new organizational cultures become established. The church must therefore rely totally on normative control of its members as, unlike working with paid employees, it has few material transactions through which to control them, except the soul, psyche and emotions. However, with the changing nature of the workplace and the shift to covenantal-style leadership, the corporate world is moving to a much greater reliance on normative control which is why it can learn/borrow so much from the religious community.

**Church identity**
The Church provides a refuge, a community away from work reinforcing a sense of self or communal identity which can be different or complementary to the work self. It provides an opportunity to reflect on the softer aspects of oneself: being a family and community member, rather than the driven and task-orientated side at the workplace.

*(Continued)*

---

*(Continued)*

### *Similarities* between Christian fundamentalism and corporate culture

**Transformational leadership**
Based on mythos, signifying powers and normative control to create conformist, homogeneous and yet dynamic cultures. Predominantly gendered as male.

**Conviction of righteousness, certainty of the truth**
Free market corporate culture believes 'there is no other way' but the free market, and fundamentalist Christianity believes that 'there is no other way' but their form of Christianity.

**Intolerance of difference, refuting pluralism**
Again, both believe 'there is no other way'. The only pluralism accepted by corporate culture is the pluralism within the bounds of westernized market democracy. Other forms of governance and economic functioning are blasphemous. Conflict is encouraged to defeat opposing ideologies; anything which challenges the hegemony of either belief systems

**Growth**
Both fundamentalists and corporate culture aim for gaining 'greater market share' in their own terms.

**'Religious' evangelizing zeal**
Both have this in abundance and both aim to convert/conquer new markets and new believers.

**Structural organization**
Charismatic leadership with flattened hierarchies, organized around family-sized teams/groups, dispersed leadership, set within a larger homogeneous community, held together by visions, values and normative control.

---

# The Transformational leader and Christian fundamentalism in the USA

The Transformational leader became prominent in the United States during the late 1970s (Burns, 1978), at the same time as the Christian fundamentalist revival. After half a century when fundamentalists had withdrawn and become quietist, they found a new strength and confidence to become visible and politically active. Led by Jerry Falwell, the Moral Majority, formed in 1979, symbolized this growth. Karen Armstrong (2000: 308) notes that three professional right-wing political organizers inspired this movement. They wanted to build a conservative alliance to oppose the moral and social liberalism which had grown since the 1960s and they noted the strength of the evangelical and fundamentalist Protestants and saw Jerry Falwell as perfect for their needs with his 'huge made-ready constituency'. The Moral Majority went beyond Protestant fundamentalists and included other denominations and other religions, including Catholics, Jews and Mormons.

Armstrong notes that, 'Militant Christians began to colonise mainstream institutions for the next decade.'

## The New Christian Right

This religious fundamentalist revival began in the 1960s and 1970s and by the late 1970s had gained momentum and self-confidence, the Moral Majority as its symbol, headed by Jerry Falwell. The fundamentalist movement has been dominated by Protestant evangelicals but has also grown to encompass other Christian dominations and become known as the New Christian Right which, 'was declaring war on the liberal establishment and fighting a battle for the future of America' (Armstrong, 2000: 110). The Christian fundamentalists believed in biblical inerrancy and were politically radical conservatives. The Moral Majority impacted on millions and grew through expert communicators, using the media in new ways (televangelism) and offering a transformational, visionary, charismatic leadership based on strong moral 'family and traditional' values.

It has been estimated that 4 out of every 10 households in the US tuned into Falwell's TV Station during the 1960s and 1970s and the top ten Christian television empires took over a billion dollars each year, turning out a professional product (ibid.: 275). The fundamentalists interpreted this as evidence that God was on their side. Pat Robertson, a leading fundamentalist Christian preacher, claimed that in the Kingdom of God 'there was no economic recession, no shortage' (Robertson, 1982: 108–9). The movement shifted from being fearful and defensive in the late 1960s and early 1970s to going on the offensive by the late 1970s.

The fundamentalist movement has also been hugely influential on American economic, social and political institutions, including the right-wing think tanks, the Heritage Foundation, the American Enterprise Institute and the Hoover Institute. Disappointed by Christian political leaders, particularly Jimmy Carter, who as President they hoped might support them but who did not take a radical evangelical stance in office, the movement felt powerful enough in 1986 to support Pat Robertson to make a serious attempt to stand as president. The influence this movement has on American policy through the White House and the wider business community is widely discussed. The size of the fundamentalist population depends on one's definition of fundamentalism, but suffice to say that there is huge support for much of their agenda, even if these people do not define themselves Christian fundamentalists. In a recent Gallop Poll in 2000, 44% of people in the USA describe themselves as born-again or evangelical Christians. These communities are now some of the most politically active in the USA (Putnam, 2000: 161).

The Christian fundamentalist movement has been a key grass-roots support group for the neo-conservative, Republican political successes during the George Bush presidency.

The Christian fundamentalists' profile grew as they became increasingly successful. By the late 1970s the most successful charismatic leaders had celebratory status, had mass TV followings and were courted and taken seriously by the political establishment. They were also creating new churches, which stood outside traditional church governance, crossing denominations, which led to new cultures forming within these religious communities and the Christian fundamentalist movement as a whole.

# The formation of a new leadership discourse

Christian fundamentalism in the USA initially provided a site of resistance to liberal Christianity which it saw as 'caving into' modernity and liberal secularism. Western (2005) found that the religious fundamentalists' leadership had been defensive and inward-looking, maintaining rigid boundaries to keep the sinful world at bay. However, this leadership shifted their focus and rather than defend their flocks from the world, they sought to fight to challenge and change liberalism and secularism. The leaders began to slowly open their boundaries, allowing a flow of knowledge, leadership skills and culture exchange, with both the political-social environment and particularly with corporate organizations.

Likewise corporate organizations, when confronted with the new challenges of the global economy and having to face their lack of success when relying on the leadership discourses of the Controller and Therapist, opened their boundaries and imported ideas from Japan and anthropology. This book claims that they also opened their boundaries to the home-grown local Christian fundamentalist movement. The transformational leadership style and strong collectivist cultures with distributive leadership of the fundamentalists were to be found in many places in corporate America. Isomorphism helps to explain how these cultures transfer and learn from each other without a conscious or deliberate strategy.

## *Isomorphism*

It is claimed that successful organizations have forms that are isomorphic with their environments (DiMaggio and Powell, 1983). This means that the environment 'selects' successful organizational forms with characteristics which match their environment, rejecting others which are not successful (Nelson and Gopalan, 2003: 1118). For example, in the changing global environment, those organizations which hold onto hierarchical and bureaucratic forms will fail and those which become more international, flexible and responsive to change will survive. There does, however, appear to have been a very limited view as to what is defined as 'the environment' in this literature. Somehow the business world has created its own insular environment, ignoring the social-political changes brought about by religious and other social movements. Therefore, looking to the Japanese business community is an obvious choice, whereas looking to the powerful social movement of Christian fundamentalism is missed.

The isomorphic process between successful religious and secular organizations cannot be ignored within the American context. Isomorphism is more likely to occur between secular and religious organizations in countries where religion flourishes and the USA is the most religious country in the Western/developed world. Christian fundamentalism was on every American TV screen and radio show; it was entering the political stage. In every American workplace, born-again Christians, some of them fundamentalists going to the new mega-churches and house-groups, being influenced by the religious transformational leadership must have had an influence on corporate America and the arrival of the Transformational leader.

When looking for the impact of fundamentalist Christianity in the workplace, looking for evidence of explicit religious activity such as bible study groups in the workplace is not enough. The exchange between organizations and the environment is to be found 'beneath the surface' at more subtle cultural and signifying levels. Nelson (1989) also points to the non-isomorphic characteristics of organizations which states that they have to maintain defined boundaries in order to be distinguishable and not to dissolve into the environment.

## *Repudiation*

When trying to explain innovative changes in organizational leadership and behaviour, it is useful to turn to theological and sociological theory. Church sect theorists posit the idea of 'repudiation' as a challenge to the concept of isomorphism. The anti-establishment posture of many religious movements sometimes leads them to select administrative forms at variance with the institutional patterns of the general society. This anti-institutional response of religious sects has long pioneered new organizational forms, often radically different from society's dominant forms (Nelson, 1989). For example, instead of the oppressive hierarchies of the dominant society, they choose to revolt against the values of 'the world' and the sect strives for a non-hierarchical egalitarian organization. 'Instead of written rules and records, the sect relies on the inspiration of the moment, folk wisdom and so on' (ibid.: 209).

The process linking the fundamentalists to corporate cultures can be explained in two stages. First, it is through 'repudiation' that the Christian fundamentalist leaders initially pioneered new organizational forms and cultures which seemed totally alien to the dominant American culture. Championing community, strong cultures, traditional family/conservative values and being led by a charismatic, prophetic and visionary leadership, they were quietly creating new narratives, new worship forms and new organizational forms within their own boundaries.

The second stage of this process was when the fundamentalist leadership decided to become more ambitious and moved to engage with and challenge the secular world. Isomorphism took place between corporate and these religious organizations. The tools of marketing, branding and rational business acumen seeped into the fundamentalists' world, to grow their mega-churches and build a powerful and wealthy social movement, mimicking commercial business and marketing models.

As the fundamentalists achieved major success, the process of isomorphism acted in reverse. Secular businesses were looking for new leaders and new organizational forms. This chapter argues that the Transformational leader written about in management texts has a direct lineage to the charismatic authority of Pentecostal pastors who had so successfully transformed congregations and churches. The Transformational leader's task was to transform employees and commercial organizations, creating a similar culture of solidarity based on secular, rather than religious, visions, values and missions. They took on the charismatic, narrative style of the fundamentalist preachers, to lead and inspire their organizations, mimicking the strong conformist and yet dynamic cultures within the fundamentalist congregations.

There is clear evidence from the similarities between the leadership styles, the shared language and the similar organizational cultures that an isomorphic process has occurred between fundamentalist organizations and corporate organizations. Boundary maintenance also took place between the two diverse environments, preventing merger or total diffusion. If the fundamentalist churches took on too much from the marketing and business world, forgetting their primary task, they would collapse or dissolve as churches. Likewise, if the corporations became too evangelical in their approach and mythos took over completely, they too would implode.

Figure 11.2 shows this process of isomorphism and the transfer that took place between the secular and fundamentalist organizations. One of the outputs from this process is a new Protestant work ethic, which like the old one, supports economic growth, only this time within the hyper-capitalist, global milieu. It is this we shall discuss next.

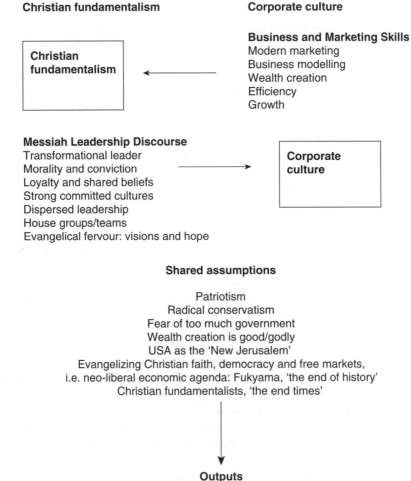

Figure 11.2   Isomorphism between corporatism and Christian fundamentalism

The exchange of culture, expertise and leadership style meant a re-alignment in values across much of the USA. Leaders who ran successful companies, like preachers who ran successful churches, became role models for the new elect, whether you were a Christian or a member of other or non-faith, this now clearly aligned itself with the American Dream. Evangelists displayed wealth and proudly boasted of their million-dollar churches and TV empires. The old Protestant work ethic did not fit this morality and so a new one emerged to accommodate it (Box 11.2). The 'eye of the needle' has widened and entry to heaven for those who follow the path is less anxiety-provoking and persecutory than through the old Calvinist route.

---

## Box 11.2 The new Protestant work ethic

*Working hard beyond one's calling*
The old Protestant work ethic meant that one worked hard at one's calling but never questioned it. The new ethic takes a developmental line. Attempting to achieve beyond one's calling, endeavouring to excel for one's own salvation and for the company vision, thereby fulfilling God's work.

*Personal salvation comes through 'working on oneself'*
Self-actualization becomes a spiritualized act. Personal salvation and personal growth merge. Working hard externally in the workplace and internally, in one's soul/heart becomes a purifying act, a way of becoming whole (at one with God) again.

*The Prosperity Gospel: Blessed are the Wealthy*
Material acquisition is a sign of God's favour. 'God's promise of abundant life becomes a promise of a life of abundance' (Gwyn, 1989). Displaying success through consumption and material wealth is now morally acceptable. The big house and wealthy church show God is rewarding the righteous.

*Conservative values*
The piety of the old Protestant work ethic now only shows itself through a political/social conservativism, e.g. supporting perceived traditional and American family values.

*The poor shall – inherit the earth*
The undeserving poor must work harder to reach salvation, only they can save themselves; to help them would be violating God's will.

*Too much governance is dangerous*
National government and especially international governance from agencies such as the IMF, the United Nations and the World Bank are viewed as infringing on individual rights, preventing free trade and as part of a liberal/leftist secularist conspiracy to rule the world, and they should be resisted. Having faith in God and/or the free-market is the way forward.

This new Protestant work ethic has grown and mutated from the Calvinist one, and has become a part of mainstream American culture, reaching beyond the Protestant Church. The radical and selective vision of this ethos uniquely supports both the corporate neo-liberal and the Christian fundamentalists' agenda. Even many non-believers or those from other faith communities agree with these broad values, (excepting the liberal and political left). Casey acknowledges what she calls the neo-Protestant work ethic, in this advanced industrial milieu: 'The corporation revives and restores the Protestant cultural forms that have been obscured and faltered under the culture of narcissism of advanced industrial society and its therapeutic salvation' (1995: 181). Casey then argues that this neo-Protestant work ethic recovers the elements of order and dedication to work (duty), rational submission to a higher authority and self-restraint from the old ethic.

## Leadership and fundamentalism

Where there is no vision the people will perish. (Proverbs 29: 18)

Leadership is paramount within religious fundamentalist movements but it is commonly an informal rather than an institutional style leadership, drawing on mythos, charisma and influence rather than institutional authority. Their authority is from within, (and God) rather than authority from above (the hierarchical church).

It is the leadership of the great evangelist, the advisor, the scholar, known to be a conservative in his tendencies, but the authority of such persons is much greater than the authority of bishops and other church leaders in institutions or churches. The fundamentalist emphasizes the guru, the teacher with his following. (Barr, 1981)

Barr (1981: xix) goes on to say that Christian 'Fundamentalism produces a psychological stress, it is intrinsically suspicious and has a need for an external authority' that can lead to paranoia and classic fight–flight responses (often increased by real marginalization and persecution). The stress that requires an external authority usually refers to an omnipotent God, and an omniscient leader who can translate God's will. The *Messianic Leaders* create cultures through which the followers voluntarily commit themselves to the leader's vision and values. The Christian fundamentalist leaders Billy Graham, Jerry Falwell and Pat Robertson, amongst others, were successful beyond their expectations and the mass support they received shocked many American commentators. They demonstrated how amenable large sections of the American public were to their leadership styles and the new cultures they created within the Christian tradition.

## Narrative and generative leadership

Susan Friend Harding, writing on Jerry Falwell and fundamentalism (Harding, 2000), re-affirms that this leadership style and the cultures they create are not dogmatic and rigid as often portrayed but dynamic and, in her words, narrative and generative. She means evangelical Christians are open to questions not defensive, and that they read their Bibles generatively. While believing the Bible to be literally true, their leader's skill is through interpreting and constantly generating new truths from the text. Falwell is a master preacher she says who is constantly in creative dialogue with his followers, both in regards to the Bible and his own life. To explain how his followers remain true and supportive after sexual affairs, monetary scandals, etc., Harding identifies that at times of 'narrative instability', it becomes clear that there is more than one version of the truth. In postmodern theory, there is a distrust of rationality, a deconstruction of texts and pluralism and multiple narratives are put forward in place of a single grand narrative. In fundamentalism, there is also a distrust of rationality. The difference between them is that at one end of the spectrum, the post-modern deconstructive theories leave us with increasing relativism, fragmentation and nihilism. There are no truths, no grand narratives (except the grand narrative that there are no grand narratives). Contrary to the simplistic explanations of fundamentalists, they also understand the notion of pluralism but from this they re-construct grand narratives. However, these are not as they seem, rigid and literal, they are narrative, generative, negotiated and dynamic and at the same time politically conservative, and built on idealized notions of the past, of salvation and of community.

Harding explains that faith traditions are inherently instable, coming from texts and claims that are contradictory and challenging. The fundamentalist leaders of these faith groups generatively create narratives, that reveal truth in the text and also link the text to personal experience. This is vitally important, the weaving of the text into personal and community meaning; in the fundamentalist churches is known as 'witnessing':

It is as if Falwell, in his varied storied manifestations, were telling his followers, 'Read me as you read the Bible. I appear in many versions. There are differences between the versions, and there are awkward silences and anomalies within them. My tales are troubled and they are troubling. Harmonize my discrepancies. Close my gaps. Overcome my troubles. Make me whole. Make me true.' (Harding, 2000)

The Messiah discourse of leadership uses the same generative technique. It focuses on weaving narratives about the company and the leader's personal script. The new Messiah leadership offers within this discourse a narrative approach, they are able to harmonize discrepancies, and to create the space for followers to listen to their speeches, read their leadership announcements and texts, and to make themselves fit the image of the company, creating solidarity. Skilful transformational leaders achieve this, to a greater or lesser extent. Brand engagement and employee loyalty are becoming an increasingly important focus of companies, who realize the benefits of branding internally and achieving identification between employee and leader/company.

This style of fundamentalist leadership is very similar to the view taken by theorists who have promoted the new Transformational leader. Consciously or unconsciously the leadership of these fundamentalist movements has influenced the world of business leaders. The guru and the charismatic aspects have been toned down, but are still very perceptible in the literature. One of the most important attributes of today's Transformational leader is creating a corporate vision that acts as a rallying point when creating a new corporate culture. The new Transformational leader is a narrative leader, generating stories about themselves, and stories which bind the company together. The Transformational leader has been created in the image of the 'great evangelist', sanitized to fit into the grey suits of the boardroom when appropriate, but in essence the Transformational leader embodying the Messiah discourse, who has learnt much from the success of the fundamentalist movement and its leadership style.

## The Transformational leadership paradox: conformism and dynamism

Freedom is Slavery. (Orwell, 1949)

Like the religious fundamentalist leaders, the secular Transformational leader aims to create strong (conformist) cultures with the paradoxical intent of releasing the dynamism of individuals and teams in the workforce. Was this a brilliant and insightful leadership project or was this a modern version of Orwell's double speak; 'autonomy is conformity'? A leadership fad which offers liberation to employees but in reality is a rhetorical device, which acts to impose greater control through culture and normative practice? I will now briefly highlight the problematic and worrying totalizing effects of the fundamentalist leader and the Messiah discourse it produced.

The challenge for leadership at the turn of the millennium was how to influence a diverse expert and knowledge-based workforce globally dispersed within multinational companies. The answer seemed to be a paradox; to create dynamic *and* conformist cultures. A dynamic and energized culture to ensure the company was innovative and competitive, maximizing individual and team knowledge and skills; and conformist cultures to ensure that the employees worked hard and with loyalty towards common company goals and self-managed this process. Religious fundamentalism offered one source of answers to this dilemma, Japanese work place culture another. However, while both had a lot of success, they both posed long-term problems and early success did not mean sustainable success.

## Totalizing corporate cultures

Individually cased, Hirst's fish swim blindly in the same direction without interaction. It's a cold and clinical metaphor for society without conflict. A Utopian ideal of a harmony that comes at an unthinkable cost of sameness and emotional confinement.

(From the Damien Hirst Collection, Saatchi Gallery, London, 2003)

**Figure 11.3**   Isolated Elements Swimming in the Same Direction for the Purpose of Understanding (right) MDF, melamine, wood, steel, glass, perspex cases, fish and 5% formaldehyde solution, 72 × 108 × 10 in. (182.88 × 274.32 × 25.4 cm)
*Source*: Damien Hirst (1991) © Damien Hirst. Courtesy Jay Jopling/White Cube (London)

When I first saw Hirst's artwork I immediately associated it with my personal experience of the corporate world and the mono-cultures that exist in that space. The open plan offices, the dark suit dress codes, the glass and steel buildings, the monotonous hotel chains and airport lounges and the marginalization of colour, diversity and difference.

Damien Hirst's artwork shows a large number of fish, each different, encased separately in a clear formaldehyde filled box 'swimming' in the same direction. The vision of 'harmony, eliminating difference' is hauntingly reminiscent of the blandness and sameness experienced within corporate cultures across the globe. Walking into a corporate business, whether in India, America, big town or small town, there is an uncanny lack of difference in the physical environment. This exemplifies the attempts to eliminate difference and homogenize the employees' beliefs within these corporations, the aim being to create strong cultures in which committed employees share values based upon a leadership-inspired vision.

Casey's research into corporate culture demonstrates their likeness to Hirst's artwork:

> The new corporatisation of the self is more than a process of assault, discipline and defeat against which employees defend themselves. It is a process of coloni-sation in which, in its completion, assault and defeat are no longer recognized. Overt displays of employee resistance and opposition are virtually eliminated. Corporatised selves become sufficiently repressed to effectively weaken and dissolve the capacity for serious criticism or dissent. (Casey, 1995: 150)

These 'corporatised selves' unite behind a leadership that subtly demands and gains an active followership and allegiance to the company's vision, goals and values.

Smith and Wilkinson's (1996) research takes us to a progressive non-hierarchical company 'Sherwood's' and provides a concise example of the totalitarian nature these cultures can produce; similar research supports these findings (Lawrence, 1979; Axtel Ray, 1986; Kunda, 1992; Casey, 1995). Smith and Wilkinson say that 'Sherwood's' is a company which shines as a beacon within the new collectivist organizational paradigm. They describe it as a hugely successful part of a multinational. Employees pursue 'furious interaction' in open plan offices with a religious fervour, job functions rotate between managers in an anti-bureaucratic milieu and consensus and cooperation have been institutionalized. Smith and Wilkinson describe this as a totalitarian culture with nightmarish qualities due to the tight control, which co-exists within a high degree of autonomy. They make the analogy with a penal institution, saying it is like an open prison. The lack of privacy precludes dissent, control is not located specifically but generically, 'everyone is at the heart of things but everybody also has several others within their gaze and everybody is clearly observed by others' (Smith and Wilkinson, 1996). There is an obsessive degree of quality control within the company and conflict is apparently obliterated. They are paid above the industry norms in order to keep them in 'golden handcuffs' and 'they are their own policemen' (ibid.). They say that when people join 'Sherwood's' they think it 'a bit funny at first, but then soon see it as normal'.

What exists is an internalized culture of control, a surveillance culture, policed by the self and the social group, in which to be different is not an option and, more worryingly perhaps, is not even a thought. This type of organization, with its many cultural variations, is one of the ascending visions within contemporary management literature for company cultures and management approaches. These cultures resonate with those of religious fundamentalist movements who win souls through charismatic leadership and as a result create self-regulating mono-cultures, which demand commitment and allegiance to the movement. Others claim that these new organizational cultures are far from totalitarian but are flexible, dynamic and non-authoritarian and improve productivity. The latter two claims are not absolute opposites.

The rise of the Transformational leader in the management world followed closely on from the success of the Christian fundamentalist leaders, and Japanese work culture. Both cultures now seem in transition, in Japan, the traditional conformist roles are no longer deemed sustainable, and a turning point may have been reached in the fundamentalist churches in USA. The misjudgements regarding the war on Iraq have put the fundamentalist Christian-supported neo-conservative vision for exporting US style democracy in serious doubt. Christian leaders are becoming disillusioned and are distancing themselves from politics, and while fundamentalism is still a powerful force, continued gaps in moral preaching and personal behaviours threaten to undermine the movement further. For example, the Rev. Ted Haggard, leader of the biggest church in the USA, the huge Evangelical Alliance, who it is claimed had a weekly phone call with President Bush, resigned in 2006 due to his long-term relationship with a gay prostitute, In Haggard's own words:

The fact is I am guilty of sexual immorality. And I take responsibility for the entire problem. I am a deceiver and a liar. There's a part of my life that is so repulsive and dark that I have been warring against it for all of my adult life (http://www.foxnews.com/story/0,2933,227568,00.html).

Also there are real concerns about the future. A leading article in the *New York Times* stated: 'Despite their packed mega-churches, their political clout and their increasing visibility on the national stage, evangelical Christian leaders are warning one another that their teenagers are abandoning their faith in droves' (Laurie Goodstein, *New York Times*, 6 Oct. 2006). Casey identifies that there has been a 'southern-style revivalism' with the sexual energy of charisma and conversion displayed by the corporations' leaders. This creates the 'magic of a turned-on workforce' (Peters and Waterman, 1982), which comes from meaningful team relationships and a loyalty to the company. However, she critiques these totalizing cultures. They do not immediately reflect a 'big brother' cultures and can be dynamic, high energy and often initially successful, with a 'charged up' 'feel great'-type culture as described by Peters and Waterman, where employees unleash their energy and talent for the company. But, as Peters and Waterman discovered, their excellent companies were not the most sustainable.

Casey states that her ethnographic research showed that these employees developed a 'new-colluded self' which she describes as 'dependant, over-agreeable, compulsive in dedication, diligent and passionate about the product and company' (1995: 191). This new-colluded self has an alter ego in which it is consistently in a state of capitulation which leads to a 'wearied surrender' because it 'implicitly recognises but denies the process of discipline, enforced self restraint and evangelical optimism' (ibid.). Messiah leaders increasingly revert to normative coercion, peer surveillance, creating fearful scenarios to galvanize solidarity and energy, to replace the waning evangelic fervour that inevitably fades. Dangerous totalizing cultures emerge within the Messiah leadership discourse.

Corporate America was searching for a Transformational leadership able to transform organizations to compete and win in the new era. At the same time an age of anxiety produced the need for psychological and social 'containment of anxiety'. This meant a radical re-think and culture change rather than incremental or structural change. The 'therapist character's' attempts to make the workplace more fulfilling failed to keep up with the speed of change; attempting to help individuals to self-actualize or teams become more collaborative, just didn't produce the results needed within the new global and changing business climate. The contractual style of management was to be replaced with a covenantal style of leadership. The transactional leadership approach was dead in the water and a much more ambitious approach was required. The Transformational leader offered a covenantal promise on behalf of the company to the employees. The covenant was that if the employees gave their hearts and soul to the company, they would be as one people, working in family groups within a larger community, pulling together for the greater good of all, under one vision with shared values. They would become much more self-sufficient and self-managing because the company's success was their success.

Transformational leaders with the ability to create covenants with employees and other stakeholders were sought in the 1980s and there was a rush to find and develop these successful leaders. They needed to win hearts, minds and souls, create visions, engineer cultures and create the environment in which 'designer employees' would emerge to compete in the global marketplace. Leadership by covenant required mythos, faith and belief rather than the diet of more persuasion and rationality. The techniques and skills of the therapist character remain evident and useful in the workplace, but the therapeutic leadership discourse alone was insufficient.

'Brand engagement' became a common phrase identifying that the most successful companies were those that didn't just sell the brand in the market place, but actually engaged their own workforce to believe in the brand. Winning business became a matter of converting the workforce to the new faith, the company brand and the leader's vision. Corporate America searched for a new leadership model, which could harness a covenantal style and was also culturally acceptable to the American people. The Christian fundamentalists provided the answers. Their leadership style and cultures were the most successful templates around and were visibly having an impact, way beyond the confines of their religious faith groups.

Within corporate and organizational life, the Transformational leader attempted to replicate this success. Their aim was to generatively produce meaning, and company narratives and be visible as a leader, signifying what leadership is, within the company narrative. Others could then take up a dispersed leadership role, becoming part of this narrative. The leader's role is to negotiate and dialogue with diverse constituents and stakeholders across functional and often international borders, attempting to find commonality and solidarity, establishing strong organizational cultures. This is the Messiah leadership character at its best.

The Messiah discourse is not simply about an individual hero, but is a character in a workplace theatre who is in constant dialogue, interaction, and negotiation with the audience. A Messiah leadership represents a signifying figure beyond the technical and incremental leaders. They are covenantal leaders rather than contractual leaders. This leadership discourse is underpinned by hope, community and solidarity and transforms through changing culture. This discourse can be either powerfully transforming, or can be powerfully totalizing and destructive.

Organizations led within the Messiah discourse can succeed in creating dynamic work forces with a sense of solidarity and community, for a short period, but so often this position is unsustainable. Too often the leadership is seduced by its early success, with leaders coming to believe that they are omnipotent. The case study, in Box 11.3 is an example of this.

---

### Box 11.3   Case study
#### *The Messiah leadership discourse: totalizing cultures*

This case study came from a piece of consultancy work I undertook as coach to senior leaders in a multinational fashion retailer.

The CEO began his career as a designer and when CEO he expanded the company to make it a globally recognizable business, believing that the success was almost solely dependent on creativity and great design.

It became clear that he personally identified with the Messiah leadership discourse; he generated enthusiasm and loyalty from a dynamic and committed workforce, created a brand followership, and in his view great design and great leadership came from creativity and passion.

*(Continued)*

*(Continued)*

Things started to go wrong, but went unnoticed, during the period of growth and success for the company. The CEO had been bolstered by his success and used his increased leadership influence to hire people with the same style as his own. He led the company with creativity and passion and he employed people with creativity and passion. They identified with him as a fellow 'creative'.

Paradoxically while the designers were creative, this approach led to a mono-culture forming. There was uniformity about the company look, which mimicked the glamorous company advertising. The age of the staff group was very young, and on visiting the company restaurant for a sushi lunch, it felt more like entering a young persons club than a work place. Cool designers are fine but the company was moving towards a totalizing, mono-culture which excluded anything else. From the outside it looked liked a buzzing creative company, to those inside there was a culture of conformity and peer pressure to tow the leadership line. There was very little independent or critical thinking. Everybody acted 'as if' they were cool designers, and the other leadership sub-cultures necessary to lead a multinational company were obliterated. In this company the CEO was renowned for saying, 'You either got it or you didn't.' Those who didn't get it or questioned 'it', didn't last long.

After a period of huge growth, the company found that it lacked the maturity and experience to balance the creative aspects with the process of leading and managing a global business. To run a huge multinational the leadership culture needed to be more mature and more diverse. They lost their way, dropping huge share price, with job losses, and eventually the CEO had to go. The leader as Messiah went from being untouchable to being 'sacrificed'.

In essence, the rebuilding job was to change the leadership culture from a totalizing Messiah leader discourse. To gain a more balanced approach, which allowed diversity into the company, some 'leaders as therapists' in middle management, some 'leaders as controllers' in production and finance were hired. They appointed an experienced leader who took a less passionate and more stable and pragmatic leadership role.

The other main reason why the Messiah discourse is flawed and leads to totalizing cultures is that the aim to build a strong culture has conformity as an inbuilt dynamic. Strong cultures try to replicate strong community bonds. Strong communities are held up as good, but under examination they too have an inbuilt tension between individualism and conformity. As Freud noted in *Civilisation and its Discontents*, there is always a tension between personal freedom and belonging to community; Bauman believes that 'community is tantamount to conformity, and therefore to the (at least potential) loss of individuality' (in Sullivan, 2003: 145). There is no utopian community, only nostalgia for such, autonomy and conformity are always in tension. The Messiah leadership discourse with its hyperbolic leadership claims, its idealized strong cultures and the pressures to grow outputs and profits, was always a recipe for fundamentalist mindsets and totalizing consequences.

The Messiah leadership discourse offers hope but the leadership within this discourse is too often ill equipped to sustain what is required for positive trans-formation to take place. The cultures began as many evangelical religious move-ments and sects, with a fervour and hope, and were often dynamic and engaging. However, to maintain this level of excitement and commitment is nigh impossible and those subjected to these cultures become conformist and jaded. To repeat Catherine Casey's observations, she refers to this state as the 'capitulated-self' which has undergone a 'wearied surrender' (Casey, 1995: 191).

These cultures aren't big brother, authoritarian regimes, more 'little brother' (Žižek, 1999) where peer and self-surveillance ensures order within family-team groups and where any real conflict is eliminated and difference is hidden or denied. This culture idealizes harmony, but within it there is a hint of paranoia and grandiosity that comes from idealizing oneself, one's team and one's organi-zation. Alongside the harmony there exists a new kind of dependency culture, different from the patriarchal and hierarchical leadership cultures of the past.

In the new cultures one appears to be much more autonomous but nevertheless a psychological dependency on the community exists. It is this subtle dependency that prevents individuals accessing real autonomy or being able to question the culture itself. Those who resist the culture are ejected or marginalized.

Most frightening is the lack of recognition of one's entrapment within this culture. Reflexivity, the ability to see oneself clearly as an individual or sub-group within these strong cultures, is very difficult, as their very *raison d'être* is to increase conformity, commitment and compliance.

## Conclusion

The Messiah leadership discourse managed to create organizational cultures which allowed for some conformity and dynamism to co-exist. Layers of hierarchy were removed, self-managing teams and dispersed leadership replaced them, greater flex-ibility and adaptability resulted under strong cultures, which were established under a Transformational leader's values and visions. However, these leaders failed to cre-ate sustainable cultures, which allowed for reflexivity and critical self-examination.

Strong dynamic cultures inevitably slide towards totalizing fundamentalist cultures. It takes a very informed and gifted leadership to counter these tenden-cies. The typical process that occurs is that at a conscious level the organization employees become tired of the evangelical rhetoric, and cynical of the visions and values which are increasingly seen as a veneer. At an unconscious level, culture control expels and marginalizes difference, and resistant employees; and the organization becomes increasingly homogeneous and totalizing and the dynamic energy begins to fade. To counter this, leaders often turn to flight/fight rhetoric in order to galvanize this draining energy. Fundamentalist tendencies not only distort organizational cultures, they also distort the leader's judgements.

The mobilizing of the workforce becomes a leadership act which is under-pinned by the psychological mechanism called splitting by Melanie Klein (1959).

Klein observed how children used splitting as a psychic mechanism to protect themselves from their own feelings of insecurity and guilt. They would create stories of good fairies and bad witches, the witches would carry the 'split off' difficult feelings they experienced. When they became more mature, they were able to see that within themselves and their parents, both 'good and bad' traits and feelings could co-exist.

This process is never fully resolved and individuals, groups and nations collectively still split off negative feelings. Some leaders (particularly fundamentalist leaders) harness this mechanism to mobilize support. An external enemy is created; for today's religious fundamentalists it is liberal secularists, homosexuals and abortion. These become a rallying point, creating a dangerous enemy, which needs defeating by the good forces. This creates a world of black and white, good and evil, them and us. George Bush's now infamous 'axis of evil' speech is a classic example of this, it idealizes 'us', the free democratic world, while denigrating the 'other', the undemocratic, terrorist world. However, as we can see, this over-simplification of the process leads to poor decision-making, colours perceptions and conflates complex situations. It is simply unsustainable.

In an extreme example, Hitler used the Jews as the enemy that unless resisted/eliminated would pollute the idealised Mother Land and the pure German race. Hitler mobilized his nation, creating huge energy and support, while openly creating a conformist and homogeneous culture; again, this was unsustainable.

Jerry Falwell and Pat Robertson, two leading evangelical and fundamentalist Christians in the USA, immediately after 9/11 claimed that America deserved this attack, due to its secular liberal lifestyle, i.e. it was God's intervention against a sinful nation (Žižek, 2002). This example identifies how the fundamentalist mindset works, identifying an enemy and then relating every event to this, it moves towards paranoid tendencies. Initially this can create a mobilized followership, but it never is sustainable and inevitably self-destructs. I am not suggesting that business leaders using the Messiah discourse are such fundamentalist leaders, but that fundamentalist tendencies are inherently part of this discourse. Beware of the leaders who are always fighting others, always denigrating others, idealizing their own company. Look carefully at any company which apparently has a highly energetic and unquestioning loyal workforce, check out the leadership discourse and culture underpinning this, and watch for its future demise (Enron was a recent example of such a company).

Transformational leadership is still relevant and popular and, despite challenges in the marginal literature, in the mainstream the Messiah discourse remains the normative way to think about leaders: individual, charismatic or inspirational, able to motivate followers and create visions and values which others will follow. The ideology of the strong conformist cultures led by visionary leaders is now being scrutinized, and the heroic leader ideal is also being questioned. As the next leadership discourse emerges, it would be a shame if the baby were thrown out with the bathwater, as a reaction to the failings and dangers of the Messiah discourse. This discourse does lead to the likely formation of conformist cultures and fundamentalist mindsets. However, it also revealed the importance of a signifying and generative leadership which can be highly effective, when stripped of the hubris surrounding the Transformational leader with their grandiose visions and idealized strong cultures.

# An Overview of the Leadership Discourses

## Introduction

Chapter 12 will summarize the leadership discourses, and show how they relate to each other and to leadership practice. It is important to highlight that while these discourses emerged at different social and economic periods, each are now familiar and have become normative. Each discourse dominated a historical period, in contemporary organizations, each one has its strengths and weaknesses, which will be explored in this chapter. Each discourse may stand alone and dominate different sectors and organizations, but they also co-exist, within organizations and within individual leaders and leadership teams. However, one discourse is usually dominant in any given situation at any given time. In leadership practice, co-existence usually means one of two things:

1  a strategic leadership synthesis of skills and culture to maximize organizational efficiency and enhancement of member engagement;
2  competing cultures and visions of how to lead the organization.

I will now summarize each discourse:

## Discourse 1: Leader as Controller

The first leadership discourse that emerged at the beginning of the century epitomized by Frederick Taylor's scientific management is the Leader as *Controller*. This character is very similar to A. MacIntyre's social 'manager' character, which he claims signifies the tension between manipulation and non-manipulation, and I would add between control and autonomy. The Controller leadership discourse is born from scientific rationalism and the industrial revolution, which, in the name of the Enlightenment and progress, relegated the worker to being a cog in a machine, mirroring standardization and mechanization within the mass production of the factory. The leader as Controller operates as a technocrat leader focusing on efficiency. In Etzioni's (1961) taxonomy of control, this leadership character is based on an overt system of coercive and utilitarian control, using reward and deprivation (transactional leadership). In the leadership discourse, covert control is applied from beyond the workplace. The political/economic and social leadership supports the drive for worker efficiency, leveraging worker productivity through class power relations and the threat of unemployment, poverty, healthcare and pension benefits. Political leadership always retains the leader as Controller discourse in the background alongside other leadership discourses, using the threat of job loss and welfare to work benefit links etc., as social control mechanism (healthcare linked to paid employment is very important in the USA).

## Discourse 2: Leader as Therapist

The second discourse is the leader as *Therapist*. This discourse signifies the dominant therapeutic culture in contemporary Western society and highlights the tension between individualism and alienation, personal growth and workplace efficiency, well-being and mental/emotional health. The leader as Therapist discourse represents the subtlety of therapeutic governance as opposed to coercive control. This leadership reflects the wider social trends of atomization, self-concern, and the post-war individualistic expectations of being fulfilled, successful and happy (Rieff, 1966; Lasch, 1979; Furedi, 2003).

The Therapist leader emerged from within the Human Relations movement and encompasses the work of theorists such as Mayo, Lewin, Maslow, Frankl and Rogers. Their focus on individual personal growth and self-actualization was readily translated to the workplace, through techniques to motivate individuals and teams, through job re-design and job enhancement to make work more satisfying and to produce work-group cohesion. Employers and theorists believed that happier workers would be more productive than unhappy, coerced workers. This approach in essence was seen as more progressive and productive. It aimed to overcome the alienation created by the machine-like efficiency under the leader as Controller discourse. Work became a site for personal growth and achievement, a place to create meaning and identity. Under the leader as Therapist, people 'went to work to work on themselves' (Rose, 1990), embracing therapeutic culture in society at large.

Personnel departments were established, management consultants and new texts, theories and a huge training and development industry flourished. The leader as Therapist still flourishes often alongside the later Messiah character; a common scenario is the HR Director acts as the Therapist character and the CEO as leader as the Messiah character. Recent examples of the therapist discourse are the interest in emotional intelligence and the huge growth of executive coaching. However, this discourse lost its potency in corporate life, as it could no longer deliver the economic benefits across global business.

## Discourse 3: Leader as Messiah

The third discourse is the leader as Messiah. The term leader has been elevated in recent years, challenging the dominance of the term 'manager' and signifying more social change. Coming to the fore since the early 1980s and most clearly articulated within the Transformation leadership literature, the *Messiah discourse* provides charismatic leadership and vision in the face of a turbulent and uncertain environment. The Messiah character signifies the tension between salvation and destruction, between the technocrat and the moral visionary, and between hope and despair. The Messiah discourse appeals to individuals and society, promising salvation from the chaotic world in which a lack of control is experienced and where traditional community is diminished. As the workplace rises in importance as a site of community, replacing institutions such as the church and family, so the manager/leader replaces the priesthood as a social character of influence.

The Messiah character leads through their signifying capacity, symbolism, ritual, myth and language. Their focus is to act on culture change and the Messiah leadership discourse relies on 'normative control', which is self- and peer-control through surveillance and internalization, emotionalism and cultural norms. Followers of the Messiah character work hard because of an internalized belief system aligned to the leader's vision and values.

The earnings of leaders graphically represent the new values and expectations on leaders since the Messiah discourse arrived. In the 1980s, in the USA, CEOs earned 40 times the average wage (as the Therapist character), in 2000 (as the Messiah character) they earn over 475 times (*Business Week*, 'Executive compensation scoreboard', 17 April 2000).

Table 12.1 shows an overview of the signifying qualities of each discourse, clearly demonstrating the differences between them and how they impact on leadership practice. This table provides a useful reference point to situate your individual leadership practice and your experience of the leadership around you. It is an interesting exercise to be playful with these three discourses, to observe leadership and the language leaders use, seeing if they fit into one or more of these discourses. Also look at vision statements, company websites, newspaper articles and try to identify these discourses. When you have identified a leadership discourse, look for any patterns and the context in which they occur. Practising this alerts you to the underlying discourses in any leadership situation, which then enables you to take a critical stance, and ask why a certain discourse is favoured, and what implications this has for the employees and the organization.

# The leadership discourses in practice

The embodiment of the leadership discourse by a leader character brings the concept of a discourse into the lived workplace. It provides a tangible and observable leadership practice to engage and negotiate with. It reveals to those who take a critical perspective how a discourse impacts and influences organizations, managers and employees. It reveals the constantly changing tensions and desires within the social realm and how this impacts on leadership at work. There is a dynamic interaction between the character (the discourse-filled role) and the actor inhabiting the character. The interaction extends also to those interacting with the leader or leadership team.

## *Discourses preference*

Individual leaders, leadership teams and organizations rarely consciously choose their preferred leadership discourse as these are hidden with normative behaviours and expectations. However, they are drawn to discourses for various reasons.

**Table 12.1** The signifying qualities of the leadership discourses

| Discourse | Controller | Therapist | Messiah |
|---|---|---|---|
| Vision aims | **Iron cage**<br>Maximizes production through control | **Comfortable iron cage**<br>Maximizes production though increased motivation and promoting personal growth and team work | **Internalized iron cage**<br>Maximizes production through belief in personal salvation via new meanings found through following the leader's values and vision |
| Source of authority | **From above** *Science*<br>The Boss/Owner passes authority down the pyramid (position power) and the techniques of management control gain authority from scientific rationalism | **From within** *Humanism*<br>Drawing on personal internalized authority and the power gained through self-actualization and collaborative teamwork | **From beyond** *The Godhead*<br>The source of authority is transcendent whether secular (through morality) or quasi-spiritual.<br>The leader embodies the particular culture they signify, from this they gain authority |
| Perceptions of workers | **Robots**<br>Work on production lines or as one of a mass of other workers, with little personal identity | **Patients/Clients**<br>Be healed and made whole through reparation at work | **Disciples**<br>Follow the leader and learn to be more like them and create a meaningful identity within a community of believers |
| Leads what? | **Soma**<br>Controller focuses on the body to maximize efficient production, via incentives and coercion (e.g. piecework and discipline) | **Psyche**<br>Therapist focuses on the psyche to understand motivation, designs job enrichment, creates spaces for self-actualizing behaviours | **Soul**<br>Messiah works with the soul. Followers align themselves to the vision, a cause greater than the self (the company). The Messiah is role model, linking success with personal salvation |
| Organizational metaphor | **Machine**<br>Takes technical and rational view of world, thinks in closed systems, tries to control internal environment to maximize efficiency | **Organism**<br>Principles of growth both personal and social (learning organizations). Optimizes growth potential | **Network**<br>Leads through connections and linking the network. Organization is seen as a network of dispersed leadership held together by strong cultures |
| Leadership style | **Cogs in wheel**<br>Ensures each individual, team, department works optimally, keeping to strict tasks. Cogs are oiled, maximizing efficiency and performance | **Relationships**<br>Managing emotions and relationships and the boundaries between individuals, teams and across functions | **Symbolic and cultural**<br>Creates images, markets and a vision. Communicates and promotes a culture using symbols, myths, morality and rituals |

*(Continued)*

**Table 12.1**    *(Continued)*

| Discourse | Controller | Therapist | Messiah |
|---|---|---|---|
| **Signifier** | **Coercion and scientific efficiency** | **Reparation, therapeutic governance** | **Personal salvation/hope and faith** |
| The social tensions signified by each discourse | Between coercion and choice, dependency and autonomy. Holds the tensions between scientific progress and humanism | Between wholeness and fragmentation. Therapeutic governance i.e. taking private emotion and utilizing it as a social tool | Between personal/social salvation and destruction. Between prophetic vision and technical jargon, hope and despair, mythos and logos. Puts faith back in business |
| **Control** Axtell Ray (1986) | **Bureaucratic** Control via manipulation and strict policing | **Humanistic** Control by emotional management and therapeutic governance: managing the need for reparation: a paternalistic overseeing | **Culture** Culture control. Workers internalize the cultural norms which become an internalized organizational ideal. Policing is via self and peers: open plan office, lack of privacy and peer surveillance |
| Etzioni (1961) | Coercive/utilitarian | Utilitarian/normative | Normative |

Sometimes leaders and organizations are 'trapped' within a discourse, others change between leadership discourses under certain conditions. Individuals and groups can be attracted to different discourses depending on their personal social location and how they perceive the world from this location.

Often individuals have an internalized 'idealized' leadership stance, which relates to their social location, and their personal experience of leadership, beginning from their parenting. If a person has a very strict mother or father, or they are brought up in a strict religious culture or a harsh boarding school, this may influence the leader they identify with later in life. They may assume that all leaders should be in the Controller discourse, as this is the norm to them. Alternatively they may internalize a view that this early experience was damaging to them and they may seek reparative leadership model that would situate them in the 'therapy discourse'. Individuals, who doted on their parents or another early leadership role model, may identify with the Messiah discourse, relating to the special leader who presents as a saviour. In psychoanalytic terms, this process is called valency, individuals carry with them a valency for certain group cultures (Bion, 1961) and I would suggest also for leadership discourses.

Change in leadership discourses often arise due to external pressures. An individual leader can be pulled by competing discourses. As British Prime Minister, Tony Blair embodied the Messiah discourse, talking passionately, with vision, with persuasion, attempting to modernize and change the culture of his political party, the country and beyond, but every so often he reverted to the Controller leadership discourse. His desire seems to be visionary, but his instincts seem to be the controller, the interventionist leader, setting a target and audit culture of micromanagement in the public sector.

Anxiety over performance often distorts a leadership team who favour the Messiah discourse and all the company rhetoric supports transformational leadership, but then return instinctively to the controller discourse, when they receive poor output figures or share prices drop.

Understanding the leadership discourses makes it easier for leaders in practice to recognize these processes. When they are recognized, leaders can act to ensure that reactivity to short-term pressure doesn't alter their strategic course.

Different geographical, historical and socio-cultural contexts will also favour different leadership discourses. For example, in my observations it appears that in the USA leadership seems more generically accepted than in Europe where it seems more distrusted. The Messiah discourse is therefore more likely in the USA, and the Therapist discourse more likely in Europe as it has less of an overt leadership feel to it. In the UK, my experience is that the public and voluntary sectors prefer the leader as Therapist discourse as it fits with the employees' public service and vocational ideals.

The British National Health Service (NHS) is an interesting example of a large public sector institution which has experienced all three discourses. It was dominated by hierarchy and control in the early years and until the 1970s was led by the leader as Controller discourse with severe matrons, rigid role definitions, a bureaucratic structure and medical personnel acting with omnipotent power. This shifted towards the leadership as Therapist discourse as new management/leadership techniques filtered in from the private sector, and it was realized that leadership and motivation were key issues as employee morale waned in an under-resourced and underpaid service. In the late 1980s, greater reforms began to take place and again following the corporate lead (public sector leadership often follows the perceived 'glamorous' corporate sector with a delay factor of a decade). The leader as Messiah discourse became prominent, with the aims of modernizing the NHS and changing the culture to enable flexible and adaptive working. Huge sums were spent on leadership development using competency frameworks designed to support the change using the Messiah discourse. Symbolic culture changes took place, which were/are hotly contested, for example, to make patients into customers with choices and create an internal market. Interestingly, while the espoused leadership was the Messiah discourse and CEOs have been given more positional power to change culture, the reality on the ground has been one of competing discourses. The health workers' favoured discourse is the Therapist discourse, which relates closely to their clinical roles and vocations, and that is what clinical leaders attempt to provide. The senior management attempts (with different success rates) to create culture change through the Messiah discourse, but complain that the government is so anxious about its modernizing reforms that it reverts to the leader as Controller discourse, micro-managing CEOs' performance. This is due to the government anxiety that if the reforms fail they would themselves lose office, this anxiety is passed down throughout the institution and the experienced leadership is the Controller discourse. An ex-colleague of mine spoke of her experience as a clinical leader:

My job used to be caring for people, now I feel like I am running a production line, all we are concerned about is getting the waiting times down, if we don't, our funding is reduced. The leadership here talks about creating a culture of trust, empowering us to do our jobs, but in reality they are the most controlling leaders we have had in my 24 years of service. (Ward Charge nurse, NHS hospital, September 2005: Anonymous)

The result of an espoused Messiah leadership discourse colliding with the experience of a Controller discourse creates cynicism and distrust, resulting in low morale.

Positions within hierarchies, and location in functions and departments, also impact on the leadership discourse. The Messiah leadership discourse is more favoured, the higher in the organization one climbs. The Therapist leader has changed from being the dominant leadership discourse, to become favoured in the realms of aspiring middle managers, HR departments and the public sector. Human Resource departments often fluctuate between the Controller discourse, when operating on transactional and contractual concerns, and the Therapist discourse, when dealing with leadership development. This split is unhelpful and many HR teams' focus is over-influenced by the former which hinders their performance in the latter. They can be perceived as Controlling characters from below, and as Therapist characters from above. Structurally within companies the HR leadership becomes split between discourses which is unhelpful as they are in a vital influencing position and should be working towards the company's strategic leadership vision.

Leadership development, often instigated through the HR function, is a very risk-adverse process, because the deliverers worry about having safe and measurable outcomes to justify their work. Also when working with senior personnel, the risk is increased because of the power held by these executives, 'Don't do anything to upset the leaders!' This often influences choices and the deliverers revert to individualist, reductionist and formulaic solutions: competency frameworks setting universal leadership goals, followed by individual 'tests' to 'scientifically' measure skills and identify gaps. The weakest part of this process is usually the follow-up, sometimes it is missing altogether or the individual is given token leadership development, other times it is more thoughtful. This approach is situated in the Therapist discourse, attempting to change individual behaviour through modification using a technician-rational approach. What is missing is a coherent systemic approach with an organizational development and strategic vision.

Leadership discourses can be used heuristically to help understand organization individual leadership assumptions. If an HR leader can understand the tensions in their roles, they can resist the pull to the Therapist discourse and take a more strategic view alongside the individualist rational approach.

To make progress in the emancipatory role of leadership in organizational life the discourses help identify normative assumptions, social relations and beneath-the-surface structural dynamics. They also help to reveal how power, authority, control and influence are exerted. The leader is as ensnared in the dominant discourse as are the followers; nobody is acting as a free agent unless they are aware of the dominant discourses which create the boundaries and norms in which we all act.

# Working with leadership discourses

Each discourse has its merits and its weaknesses. Discourses are not right or wrong, they exist, representing wider social phenomena. However, once aware of the discourse, we can make some judgement and assessment as to how each discourse affects leadership and organizational culture. While we are all in a sense captured by a particular discourse, we are also able to negotiate, individually and collectively, to change the discourse and our relationship to it. Collectively, the discourse can be transformed, and with it the power and social relations that emanate from it. It is through this social construction (of which we are all active agents) that negotiation takes place and social change occurs.

Boxes 12.1, 12.2 and 12.3 offer examples of how each leadership discourse might impact within different work situations (which often reflects how they emerged). These boxes are not finite or definitive but there to open dialogue as to which leadership discourses, and the accompanying assumptions, fit to different situations and contexts. As stated previously, discourses can and often do co-exist within organizations, sectors, but one is usually dominant.

## Box 12.1  Controller leader discourse

| Strengths | Weaknesses |
|---|---|
| Focus on output and task<br>Results driven<br>Improves efficiency<br>Empirical and measurable targets<br>Decisive leadership in a crisis<br>Creates clear boundaries between work and home identity | Creates employee alienation, resentment and resistance<br>Poor use of human resource: Does not utilize employees' knowledge, skills and creativity<br>Creates inflexible and rigid 'them and us' workforce relations<br>Often leads to disputes |
| **Useful settings** | **Less useful settings** |
| Production line, old manufacturing<br>Workplaces where efficiency and control are vital<br>Nuclear industry, projects which require high security, and high levels of checking<br>Accounting departments<br>Construction industry<br>Task-focused project management<br>First line leadership | Post-industrial workplaces<br>Knowledge-led industries<br>Education sector<br>Entrepreneurial business<br>Innovation and creative sector<br>Senior strategic leadership |

## Box 12.2    Therapist leader discourse

| Strengths | Weaknesses |
|---|---|
| Individual and team focus<br>Emotional awareness<br>Builds trust<br>Empowers through engaging<br>individual and team through building<br>rapport, listening and finding ways<br>to offer personal growth and<br>development opportunities | Lacks big picture, strategic focus<br>Lacks dynamism and energy<br>Doesn't build strong cultures<br>Individual focus rather than<br>systems focus<br>Organization can become<br>introverted and narcissistic,<br>focusing on employee needs<br>rather than an external focus |
| **Useful settings** | **Less useful settings** |
| Steady state organizations<br>Education, health, public and<br>not-for-profit sectors<br>Value focuses in organizations with<br>an ethos of human development<br>Middle management-leadership roles,<br>supporting individuals and teams<br>Human Resource function | Fast changing organizations<br>Multinationals with complex<br>structures, requiring more of a<br>systemic and culture-led approach<br>Manufacturing sector, building<br>industry which require robust<br>task focus<br>Senior leadership requiring<br>strategic focus<br>Asian cultures which are less culturally<br>embedded in therapy culture than<br>Western cultures |

## Box 12.3    Messiah leader discourse

| Strengths | Weaknesses |
|---|---|
| Builds strong aligned companies<br>Dynamic energized cultures<br>Innovative, dispersed leadership<br>Builds in dispersed leadership and<br>autonomous teams<br>Strategic and visionary | Unsustainable over long periods<br>totalizing-fundamentalist cultures<br>Leaders can become omnipotent,<br>dependency then becomes an<br>issue<br>Conformist homogeneous cultures<br>can stifle innovation and creativity |

*(Continued)*

*(Continued)*

| Useful settings | Less useful settings |
|---|---|
| Post-industrial companies<br>Knowledge-based companies<br>Global multinationals, large<br>corporations<br>Senior strategic leadership | Steady state organizations<br>Industrial, manufacturing sector<br>Organizations reliant on<br>continuity rather than<br>transformation, e.g. health-care,<br>banking<br>Middle management/leadership<br>Organizations with resistance<br>to 'leadership cultures' (public<br>sector organizations) |

When thinking about leadership in one's own workplace, or when visiting another organization, these boxes can highlight a few of the relevant issues to consider. If a discourse exists in the wrong context, there will be increased tension, and the leader character will experience the full effects of this tension. If as a leader, you experience such tensions, then look at conflicts in discourses as a potential way of understanding and getting to the source of the problem.

# Conclusion

The discourses outlined can be an important factor in how a company is led, how change takes place, and why tensions occur in organizational cultures emanating from these leadership discourses. Equally, working in the most appropriate discourse, and using the leadership discourse to offer the appropriate leadership in practice, and create the best culture for a department or an organization is vital to organizational success. Critical theory helps leaders, followers and participators understand these underlying discourses and from this informed position, members of an organization have more freedom of choice as to how they act.

The following questions are to help you think about the discourses in your own workplace:

- What is your leadership valency (your internalized preference and assumptions)?
- From which leadership discourse do you operate?
- Does this discourse emanate from your valency or from the organization in which you work?
- How does the leadership discourse inform your leadership approach?
- How do you notice others engaging with the leadership discourse you or your senior executives inhabit?
- What expectations and what responses do they have?

- Who at your work are powerful and who are marginalized and how does the leadership discourse empower and disenfranchise them?
- How are boundaries, limits and control applied at work? Through normative and peer control, coercive control, or therapeutic governance? Or perhaps a mix?
- What happens to those who resist the leadership discourse?
- See if you can identify different leadership discourses in your organization, e.g. in the finance department and the sales department. If there are differences, why is this and what effect does this have?
- What leadership discourse would best fit your organization to achieve success?
- Watch the news and read the newspapers and try to identify in political and business leaders the different leadership discourses they operate from.

# Emergent Leadership: The Eco-leader Discourse

## Introduction

The continuous search for new leadership ideas is driven by two main urges: (1) the need to find contemporary leadership solutions to the changing social, political and economic conditions; and (2) the need to keep the huge leadership/management development industry afloat, through selling the latest ideas through books, consultancy and training, business and management schools, etc. These two drivers are not always compatible. The hubris and the marketing of leadership sometimes get in the way of supporting a legitimate search for successful leadership. New leadership is often 'mutton dressed as lamb', that is the old is dressed up as the new in order to sell the book or course. Continuity and experience can be dismissed and overlooked simply because they are not new. Tradition and orthodoxy are not the marketer's favourite words; new sells, old doesn't. Leaders themselves when new to post are under huge pressure to generate some signature change in order to prove their worth, often to the detriment of continuity to the organization. Politicians also scramble to modernize public institutions and to find ways to demonstrate their credentials as change agents. The Labour Party in the UK became successful when they re-branded to 'New Labour' (this was true of many other leftist European parties). In academia, modernizing and modernity are now passé as we fly into the future of the latest 'new' which usually involves the word 'post', the post-modern, post-structural, post-industrial, etc. The fetish of the new is nicely captured by the phrase 'I Pod therefore I am' (Jones, 2005) suggesting you only exist if you follow the latest trend; many parents will fully understand this sentiment. Leadership itself can become what Marx called a 'commodity fetish' whereby the thing itself once commodifed, i.e. is changed into a product to sell, takes on a fetishist presence with little relation to what it actually is.

However, beneath the hubris, there are signs of a new leadership discourse emerging which I call the Eco-leader discourse.

## New discourses in leadership

Therefore, from a critical perspective, new leadership theories and models should be treated with care. One helpful way to identify what a new leadership model is really offering is to think about it in terms of its underlying discourse. Is it repeating old news, does it bring subtle changes showing signs of an emerging new discourse, or perhaps it merges discourses? I will briefly look at new developments in leadership to see if there are signs of new leadership discourses emerging. Right now no clear discourse has overtaken the Messiah discourse. Although the fervour for transformational leaders has died down (after 25 years this has had a good run) and there is now a vocal minority who critique transformational leadership, the Messiah leadership discourse remains strong. Take a look at the package offered to Ford's new CEO, Alan Mulally: 'Ford said Mr Mulally would receive a salary of $2 million a year, plus a $7.5 million signing bonus. He will also receive $11 million to offset performance awards and stock options forfeited by leaving Boeing' (Maynard, 2006: B3). At just short of US$20 million, this initial package suggests that the company are expecting a high return from this leader. Perhaps to act as saviour and resurrect Ford (a company of national symbolic importance) and with it American manufacturing industry, hence the call from the US President to the company chairman regarding this appointment. This is an example illustrating that the belief in the Messiah discourse is alive and well.

A new discourse will emerge but has not done so yet, however, I will briefly note three areas in which there are signs of change in contemporary leadership thinking which could herald a new emergent discourse:

1   post-heroic leadership;
2   leadership spirit;
3   systemic and emergent leadership.

These three leadership frames often refer back to the previous discourses I have already described and they also overlap and merge with each other. Together they may also point towards a new emergent discourse.

## Post-heroic leaders

The Messiah discourse is not the final word, but it remains the contemporary dominant discourse in the mainstream literature and practising leaders' mindset. My personal field experience, working in different sectors and continents, finds that when people generally talk and think about leadership, they think of the transformational-charismatic-inspirational leader, someone who influences followers. However, there has been a small but growing backlash against the Transformational and hero leader.

Binney et al. (2004) agree that the Messiah discourse which they call hero-leadership remains so pervasive that people don't even recognize it; however, their analysis of the hero leader misses the important points raised under the Messiah discourse, which differentiates this leadership from the traditional 'Great Man' version of the leader. Huey (1994) who coined the term post-heroic leadership, and Mintzberg (2004b) in his *Harvard Business Review* (HBR) article 'Enough leadership' berate the recent glut of leadership hype and wisely counsel moderation on the subject. Badarraco (2001) in his HBR article 'We don't need another hero' makes the case for quiet moral leadership 'modesty and restraint are in large measure responsible for their extraordinary achievement'. Binney et al. (2004) set up a false dichotomy, taking the Transformational leader as an individual figure and ignoring the discourse and the broader aims as discussed in the Messiah discourse. Many authors in this vein establish yet another binary split: positing (bad) hero leader versus (good) post-heroic leader. The hero depicted is the tired 'Great Man hero', a solo character, with formal power, who exerts charismatic control over a dependent, passive workforce. Their answer is the post-heroic leader, but under examination we find regurgitated leadership approaches, taken directly from the Therapist leader discourse.

Their analysis ignores a generation of leadership literature and practice, and fails to address what was new about the Messiah discourse. They do not address the covenantal leadership, the narrative, generative and dialoguing approaches or the efforts to lead through strong cultures in order to overcome traditional hierarchy, dependency and control. The post-heroic leader does, however, show some signs of change, it is a reaction to the noise and bells of the 'tub thumping' evangelic style of the Transformational leader. The leader is toned down, forceful but with humility and quiet but focused influence. Examples of this approach are Badarraco's (2001) quiet leader, and Jim Collins' (2001) Level 5 leadership 'who blends extreme personal humility with intense professional will'. Binney et al. summarize the effective post-heroic leader:

> If leaders are to connect with others and understand the context, they need to bring themselves to the job of leading. Leaders can do this in the following ways:
>
> - they come across to others as genuinely human, and don't wear any kind of mask
> - they draw on all their humanity, their intelligence, their emotions and their intuition. They don't stay in their heads and draw solely on their rational selves. They make use of all their senses and intelligence
> - they remember what they know from their life experiences and make use of them in the world of work
>
> (Binney et al., 2004)

As can be seen, the leader needs to be authentic, emotionally intelligent, sensitive and less rational, privileging the emotional and internal self. They describe the post-heroic leader as relational, as about people, the classic 'leader as Therapist' discourse. The post-heroic leadership literature also includes the recent idea of leader-coaches, advocating that leaders should be coaches to their followers and should create 'coaching cultures' in the workplace; the leader-coach is the archetype leader-therapist. Much of this literature represents ideas from democratic and the Human Relations movement, it is particularly close to Greenleaf's 'servant leader' (1977) which pioneered post-heroic leadership under a different name, over 30 years before the latest post-heroic, new idea. Servant leadership is again ensconced in the 'therapist discourse'. Larry Spears, the CEO of the Greenleaf Center, describes servant-leadership:

> As we near the end of the twentieth century, we are beginning to see that traditional autocratic and hierarchical modes of leadership are slowly yielding to a

newer model – one that attempts to simultaneously enhance the personal growth of workers and improve the quality and caring of our many institutions through a combination of teamwork and community, personal involvement in decision making, and ethical and caring behavior. This emerging approach to leadership and service is called *servant-leadership*. (Spears, 1995)

This language identifies personal growth within a 'caring community', positioning the organization as some kind of therapeutic clinic, led by a 'therapist leader'. This resonates with Rose's (1990) comments about therapeutic culture at work: 'The management of subjectivity has become a central task for the modern organization.' The post-heroic leader literature also calls for dispersed leadership, networking and matrix organizations and advocates greater collaboration, in line with much of what the Transformational leader set out to achieve.

Observing this from a discourse perspective, there appears to be a contemporary synthesis and a tension between the Therapist discourse and the Messiah discourse. It is as if the Therapist discourse is pulling leadership in one direction, and the desire/need for the Messiah discourse in another. Attempts have been made to harness the Therapeutic character to serve the interests of the Messiah discourse. For example, Jim Collins' 'Level 5 leader' retains the heroism but inverts it. Rather than acting with machismo and visionary language, the Level 5 leader advocates humility, focus and resilience as tools to achieve the same outcome. 'The most powerfully transformative executives possess a paradoxical mixture of personal humility and professional will. They are timid and ferocious. Shy and fearless, they are rare – and unstoppable' (Collins, 2001: 1). The post-heroic leader literature also leans towards spirit(ual) leadership, which is both explicit and also implicit in the tone of their claims.

## Leadership spirit

I would like to use the term 'leadership spirit' rather than 'spiritual leadership' as it is not possible to succinctly define what is spiritual and how 'spiritual leadership' impacts in the workplace. Leadership spirit implies that leaders act with spirit, or there is a spirit of leadership. This spirit can be generically acknowledged as the human spirit. For some people, the divine informs this human spirit and they may speak of being spiritual. Some may wish to go further and say that their spirituality is informed by an organized religion, 'I have Catholic spirituality or a Buddhist spirituality, or I am a Muslim, or a Hindu'. For others, the human spirit is informed by the natural environment, deep ecologists, for example, and some New Age religions and pagans. For others, the human spirit is informed by an inexplicable but universal transcendent spirit, for atheists and humanists the human spirit comes out of a deeply human experience. For others, it is a mystery or a mixture of the above.

In this context, it matters little what informs or underpins the leadership spirit, however, the spirit must support the joy, creativity, the positive life-force and the underlying ethics and holistic approach of the Eco-leader discourse. Practising how to leverage this leadership spirit is more important than finding its source.

I will now take a critical look at some of the literature on spiritual leadership.

## Spiritual leadership: compassionate corporate Bodhisattvas

(A Bodhisattva is a Buddhist saint, one who attains perfect knowledge but resides on earth.) There is a growing interest in spiritual leadership in the literature. I don't intend to cover this subject in depth in this book, although it is important in this context as it helps to signify the next emergent leadership discourse – Eco-leadership discourse.

A recent article in *Business Week* (Conlon, 1999) estimated that at least 10,000 Bible and prayer groups meet regularly in US workplaces and the Academy of Management now has a Special Interest Group on Management, Spirituality and Religion at its conference while management books and journals are full of references to spirituality.

Patricia Aburdene lists seven new megatrends for 2010; all support the formation of the Eco-leadership discourse:

1  *The power of spirit*: In times of change and turbulence people seek the journey inwards: 78% sought spiritual practices (meditation and yoga).
2  *The dawn of conscious capitalism*: Top companies and CEOs are re-engineering themselves to fulfil all stakeholders' needs (not just the bottom line).
3  *Leading from the middle:* Leadership not just at senior level. Leadership at middle levels where values and morality are carefully considered and driven throughout the organization.
4  *Spirituality* in business is a growing trend.
5  *The value-driven consumer*: They buy from companies that respect the environment, their people and the community.
6  *The wave of conscious solutions*: They are tracking their results of spirituality in business. As an example, hybrid cars (sensitive to resource usage) are being developed and offered on terms of 0% interest.
7  *The socially responsible investment boom*: Investment analysts are placing funds and faith in companies that respect the environment, their people and communities. Globally, labour forces are not being exploited as they were 10 years ago (e.g. Nike).

(Aburdene, 2005: xxi–xxii cited in Katz, 2006)

Mitroff and Denton in their book *A Spiritual Audit of Corporate America* write: 'If one word best captures the meaning of spirituality and the vital role it plays in people's lives, it is interconnectedness' (1999: xvi). Their spiritual audit finds these responses to how corporate employees define their personal spirituality:

- Highly individual and intensely personal
- Belief that there is a supreme being that governs the universe and that there is a purpose for everybody and everything
- We are all interconnected. Everything affects everything else
- Being in touch with your interconnectedness
- No matter how bad things are, they will always work out

- We are here to serve others/mankind
- Connected to caring, hope, kindness, love and optimism.

With the following definition of spirituality:

- Is not denominational
- Is inclusive and embraces everybody
- Is universal and timeless
- Is the ultimate source of meaning and purpose in our lives
- Expresses the awe we feel when we are in the presence of the transcendent
- Is sacredness and everything, including the ordinariness of everyday life
- Deep feeling of interconnectedness of everything
- Integrally connected to inner peace and calm
- Provides one with an inexhaustible source of energy, faith and will power
- Spirituality and faith are inseparable.

(Mitroff and Denton, 1999: 23–5 cited in Katz, 2006)

Their findings are interesting as they blend the Christian-Judaeo tradition finding that spirituality is individual and transcendent, with the Eastern and perhaps indigenous Native American tradition, focusing on the ecological ideas that 'We are all interconnected. Everything affects everything else'. I will return to this point later.

It is rare in other literature to find the transcendental idea that there is a supreme divinity. Much of the spiritual literature is difficult as it merges with humanism, individualism and rationalism. For example, Zohar and Marshall use the term Spiritual *Intelligence* which clearly demonstrates the 'stickiness' of the Controller discourse and its underlying message of management efficiency and rationality. Spirituality paradoxically becomes linked to cognitive intelligence and rationality, for no other reason except to sell to the management market which means keeping it within the normative, rational discourse. I was listening to a leadership lecture recently on spiritual development for business leaders, where participants were offered 'executive yoga' in the morning and 'executive meditation' in the evening. I laughed: how does 'executive yoga' differ from yoga?

The paradox is that these techniques are supposed to move leaders away from the ego and the rational and yet making yoga and meditation executive attempts to make it elite in some way for the 'special executive'. The language used signifies and reproduces the existing normative management discourse and the power relations and structures that accompany it.

Zohar and Marshall describe Spiritual intelligence (SQ) as 'the intelligence with which we access our deepest meanings, values, purposes and highest emotions' (2004: 3) They state:

In understanding SQ and Spiritual Leadership it is important to list the twelve transformative processes of SQ (these are characteristics displayed in a person of high SQ):

- Self-awareness
- Spontaneity

- Vision and Value led
- Holistic
- Compassion (feeling with)
- Celebration of diversity
- Field-independence
- Asking why?
- Reframe
- Positive use of adversity
- Humility
- Sense of vocation.

(ibid.: 80)

Taking these 12 processes, I would argue that not one of these could be separated from the characteristics of a leader with a value-based, humanistic stance. This begs the question, what separates the spiritual leader from an ethical 'good' leader? Being religious or spiritual doesn't always lead to positive outcomes; many a spiritual leader has failed due to their immoral and unethical acts.

Reflecting wider social trends, some employees are seeking a deeper meaning from their work life and attempt to integrate a 'spiritual-work' identity (Giacalone and Jurkiewicz, 2003). Attempts to claim spiritual cultures increase productivity, are now being made (Becker, 1998; Altman, 2001). How does an organization promote spirituality in the workplace? According to May (2000), the most important influence is leadership.

Pantoja describes how the Servant-Leader idea was born from Christology and is very much situated in the Messiah discourse as well as the Therapist discourse:

> Servant-leadership is symbolized by *the throne* and *the towel*. He (Christ) knew his cosmic authority: 'that the Father had put all things under His power' (Jn. 13:3). That was the *throne-symbol*. Because of that ultimate sense of security, He was able to humble Himself to 'wrap a towel around His waist' like a lowly servant, 'to wash his disciple's feet, drying them with the towel that was wrapped around Him' (Jn. 13: 4-5). That was the *towel-symbol*. (Pantoja, 1999)

The Servant-Leader presents us with is a classic paradox of a super-heroic/post-heroic leader. As Pantojoa's example shows, what better symbol of the Messianic discourse than a Messiah? These humble post-heroic leaders are presented as more heroic than the Transformational leader they criticize. Post-heroic leaders retain their impact as forceful leaders and yet are wonderful people, with humility, relational skills, servitude, compassion, authenticity and humanness. The post-heroic/servant-leader is not new, there have been many religious and spiritual teachers following this path in the recent and the very distant past.

The recent interest in spiritual leaders seems to be linked to modernity's alienating characteristics and the quest for meaning and answers when traditional religion and community have faltered in the West (Handy, 1997; Goffee and Jones, 2006). This spiritual movement in the leadership literature parallels the rising interest in New Age Eastern spirituality, which grew from the 1960s and has been linked to therapy culture, mixing personal and spiritual growth. The language used to describe the post-heroic leaders creates an image of a Therapist leader with spiritual and moral intent. These post-heroic leaders, however, are often more idealized, more of a fantasy, than charismatic leaders of the past. Reading some of the post-heroic literature, one gets a vision of a new breed of corporate leader; the *compassionate corporate Bodhisattvas*.

A glance at management literature shows books and journals full of references to these subjects, writings on Zen and Taoist management techniques, Benedictine monks and Gaia management books and courses, American Indian symbolism and rituals in training and development for managers. Spirituality is now entering the leadership literature and practice: 'For at least a decade the press has reported company leaders speaking about spirituality and business, while multiple publications have advocated links between corporate success and issues of the soul' (Calas and Smircich, 2003: 329).

According to May (2000), spirituality is the most important influence in leadership. But as Tourish and Pinnington point out, 'Ironically, this effort is often driven by a very non-spiritual concerns – the desire to increase profits' (2002: 165).

> The goals of SMD are personal growth and self-creation i.e. a state of being rather than skills or knowledge about the organization. In addition, SMD provides a context in which individuals are able to search for meaning and explore feelings of solidarity and re-identification with their work rules and work organization. (Bell and Taylor, 2004)

Ackers and Preston claim that a new priestly cadre is being 'developed':

> Arguing that a new evangelical, revelatory form of management development is making its way from the margins to the mainstream, wherein managers are treated as a 'priestly cadre' whose spiritual needs must be satisfied through semi-monastic retreats to recharge their batteries. (1992: 697–8)

Žižek suggests why New Age and Eastern spirituality are popular with global business, his claim is that the effects are similar to the impact of the Messiah discourse when it becomes dysfunctional leading to fundamentalist and ultra-conformist cultures:

> The Buddhist stance is ultimately that of indifference, of quenching all passions that strive to establish differences … Here, one is almost tempted to resuscitate the old, infamous Marxist cliché of religion as 'the opium of the people,' as the imaginary supplement of real-life misery. The 'Western Buddhist' meditative stance is arguably the most efficient way for us to fully participate in the capitalist economy while retaining the appearance of sanity. If Max Weber were alive today, he would definitely write a second, supplementary volume to his Protestant Ethic, titled The Taoist Ethic and the Spirit of Global Capitalism. (Žižek, 2002)

Žižek (2003) describes how Ichikawa Hakugen thoughtfully criticized the disastrous Japanese Second World War experience. Hakugen believed that the Zen focus on inner peace, the lack of a focus on social justice, the doctrine of no-self and other Buddhist traits all contributed to sow the seeds for Japan's militaristic aggression and which led to huge cruelty and a terrible defeat (see Victoria, 1998).

Žižek claims the doctrine of no-self and non-attachment means that individual responsibility is minimized. In the case of the workplace, if a leader can espouse these westernized versions of Eastern values, they can also expect a workforce to become indifferent, to focus on their inner peace and get the job done, with a sense of indifference to other concerns. The individual has a sense of non-attachment which frees them from ethical engagement, they are able to use their private inward spirituality as a coping mechanism which supports them but it does not encourage external engagement (Bell and Taylor, 2004).

The therapeutic/spiritual cultures espoused can also lead to an increased sense of focus on one's self, further embellishing a leader's narcissistic ego. This approach can also undermine the solidarity of collective agency by increasing a detached inward attitude that ends up being in servitude to rather than engagement with the corporate machine. So while on the surface the values of post-heroic and servant-leaders seem 'obviously good', when we deconstruct them, place them in the context of a corporation, in a capitalist workplace, or a public sector large organization, and ask questions of power and influence, the *new* post-heroic leader poses problems. Asking critical questions reveals more:

- *Who are these servant leaders serving?*
  In most cases of senior leaders, the answer is self-evident by checking their benefits packages, they serve themselves and also serve their shareholders, and funding stakeholders. As Freeman advocates: 'The more we can begin to think in terms of how to better serve stakeholders, the more likely we will be to survive and prosper over time' (1984: 80).
- *What are the structural hidden power relations?*
- *Does this 'post-heroic' leadership style embellished with spirituality enhance autonomy or undermine it?*
- *Does it increase the dependence of followers on the humble yet powerful leader?*
  Thomas Merton warns of the dangers of monastic novices idealizing him when he was their spiritual guide, with very damaging results, as they lose their autonomy aiming only to please and mimic him, and he lost his bearings as their spiritual director for a while: 'Penitents (Novice Monks) seduce you into taking the role of omnipotence and omniscience and in this situation while you are deluding' (Merton, 1966: 55). This is called transference and counter-transference in the psychoanalytic world, and any leader or person with influence (therapist, guru, teacher) should be alert to this danger. A leader who claims divine or spiritual qualities create a bigger danger as their followers may idealize them even more. These dangers are rarely discussed in the spiritual management literature.
- *Does this style increase or decrease personal power of a leader?*
  A wonderful person, a humble servant-leader will hold more power than the omnipotent high and mighty hero leader. When asked about great leaders, Ghandi, the Dalai Lama, and Martin Luther King are often cited, but their leadership relates to the betterment of humanity, not using their leadership power for company profit or personal success. The context can make a big difference. Non-attachment from material concerns is contradictory and inauthentic in most workplaces, unless the leader is very clear as to their authentic vocation, and how they use their leadership spirituality.

## *Merging discourses*

Using the lenses of the discourses the post-heroic leaders waver between the Therapist characters and Messiah characters depending on the author, but encompass both aspects. What is interesting and different about this model is how the Messiah discourse is changing, taking on more contemplative spiritual-human values rather than the evangelical preacher values of the fundamentalist. This fits with social change and the rise of Western Buddhism, and Eastern spiritual influences and the demise of Western Protestant culture.

From a discourse perspective, the Messiah discourse is shifting towards the Eco-discourse whereby the leadership style is to focus more on immanence than transcendence, i.e. it is looking towards the inward transformation of leaders and followers rather than the Transformational leader's ability to outwardly change their followers. A key differential point is perhaps that a post-heroic leader can be inspirational without being charismatic.

What seems evident is that the post-heroic leader with a spiritual edge is very much a product of both the therapeutic and messianic discourse. The therapeutic discourse focuses on individual and team performance (close leadership) while the Messiah discourse supports culture change (distant leadership). There are really dangers of a 'sheep in wolf's clothing', super-powerful leaders presenting a veneer of humble/spirituality creating ever more conformist cultures though evoking increased employee detachment that reienforces the colluded-self.

In reality, leaders with such developed spirituality and whose egos are so 'other-centred' are so exceptional that they won't be flooding the corporate market in the next decade, and these qualities are difficult to train even in committed novitiates in religious seminaries.

However, the shift in emphasis to a more compassionate, ethical and socially responsible and connected leadership does resonate with increasing concerns about contemporary environmental issues. The rising interest in 'new' forms of spirituality and social activism is raising corporate social responsibility to the fore. Political and business leaders are adopting such a change. To many people's surprise 'The Terminator' has turned green. Arnold Schwarzenegger, governor of Californias, the world's twelfth biggest greenhouse polluter, has taken some radical steps to improve the environment. Philanthropy and social responsibility are high on the leadership agenda, with the Bill and Melinda Gates Foundation, the Clinton Climate Initiative, and other leaders giving substantial sums of money and commitment to these causes. Many companies have also realized the damage it does to their business if they ignore environmental issues, sustainability and social responsibility. The large oil and clothes companies are having to pay attention to the environmental concerns, critics call this 'greenwash' and I am sure some of it is, but awareness is rising and there is a tangible change taking place; see the websites of Gap, Nike, Shell and BP as examples of the attention given to these issues. Another example is that Tescos have announced that all of its delivery trucks will be fuelled by bio-diesel, and McDonalds has plans to recycle its cooking oil and use this to fuel its delivery fleet.

Environmental and social responsibility leadership is an example of leadership initially coming from grass-roots environmental and social activists, who once were deemed an eccentric fringe, pressurizing corporate business to face its responsibilities, and their agenda being taken up by progressive leaders of business and politics.

Leadership seems to be moving in the direction away from the transformational evangelist and towards a more contemplative, connected leadership, favouring engagement rather than loyal followership.

However, the dangers of leaders performing rather than authentically embodying values such as niceness, compassion, morality, humility and spirituality are clear. Another problem is that there is a need for a radical vision to address the social and environmental issues and the new commercial conditions. Without a Messiah leadership, where will this come from?

The spiritual leader can evoke the ideal of inward calm, retreating from the world, rather than drawing on leadership spirit to address the urgent need for change. Without the visions and the grand narratives to inspire and align culture from the existing Messiah discourse, how organizations will hold together is yet to be articulated. What will create a common bond to prevent fragmentation without strong culture control? There are claims that the big picture will emerge from many smaller emergent successes, and there will be continuous flux. This takes us to the new emergent discourse of the Eco-leader discourse.

## The Eco-leader discourse

The Eco-leadership discourse encompasses the systemic and emergent leadership I noted as the third leadership trend. I use the term 'Eco-leadership' to refer to an emerging leadership discourse which is immersed in leadership practices, values, metaphors and language which resonate with the term ecology. Ecology originates from biology and is a study of the inter-relations of living systems and the environment. Human ecology is the study of humans and their relationship to the environment.

At the heart of this discourse is connectivity, what Fritjof Capra called *The Web of Life* (1996). In this view of the world, ethics shifts from a purely anthropocentric (human-centred) worldview to an eco-centric view. There is an emerging sense that leaders of business, as well as social and political leaders are becoming (and need to become more) eco-literate, which means applying systems thinking and 'spirit' to their organizations and beyond. This leadership discourse is not just about going green or taking an environmentalist stance, although once in the Eco-leadership discourse, these issues become a natural extension of one's leadership thinking.

The Eco-leadership discourse is about a new paradigm of leadership which takes an ecological perspective. A leadership perspective which understands that solutions in one area of business may create problems in another. That growth in one industry causes decline in another, with social consequences. That short-term gains may have immediate benefits, but may have longer-term consequences which may damage the business and the environment. Eco-leadership recognizes that within an organization there are inter-dependent parts which make up a whole, this goes for all stakeholder relationships, and in ever widening circles that eventually reach the air that we breathe. It is about connectivity, inter-dependence and sustainability underpinned by an ethical socially responsible stance. The Eco-leadership discourse takes ethics beyond business ethics into social concerns; it takes ethics beyond human concerns and recognizes a responsibility and relationship to the natural world. It also focuses the connectedness within each of us, and between each of us. The Eco-leadership discourse is fuelled by the human spirit. For some, this is underpinned by spirituality, for others not. Either way, the Eco-leadership discourse is a spirit-filled leadership, and a connected leadership. Eco-leadership has a tradition that can be traced back to many sources, to many of the great religious leaders, spiritual teachers, and philosophers and to pre-modern societies. In contemporary times, there is a rising momentum that suggests that the next discourse will be that of the Eco-leader. 'No man is an island entire of itself; every man is a part of the main. Any man's death diminishes me because I am involved in mankind, and therefore never send to know for whom the bell tolls; it tolls for thee' (John Donne, 1572–1631). Donne's words are an early expression of our co-existence and our common humanity. It points to the connectivity and responsibility we have for each other. This way of thinking is becoming prominent again in the twenty-first century and now goes beyond humanity as our connectivity to nature and the environment once again becomes topical. Rationalism and the Enlightenment proposed that we could be masters of our future, and yet we are unable to be masters of our own destructive forces. Science, rationalism, knowledge, liberty and democracy and a discourse of progress have brought many positive social changes but there are also many discontents. Following the last century of destructive wars, which continue into the present, and the fragility of the environment, with global warming no longer a distant threat but upon us, a new realization of our fragility and connectedness to each other and nature is emerging and with it a strong new social discourse and a new paradigm of thinking. Leadership is not immune from these social forces, and as globalization and new technologies make the world 'smaller', our connections seem more important, and our vulnerability and reliance on each other and on safeguarding the natural world are rising concerns.

On the fringes of the leadership literature exists a growing interest in systems thinking, complexity theory, narrative approaches, and also the environment as metaphors for leadership and organizing company structures. Within this diverse literature, spirituality (usually in New Age, Eastern and environmental forms) again raises its head.

Two key themes that arise are emergent leadership and generative leadership (Senge et al., 2004), that is, the attempt to find new ways to lead complex organizations within networks of suppliers, consumers and other formal and informal influences which are not in the direct 'control' of the company leadership. This complexity requires a new leadership discourse, which is in its infancy.

As with any discourse, they are never new, there is never a distinct line in the sand where a discourse begins and ends, the present always refers back to the past and looks to the future. I now wish to briefly situate the Eco-leadership discourse in a socio-political context.

This current interest in Eco-leadership arises from three key areas:

1  New scientific discoveries such as quantum physics, 'the new concepts in physics have brought about a profound change in our worldview; from the mechanistic worldview of Descartes and Newton to a holistic and ecological view' (Capra, 1996: 5).

2   The sharp rise in awareness of our finite natural resources, global warming and the destruction of the earth's biosphere have abruptly re-awakened our connectedness and interdependence on the environment (Lovelock, 1982).

3   Technological advances and globalization that have, on the one hand, made the world a smaller, more connected place. On the other hand, the experience of modernity's alienation, and displacement. Whether as a refugee, an immigrant or whether the disconnectedness is within the modern self, atomized within fragmenting communities.

There is an ever-growing complexity of connected networks of organizations, suppliers, producers and consumers, forming webs of interaction with no single leadership, no planned strategy, set in a constantly emerging and changing political and social environment. From this arises new organizational forms and leadership approaches. Activist groups and new social movements have used new communicational capabilities to their advantage, taking on multinational corporations over issues such as their treatment of outsourced work in the Third World. Religious fundamentalist terrorists use dispersed leadership and de-centralized organizing to great effect as this USA National Intelligence Report demonstrates:

> We assess the global Jihad movement is decentralized, lacks a coherent global strategy and is becoming more diffuse. New Jihadist networks and cells with Anti-American agendas are increasingly likely to emerge. The confluence of shared purpose and dispersed actors will make it harder to find and undermine jihadist groups. (cited in the *New York Times*, 27 Sept., 2006)

Leaders of multinational corporations are also finding that they have to find ways to increase the emergent capabilities within their companies to have any chance of keeping pace with change and the de-centralized forces impacting on them.

Within organizational leadership there are attempts to find ways of working with the unpredictable and uncontrollable patterns, as the contemporary leadership discourses refer back to forms of control, whether it is coercive or normative. They bind the leader and leadership to operating within either the technical discourse of the Controller and Therapist, with both relying on technique and a technical worldview. The Messiah discourse guides the leader to evoke strong organizational cultures. Each of the three discourses acts as the leaders operate within closed organizational systems. In the wider sphere of management, the business world also acts as if there is a closed-system governed by neo-liberal economic laws. The problem with this view is that external factors, social political and the environmental are not accounted for. External costs, the damage to the environment, polluting the air we breathe, the social consequences of corporate business on local communities; these externalities are treated as cost-free. A moral economics as well as a market economics is necessary and the emerging Eco-leadership discourse is beginning to raise these questions.

Theories from biology have been applied to human organisms and systems, for example, von Bertalanffy (1968) pioneered Open-Systems theory, Trist and Bamford (1951) pioneered new 'open socio-technical' systems at the Tavistock Institute and Gregory Bateson's work (1972, 1979) is of huge importance and his work on communications and systems thinking is found within many disciplines.

If one takes a systemic analysis and looks at the Messiah discourse through an open-systems perspective (von Bertalanffy, 1968), one can account for the un-sustainability of this leadership as the organizational boundaries are ever-closing and become increasingly rigid. When an organism's (or organization's) boundaries get too closed and don't allow inputs and outputs to flow (in human systems this includes communications), the organism starts to atrophy and will die. A plant, for example, which can no longer take in sunlight or water will die. The plant's boundary must be semi-permeable, and healthy living systems self-regulate to allow the correct amount of inputs and outputs to survive, and to adapt to changing environmental conditions. However, if the self-regulatory system fails, and the boundaries become too permeable or too closed, the system becomes dysfunctional and dies.

From an open-systems perspective, this explains what happens when the Messiah discourse leads to totalizing fundamentalist cultures, rigid boundaries are set, homogenized belief systems form within the company, the focus becomes on protecting the internal culture and the world outside seems increasingly daunting and threatening, ideas and communications (inputs and outputs) stop flowing and the company falls into decline. The Messiah leadership discourse can bring early success but often leads to an unsustainable system for these reasons. Open-systems thinking teaches us that we have to interact with the environment, and to achieve this successfully requires adaptive and self-regulation. In terms of leadership, self-regulation and adaptive practice can only occur when there is dispersed leadership able to act and react to local change.

Leadership becomes less about control and more about navigating through complex and diverse business eco-systems. It was realized long ago that hierarchical leadership and the Controller discourse was not appropriate for contemporary workplaces. Leadership styles relying on the Therapeutic discourse can help at an individual and team level but this discourse has little to offer leaders in the way of predicting the global market, or how to make sense of running an international multinational which has such a multitude of political, social, environmental, economic, etc. influences on its success. How does a company leadership navigate their company strategically and operationally through these waters?

Eco-leadership is a discourse, which creates self-organizing and emergent properties arising from dispersed leadership, which build into organizations the ability to be adaptive to fluctuations and constant change.

One of the focuses of Eco-leadership is to find ways to harness the human spirit, and our intuition, connectedness to each other, to nature, and our non-rational ways knowing. Senge et al. (2004) promote the idea of Presencing and the *U Process* as a methodology for working with new collective awareness:

> The leadership of the future will not be provided simply by individuals but by groups, institutions, communities, and networks. One of the road blocks for groups moving forward now is thinking that they have to wait for a leader to emerge; someone who embodies the future path ... but I think what we've been learning with the U process is that the future can emerge within the group itself, not embodied in a hero or traditional leader ... we have to nurture a new form of leadership that doesn't depend on extraordinary individuals. (Senge et al., 2004: 185–6)

Findlater (2006) writes that the U process is aligned to spirituality. Part of this process is the solo-wilderness experience. After initially meeting and defining important issues in a group, individuals go into the natural wilderness alone to 'open up one to the deepest inner self' which is followed by attempts to reach collective awareness through what Senge refers to as Presencing and reflections to try and ascertain the future direction:

> This pursuit of personal spiritual growth to enhance the meaning derived from their work and to improve their effectiveness though engagement with an inner self and their relationship to the world relates to the Presencing phase of the U-Process, and the description of the solo (an outdoor wilderness experience) in the U-Process as working to give space to our deepest and quietest voices, which are in turn connected intimately to the whole (Hassan and Kahane, 2005). It encourages an internalised, implicit form of religiosity where the search for self-understanding and the search for meaning of closely aligned (Bell and Taylor, 2004). This also relates to the U-Process where Hassan and Kahane suggest that meditative practices can be foundational to the work at the bottom of the U. (Findlater, 2006: 4)

The literature on emergence is still in its infancy. Within the leadership literature there is a tendency to conflate therapeutic culture with New Age spirituality and systems or complexity theory. When this occurs, the mish-mash is often difficult to use in practice, and the dangers are that it becomes 'fluffy' and comforting but without depth or content.

There are other serious attempts to create frameworks for an Eco-leadership discourse which have practical applications. Tapping the spirit and non-rational knowledge as a way to get beyond the rational and obvious and move to a more connected way of leading is not a newly discovered enterprise. There are good examples of where this has been tried in other fields which could be translated to managememt practice. When discussing some of the key features of U-theory, or other leadership development notions of inward-bound training (Bell and Taylor, 2004), I immediately associate them with psychoanalytic techniques which access and make sense of the unconscious. In psychoanalysis, the analyst and the client both access their unconscious worlds; the client is asked to free associate and the psychoanalyst enters what Bion (1962) called a state of 'reverie'. Chris Bollas, a prominent writer and psychoanalyst, describes this reverie process:

> There are always levels of thought, levels of engagement, levels of response to a question, levels of thinking about something. I can think off the top of my head. I can provide a certain level of response to what you might be discussing, or to what a patient might be saying to me. But for reverie to take place, I have to be able to drift inside myself ... in a more associative way ... in a less reactive manner. I also have to be relaxed inside myself for this to take place, creating a containing space for the analysand [client]. (Bollas, 1997: 39)

Chris Bollas goes on to refer to the 'unthought known' (Bollas, 1987) which equates to tapping into one's own or a collective unconscious knowing. He describes how we know something but have not yet thought it. When it becomes a thought, we recognize that we already knew of it. Being able to tap into this knowledge is vital to avoid huge mistakes: 'When I looked back it was so obvious ... Why didn't I see it!'

Bion (1962) also identified attaining 'negative capability' (Keat's term) which is a 'particular kind of attention, where we reach a state of being capable of "not-knowing"'. This opens a space for us to access and learn something new. In the rational world of business leaders, the idea of not-knowing is totally counter-cultural and scares the daylights out of leaders operating from normative practice.

Using these psychoanalytic methodologies and drawing on my psychoanalytic training and my practice as a psychotherapist, I have developed a leadership training technique called the Free Association Matrix (drawing on the work of Gordon Lawrence's Social Dream Matrix [Lawrence, 1999] ). Lawrence's work is similar to the ideas of Senge's 'presencing' and preceded it. He uses individual dreams as a way for a group to intuit and infer what might be happening organizationally and socially. The Free Association Matrix performs a similar task but links the traditional psychoanalytic method, free association, to the social and organizational. It is set within a critical pedagogy which challenges the rational-knowledge pedagogies of learning. The aim is to help leaders to do the following:

1   Move to a space of not-knowing and open a space for the new to be discovered.
2   Allow them to re-connect with their own body and unconscious and with each other, and with the social world, in a different way.
3   Reflect on this process and to share what can be learnt and applied in their roles as leaders.

The Free Association Matrix creates a liminal or transitional space, which later becomes a containing space in which a group of leaders can explore their free associations, i.e. whatever 'comes to mind'. This is done not in a group, nor individually but in a matrix; a formation of chairs assembled in an ad hoc fashion. The time is usually 30 minutes to an hour. Box 13.1 shows the instructions I give to the group. In a coaching course I lead, each day begins with yoga, then we go straight into a Free Association Matrix, the idea is to ground individuals in the group in their bodies, and then move into the transitional space which allows new thinking to emerge.

---

## Box 13.1 Free Association Matrix

Discard your memory; discard the future tense of your desire; forget them both, both what you knew and what you want, to leave a space for a new idea.

(W. Bion)

**The aim:**
To emancipate thoughts which are not easily accessed, releasing new creativity.

Free association is a bridge between experience, thought and knowledge.

*(Continued)*

*(Continued)*

**The object we are studying is the individual and group unconscious.**
This is a counter-point to the daily focus on the rational, and on goals and outputs.

This session is about pausing and hesitating, and letting go of the desire to present intelligent, well-thought–out ideas.

**How we do it:**
Free association means to talk about whatever comes into mind trying not to censor or edit your thought flow.

We observe our stream-of-consciousness – as it emerges, individually and collectively.

Take your time – allow your thoughts to rise to the surface.

This is not a word-association game, don't be afraid of silence.

Observe what arises, some thoughts you have (or the silence) may make you uncomfortable; stay with the process and let the discomfort pass.

We are not attempting to analyse individual offerings but to access our collective wisdom through the connections we make.

## Ground rules

- **Do not ask questions:** your normal reactions to somebody's associations are to want to ask, to clarify, to comment or to disagree. Let go of this need. Simply associate your thoughts to any comments made, and, if you choose to, share your associations.
- **Stay present:** when you drift, catch yourself and bring your attention back to the matrix and your present experience.
- **Be curious** about yourself, others and the matrix you are in. Why are you feeling, angry, happy, sad, giggly? What does your body feel like?
- **Associate** to yourself, your own thoughts and feelings, and associate to each another.
- **Amplify** and open up, rather than close down. Do not look for interpretations, answers, solutions or closure.
- **Dreams** are an excellent source of the unconscious data – share your dreams, they allow us to access ideas we can relate to our learning.
- **Non-sense is good sense. Do not be tied to logic:** sense-making comes later. Just say whatever arises in your mind, you don't have to understand it

## Role of Focuser

Each matrix will have at least one person who is trained in this process and assumes the role of focuser.

*(Continued)*

---

*(Continued)*

The role of the focuser is:

- to hold a safe space, to make connections and links when appropriate;
- to keep the group on task and to open and close the matrix on time.

## Sense-making

After the matrix: sense-making in pairs, small groups and plenary takes place. This is an opportunity to reflect on the content and the process that occurred, and to make links to one's workplace experience.

---

The idea is to create a liminal space which breaks the social norm of a group dynamic, and normative group behaviours and expectations. When entering the matrix chairs set out in this jumbled fashion, facing all directions, it signifies a different space, a discontinuity from the norm. This is like entering the therapist's office and lying on the couch, a new and different space is established, and a transitory space is evoked within participants who are open to new experiences. This space allows free associations to occur. These are not analysed or interpreted as happens in individual therapy; the associations are accepted as data for the information of the group. After the Free Association Matrix, sense-making takes place but often it is the next day, during the week or over longer period of time that important links, deeper connections and understandings are made. One of the important aspects of this work, like the U-process, is that it connects people to themselves and to each other, it focuses on emotions and experience rather than knowledge and cognition or thinking. During the sense-making the associations are discussed, and the personal experience of the Matrix is pooled with surprising results. In one session we worked with a leader who discussed an association he had of a ladder which he was constantly climbing higher and higher. During the sense-making the ladder was deemed to represent his career and the growth of his company, however, when he drew this on a flip chart he suddenly became aware that at the end of the ladder was nothing, nowhere to go, an empty space. He realized that he had been caught up in a rush to growth, and promotion, damaging his health on the way, and to what ends? This insight allowed him to stop running around manically, and to focus on what he wanted for himself, he received personal coaching, re-balanced his home–work life balance, and it led to a strategic review of what his organization's goals were. Growth alone was no longer the endgame.

In another Free Association Matrix session held with the Principals of FE Colleges, the associations led to playful ideas as to what it felt like to be a leader:

## Leadership is ...

*A Sponge,* soaking up pressure from above, below and the outside environment.
*An Essence,* the leader is the essence, epitomizing the company.
*A Mediator,* resolving conflicting tensions and conflict itself.
*A Translator,* translating between stakeholders and departments, etc.
*A Buffer,* protecting the internal organization from external pressures.
*A Mirage,* how much actual influence or control does a leader really have?
*A Dynamo,* generating energy to the employees and customers.

These highly insightful associations were only possible when the leaders were freed from their normative expectations. It allowed them to rethink how they took on their roles and what was expected of them. We then did some work using the leadership discourses I have written about, so they could work on what leadership discourses were operating in their organizations and departments.

Senge et al. and the U-theory also turns to nature, solo-wilderness trips in an attempt to tap the unconscious/spiritual and to experience what is unavailable through the rational conscious thought process. At Lancaster University Management School research is being carried out on 'Wilderness Thinking', an inward journey for leaders that claims to use SMD, and that anecdotally has been very successful over a number of years (Watson and Vasilieva, 2007). This work again raises the question of what constitutes spiritually. How does spending time in nature constitute spiritual management development rather than simply time for human reflection? Do managers get more from this activity than a day's hiking? The sale to organizations suggests links between better performance and this type of 'spiritual' development. Using spirituality with the aim of getting ever-greater efficiency is in itself problematic. Improved performance to increase productivity of what? For what purpose? With what spiritual and ethical purposes? When spirituality and religion are used for the wrong purposes, linking them with nationalism for example, has let to very disturbing outcomes, and we should be wary of breaking the taboo of serving 'God and mammon'. Great religious and spiritual teachings from all traditions lead us away from material gain and towards a non-material transcendent ethic. Unlesss reflective and 'spiritual' development are clearly linked with deeper questions on ethics, values and the wider environment and social responsibility then there seems to be radical dissonance that requires challenging. The concept of SMD has not as yet addressesd this in earnest.

These trips are similar to deep ecology 'therapeutic' techniques where people go into nature to heal and renew themselves and become reconnected with nature, themselves and the universe, this is posed as an alternative to talking therapy. These leadership training techniques using the environment are further evidence of the emerging Eco-leadership discourse. This is not new of course, and it is worth briefly looking at examples whereby pilgrimages and journeys into the wilderness and nature have been a place of refuge, revitalization and of spiritual renewal. Different cultures around the world have examples, such as the westernized Judaeo-Christian perspective, the Garden of Eden represents a place whereby perfection existed before man's search for knowledge destroyed this utopian experience. Re-visiting nature has always been a cleansing, spiritual, time of seeking a different kind of knowledge from worldly or rational knowledge. Examples are Moses' time in the desert and his visits to Mount Sinai, Christ's 40 days in the wilderness and the Desert Fathers, all are archetypal images of the human search for other-worldly, divine experience, spiritual cleansing and prophetic inspiration through nature, and isolation. In a sense the wilderness represents a liminal space where God can be accessed away from worldly contamination. In more contemporary times the Romantic movement in late eighteenth-century Britain, for example, Lord Byron, William Wordsworth, William Blake reacted against the Enlightenment, rationalism and industrialism by returning to nature as an inspiration. Whereas the Enlightenment emphasized reason, Romanticism emphasized imagination and feeling. Early nineteenth-century 'American Transcendentalism' (for example, Ralph Waldo Emerson, Henry David Thoreau, Margaret Fuller) was also influenced by Eastern thought, inspired by nature and the transcendental spirit. Thoreau in his classic book *Walden* spoke of Vedic influences, and is regarded as a fore-father of the ecology movement.

The Beatnik generation of the 1950s also turned to Zen Buddhism and nature as inspirations; Jack Kerouac describes his trip to the mountain in Yosemite in 1955 to discover spiritual enlightenment in his novel *Dharma Bums* (Kerouac, 1958).

Most recently there has been a huge growth in environmental interest underpinned by a re-awakening of our connectedness to nature. Deep ecology (Naess, 1989) is emerging as a powerful philosophy. Michael E. Zimmerman, Professor of Philosophy at Tulane University, explains deep ecology philosophy:

Deep ecology is founded on two basic principles: one is a scientific insight into the interrelatedness of all systems of life on Earth, together with the idea that anthropocentrism - human-centeredness - is a misguided way of seeing things. Deep ecologists say that an ecocentric attitude is more consistent with the truth about the nature of life on Earth. Instead of regarding humans as something completely unique or chosen by God, they see us as integral threads in the fabric of life. They believe we need to develop a less dominating and aggressive posture towards the Earth if we and the planet are to survive.

The second component of deep ecology is what Arnie Naess calls the need for human self-realization. Instead of identifying with our egos or our immediate families, we would learn to identify with trees and animals and plants, indeed, the whole ecosphere. This would involve a pretty radical change of consciousness, but it would make our behavior more consistent with what science tells us is necessary for the well-being of life on Earth. We just wouldn't do certain things that damage the planet, just as you wouldn't cut off your own finger.

(http://www.context.org/ICLIB/IC22/Zimmrman.htm,accessed 27 September 2006)

The Eco-leader discourse is emerging, the ideas are formative but are gaining mainstream acknowledgement. There are tangible examples of leaders raising human and ethical concerns relating to social responsibility and sustainability. Anita Roddick was an early pioneer of this Eco-leadership discourse, and she claims her ideas were part of the Green Revolution: 'Businesses have the power to do good. That's why The Body Shop's Mission Statement opens with the overriding commitment, "To dedicate our business to the pursuit of social and environmental change"'(http://www.anitaroddick.com/aboutanita.php, accessed 28, September 2006).

More recently, Richard Branson's announcement at the Clinton Global Climate Initiative suggests he too has joined the Eco-leadership discourse:

> British business mogul Richard Branson on Thursday pledged to invest about $3 billion over the next decade to combat global warming and promote alternative energy, saying that it was critical to protect the environment for future generations. Branson, the billionaire behind the multi-platform Virgin brand, said the money would come from 100 per cent of the profits generated by his transportation sectors – trains and airline companies. It will be invested in efforts to find renewable, sustainable energy sources in an effort to wean the world off oil and coal
>
> (http://www.cnn.com/2006/TECH/science/09/21/branson.global.warming.ap/index. html)

In one of the many newspaper articles on the subject of sustainability, Murray Armstrong of *The Guardian* headlines 'Leaders Challenge Business as Usual' (6th November 2006) and in spite of valid reservations, 'Jonathan Porritt is concerned that it's business as usual with CSR retrospectively welded on', he writes that sustainability is central to survival, citing Mervyn Davies, chief executive of Standard Chartered bank and a director of Tesco, saying:

> There isn't a management meeting in Standard Chartered where we don't talk about corporate responsibility and sustainability ... you won't survive in business if you are not environmentally responsible ... Every company in the FTSE 100 now produces a corporate responsibility report ... 80 of them have identified climate change as a business risk ... US vice president Al Gore appointed as an environmental advisor to the British Government by Gordon Brown has challenged businesses to put sustainability at the centre of their activities. Gore said, 'The old way of measuring value is becoming irrelevant'. (*The Guardian*, 6th November 2006: 24)

Being green is part of this discourse, but it is also about changing the way leadership is conceived of. Holism is vital to this discourse, leadership is always conceptualized as fluid and dispersed throughout an organization. Leadership may emerge from surprising places given the right conditions. It is about acknowledging diversity and connectiveness rather than attempting to homogenize company cultures. It is about a leadership which looks for patterns, emerging in and outside of the company, and creates an adaptive culture and a localized and dispersed leadership which can both react more quickly and notice the changes occurring at grassroots level.

## Ethics and Eco-leadership

I wish to highlight a few issues which arise with regards to the Eco-leadership discourse. If the purpose of ethics is to inform moral conduct, then two clear questions arise when thinking about contemporary leadership. The first is well rehearsed, how can ethics inform the moral conduct of leaders, as individuals and as collective groups such as corporate boards? When business ethics are taught and discussed, the focus is often at this 'close level'. By 'close' I am referring to ethics of proximity, of our actions which affect others near to us, those we are in contact with or those we are responsible for.

For individual leaders and those with clear collective leadership responsibility, Aristotle suggests that ethics and moral actions can be cultivated through 'doing ethics' in practice 'just as we acquire crafts, by having previously activated them, we become just by doing just actions' (Aristotle 1985: 34).

The second question is less well rehearsed in leadership circles, but is becoming more prominent. This ethical stance takes ethics beyond the 'close' relationships and takes into account the 'distant' relationships, those we are engaged with indirectly, for example, outsourced workers in Asia; or our damaging impact on the environment that affects all humanity. This ethical responsibility goes beyond being responsible only for what is directly in your control, and takes ethics to mean that we all share a responsibility for the planet, and for the indirect consequences of our individual and collective actions.

Bauman says that morality becomes neutralized in three ways:

1 Denial of proximity.
2 Effacement of face.
3 Reduction to traits.

The denial of proximity directly relates to corporate leadership's dismal record on social and environmental responsibility in the past century. It is only recently, and only due to pressure from grass-roots activists, that working conditions in developing countries and the damage done to the natural environmental are high on the corporate agenda. Just because it is not on our doorstep, doesn't mean we can ignore our ethical responsibilities.

The effacement of face (the removal of face) means that leaders lose sight of their ethical concerns even if it is close by. Leaders need to be aware of bureaucratic mentality that Bauman (1989) claims did not lead directly to the Holocaust, but did not preclude it. Bauman's central argument is that bureaucracies instrumentalize morality by focusing on the organization's goals and totally disregard the moral substance of the goals themselves. Defence mechanisms such as rationalization are key to this process. In contemporary organizations Rene ten Bos (1997: 999) contends that: 'The façade of anti-bureaucratic rhetoric that is typical of this world cannot conceal the basic fact that goal orientation, rational problem solving, group and task loyalty and so forth are still held in high esteem.' He continues by suggesting we need to pay attention to Bauman's work if bureaucracy is still a dominant force. Morality is neutralized in bureaucratic organizations because it diminishes autonomy, which is the source of morality: 'The moral impulse is the source of the most conspicuously autonomous ... behaviour (Bauman 1993:124) and therefore cannot be a very welcome guest in organizations' (Rene ten Bos, 1997: 1000).

This book has identified that it is not only bureaucracy which can lead to the loss of autonomy and with it morality; the powerful cultures emanating from the Messiah leadership discourse also have this totalizing function.

The reduction to traits is a warning to all leadership theorists not to be reductive. When leadership is reduced to individual traits and competencies, then humans themselves are reduced to 'cogs in a machine' and leadership development becomes merely the apparatus to oil these cogs. This approach is functionalist and annihilates systemic thinking, depth analysis and relationships. The reduction to traits creates structures which provide an excuse that each of us plays a part without being responsible for the whole. This is evident when corporate leaders claim that their role is to make shareholder profit, while the culmination of this process adds to the environmental crisis we now face.

The Eco-leader discourse is beginning to recognize that leadership now means re-negotiating what success means for an organization or company. There is a need to look awry at this question, and not take the macro-economic and neo-liberal agenda for granted. Delivering growth and short-term shareholder value is no longer acceptable as the sole measurement of success if we are to act ethically and responsibly. Corporate Social Responsibility, ethics and environmental concerns are now on the agenda (for more information, see Maak and Pless (2006) and Parker (1998)).

To take an Eco-leadership stance, business firms need a leadership which involves them in becoming active and responsible actors in the socio-political arena. The present situation where they are powerful global actors but without political responsibility through claiming to be separate entities, working only in the economic sphere, is no longer tenable. The social world and the natural environment do not operate with such false boundaries; everything is inter-related. A new level of Corporate Social Responsibility which gets beyond 'greenwash' and enlightened self-interest and which embraces a new pragmatic and 'deliberative democracy' is required (Bessette, 1980; Habermas, 1996,1998). This is the key difference between the Transformational leader and the Messiah leader (transforming employees and followers, creating strong cultures within organizations) and the Eco-leadership discourse (creating connections, contexts to communicate, building alliances and networks across and beyond organizations).

A new agenda, a new paradigm needs to evolve and is evolving; provision rather than profit has to be accounted for. Provision means that the loop of profit, and success has to be linked to social justice and environmentally sustainable actions. Leadership success will be to harness technological advancement, knowledge, and our global trading platforms, to 'provide' for a better quality of life, and a sustainable future.

Ethical leadership is to take a critical stance, to look awry, to think holistically, to be accountable for your own actions and for the systems and networks you inhabit, both locally and globally. It places social justice and the environment first;

Milton Friedman (1962) is wrong, so wrong in his claim that a company's only role is to make a profit – this blinkered worldview should be condemned to the history books of the past century. The new leadership discourse demands more, it will continue to keep demanding more from leaders. Leadership without ethics is a non-starter. What is required is for leaders to practise ethics, to engage with ethics from a critical perspective and with what Foucault refers to as an ethical imagination: 'Ethics need not necessarily be associated (but may be) with reference to religion, law and science but be researched using an, "ethical imagination" ' (Foucault lecture given at Berkeley History Department, University of California, 1983).

# Conclusion

This new Eco-leadership discourse is an emergent discourse that has both continuity and discontinuity with the previous discourses, and is aligned to other leadership approaches (see Appendix 1). It is least connected to the leader as Controller discourse, it is a paradigmatic shift away from this discourse and perhaps from modernism itself. However, the continuity resurfaces when it comes to how we limit our resource usage. For example, some leaders are advocating rationing of carbon, using carbon cards to measure and control and limit our individual use. It is an example of how Tayloristic principles of scientific management might be applied. The Therapist discourse will continue to support the Eco-leadership discourse in the area of ethics, finding reflective thinking space, and leading local teams, working on team dynamics and morale. The Messiah discourse is also to be found in regards to the vision and the ability of leaders to communicate the urgent need to undertake the paradigm change necessary to embrace the Eco-leadership discourse. The shift in focus is from functions and outputs and profits looking only at the closed system of the organization and business economy, to an ethical, socially responsible and sustainable ecological view. The discontinuity is that the Eco-leadership does not try to create strong cultures with homogeneous loyal employees, but the opposite; strong networks which enable difference to flourish.

The Eco-leadership discourse has three key qualities:

1 *Connectivity (holism):* It is founded on connectivity; how we relate and inter-relate with the ecologies in which we work and live.
2 *Eco-ethics:* It is concerned with acting ethically in the human realm *and* with respect and responsibility for the natural environment.
3 *Leadership spirit*: It acknowledges the human spirit, the non-rational, creativity, imagination and human relationships.

The Eco-leadership discourse moves away from control and towards understanding emergence, connectivity and organic sustainable growth. The leader character exemplifies tension between central regulation and self-regulation, between emergence and direction, organic growth and strategic planning. For the highly rational management world, many of these ideas are challenging and truly create a new paradigm. How do you invest in a business whose leadership talks about not-knowing and emergence as strategy?

Leaders are realizing that inter-connectivity is a reality and feedback systems affect them and their business as well as the rest of the planet. Training leaders to think in this way, to understand ideas of self-regulating and self-managing systems, and emergence rather than planning, then linking these to the human skills from the therapeutic discourse might support a powerful new discourse (Appendix 2, 'Lead2lead', offers a case study of a leadership development approach to help promote an ecology of leadership in a company).

This Eco-leadership discourse privileges respect for all living things, for connectivity and influence rather than leadership by control. It creates a further push towards an ethical leadership position, which is accentunted by the knowledge of the fragility of the global system itself. Paradoxically, this discourse finds that the real vulnerability of leadership lies in control, hierarchy and omnipotence. The real strength of leadership lies in devolved power, dispersing leadership and having the confidence of not-knowing, of being able to follow emergent patterns, rather than fixed plans. It will be fascinating to see how this Eco-leadership discourse will emerge.

# 14

# Reflections:
# Leadership Formation

This book set out to promote critical and curious thinking about leadership, with the aim of supporting improved leadership practice. Reflecting on this, it has become clear that making the link between theory and practice is not easy through the medium of a book. As I wrote, I realized that in order to do justice to the theoretical discussion, practical examples would have to be minimal. I make no apology for this, as my first concern was to promote critical thinking and as the anonymous reviewer of this book helpfully pointed out, it is the reader and any programme leaders/lecturers who are best placed to make the links to practice, drawing on personal experience and situating the discussion within their relative contexts. My hope is that this book has seeded ideas and questions, which will grow in the classroom, but more importantly, will find fuller meaning and come to life when the reader is engaged in the practice of leadership at work.

Leadership is a vast subject which presents any author with a multitude of options when addressing it. After establishing the ground rules for a critical approach to leadership, and setting out the book's critical agenda: Emancipation, Looking Awry, Systemic Praxis and Depth Analysis, I journeyed into some key areas of power and diversity and along the way attempted to critique some of the main debates in Leadership. Chapter 5 on asymmetrical leadership set out my belief that leadership should neither be discussed as the sole property of an individual, nor should the agency of the individual leader be derided or dismissed. Leadership has many facets, but this does not mean that the agency of leaders and leadership should be deconstructed and theorized out of existence.

Chapter 5 clearly identifies seven aspects of leadership in one social movement:

1  Intellectual leadership
2  Unconscious leadership
3  Corporate leadership
4  Dispersed leadership
5  Individual leadership
6  Social movement leadership
7  Symbolic leadership.

This offers a transferable example which can be tested and applied to your organization. When at work, look for the obvious leadership, e.g. the CEO and others with formal positional leadership, and then ask yourself, how are they taking up their leadership? Is it through intellectual leadership or perhaps symbolic leadership? Where else can leadership can be found? Is there dispersed and unconscious leadership taking place? Is the organization part of a social movement which is taking a lead in social change? What really makes the organization tick? Where are the less obvious leaders and leadership groups? Are there other leadership aspects you can see, not found in the example given?

Practise and train yourself to be a participant-observer at work; this is both interesting but also practical, and is an important high level leadership capability. When working, take moments to ask, where is the leadership? Who has influence, who defers to whom? Who takes a lead, and on what authority do they draw? What groups are powerful, who is marginalized? How can I take up an ethical leadership position in this meeting?

Leadership is not symmetrical but attempts to standardize it are seductive and common.

The book then explored the leadership discourses which account for the main underlying (unconscious) and normative assumptions that are held about leadership. These are vitally important as they define the boundaries and unspoken expectations as to how leadership is enacted on a daily basis, how different actors perceive it, and how it is responded to. The discourses underpin how we think about leadership, they define our expectations, they determine on what premise leaders are selected, and how leadership development is planned. Discourses are not rigid or set in stone, and they are not exclusive to each other. Observing which discourse dominates, how they clash, how they work well in different parts of an organization, is the skill of an aware leader. Discourse analysis is too precious to be confined only to the university classroom, but should be practised within the work setting by practitioners, leaders and followers (of which we are usually both).

The three discourses emerged from my doctoral research into leadership. I didn't set out to find these or any discourses, I set out to write about leadership and the Quaker movement. Nor did I set out to make links with religious fundamentalism; this too emerged from the literature and jumped out at me as the theoretical connections also matched my experience of corporate and organizational life. It was through using the critical lenses set out in this book, which alerted me to these new resources which can help us to grasp and understand leadership.

In my personal experience of being a leader, teaching leadership, developing leaders and developing myself, being able to *look awry*, think *systemically*, or use *depth analysis* are not tedious tasks to undertake and learn; they are jewels! Different worlds are discovered within existing worlds when unconscious processes are engaged with. When we look from a completely different perspective and when new links are made, the connectedness of the world is revealed. A critical approach increases the potential for leaders to co-create with others the social conditions which lay the foundations for emancipatory work environments.

## Critical theory and leadership: working assumptions

To briefly summarize, a critical leadership approach:

1   Leadership exists within all forms of organization, whether this is overtly or
    covertly recognized. It is therefore important to understand how leadership
    works in practice. The task is to look beyond and beneath the norms and
    assumptions espoused about leadership in popular culture and the main-
    stream management literature.
2   Mainstream leadership assumptions and discourses reproduce the organiza-
    tional power structures that already exist. To address this, critical theorists pay
    particular attention to the systemic and structural aspects of leadership that
    privilege some and marginalize others. There is a tendency for organizations
    to drift blindly and unknowingly towards seductive but dangerous totalizing
    cultures. Understanding and revealing the role leadership plays within social
    processes can help prevent this from occurring.
3   There is no leadership without followership and participation. There is no
    leadership without power, influence and authority. Individual and collective
    autonomy and liberty therefore rely on organizations with non-authoritarian
    leadership approaches. It is possible and necessary to take up leadership
    authority without being authoritarian. It is a utopian error to try and eliminate
    power relations. Critical theory attempts to make transparent and address
    (rather than eradicate) the relations between leadership and followership,
    authority and power.
4   Contemporary workplace organizations are increasingly important sites of
    social activity and community, replacing traditional communal structures such
    as the Church. What happens in the workplace has a reflexive relationship
    with the wider environment. Understanding and improving the dynamics of
    leadership in the workplace is therefore essential to society in general.

In spite of the rise in critical and post-modern critiques of leadership, and the
emergence of the Eco-leadership discourse, the mainstream leadership band-
wagon rolls on peddling its wares of new leadership models, and competency
frameworks. These are very seductive; like a child's safety blanket, they offer comfort and reassurance, but aren't much use in the real world. I had to restrain
myself from the seduction of writing a conclusion with tidy models and frameworks in order to provide a neat closure and leave the reader (and myself) with a
feeling of false comfort.

To understand leadership in practice, really is to *look awry*, at leadership and at
oneself, and to keep looking awry. Taking up our agency, our individual and collective power and our authority appropriately in leadership and in participative
roles, and working collaboratively towards emancipative ethical ends, is a liberating and rewarding journey.

So instead of finishing with a neat definitive leadership summary, I would like
to acknowledge that there is no final word on leadership, 'no golden bullet', no
seven-stage framework and no set of leadership competencies that are universal.
A valid question asked of critical theorists is, how then do we develop leaders?
This would take another book on leadership development to do this question
justice, but I would like to end the book by suggesting that:

1   Emancipatory leadership is developed through the application of a critical
    approach to leadership practice, which is the task for each one of us.

2   My reflections on this book have led me to muse that a process of Leadership Formation should be constructed to support the emergence of tomorrow's leadership and the Eco-leadership discourse.

## Leadership formation

I hope these thoughts provoke an engaged response which adds to the discussion on how organizations can become creative, ethical, progressive and emancipatory. To achieve this, they need a radical and dynamic leadership, to help breathe life and form into the new emergent Eco-leadership discourse. Radicalism, however, is not always found where it is expected. G.K. Chesterton in his 1908 critique of modernity, in his book *Orthodoxy*, observed that, 'I did try to found a heresy of my own; and when I had put the last touches to it, I discovered that it was orthodoxy ... I did try to be 10 minutes ahead of the truth. And found I was eighteen hundred years behind it. (Chesterton, [1908] 2004: 4 )

Burrell argues for a 'retro-organization', that organizational theory needs rejuvenating by looking not only at modern organizational forms but also at those with longer histories:

> In recognizing the centrality of the Enlightenment to the modern world, this book argues that it is in need of rejuvenation through the medium of dawn-picked extracts of the pre-modern period in European thought and seeks in the pre-scientific era ideas and themes of relevance for today. (Burrell, 1997: 5-6)

I agree, and in recent years I too have found radical thinking in tradition and orthodoxy. In this light, I will turn to a radical tradition which dates back more than 1,700 years. Chapter 13 stated that the Eco-leadership discourse is underpinned by connectivity, leadership spirit and ethics. The phrase 'Leadership Development' too quickly resonates with the normative approaches of developing an individual's competencies and behaviours, based on functional and rational ideology. This immediately disconnects and disengages leadership from the wider ecology; systemic thinking, leadership spirit and ethics, focusing on micro-development rather than macro-development. Individual leadership development is not incompatible with a systemic approach, but too often is treated as such, hence I turn to the idea of Leadership Formation.

Leadership Formation emanates directly from the religious idea of spiritual formation, and I turn to the Christian monastic tradition that has developed over the past 1,700 years since the early Desert Fathers. Sustainability is key to the Eco-leader discourse and this monastic tradition has proven to be sustainable; the Benedictine monastic tradition itself dates back over 1,400 years (Merton, 1966).

Having recently stayed in a Camaldolese (Benedictine) Hermitage in Big Sur, California, I can verify to the power of this community, their leadership spirit, and the paradoxical radicalism entwined with orthodox tradition which is embedded in their religious practice. Spiritual formation within a monastery is obviously not directly transferable to secular organizations but it does provide a further resource, a sustainable case study that can stimulate and support how we think about leadership development.

The idea of spiritual formation is straightforward; the monastic tradition does not place an emphasis on the monks' spiritual life being learnt through teaching, training or personal development. To undergo formation as a monk is not to undergo a series of separate developmental acts, but is a holistic experience which arises from living in the community. It is an ongoing process of formation, and each monk is continually formed by, and also contributes to, the living tradition and formation of the community. Likewise, I would suggest that to become a leader, and to develop leadership within an organization, will also be better achieved through a process of collective and individual formation rather than an ad hoc set of developmental opportunities and experiences. Leadership development suffers hugely due to the inability to hold the whole organization and wider environment in mind, to take a holistic view creating a consistent context and learning process which supports leadership.

The monastic communities have mastered and tailored the ability to create successful and sustainable contexts in which the lives of their monks are formed. A novitiate monk chooses to join a monastic community having discerned a certain charism (a God-given gift) and takes a vow to follow the Monastic Rule of the particular order they join. The Monastic setting, the Rule and the community, overseen by an Abbott, provide a Paternal Container (Western, 2005). A Paternal Container is a safe containing space that is a prerequisite for 'developmental or formative' activity to take place.

This work is drawn from psychoanalytic theory, particularly from the Tavistock tradition that applies object relation's theory to organizational dynamics. Maternal containment is a well-known concept in this tradition (Bion, 1961) but when applying this theory to practice while studying the Tavistock Centre, I found that maternal containment alone was problematic when used to bring about organizational change. I proposed and tested a new framework drawing on paternal and maternal metaphors (Western, 2005) to support developmental activity. Box 14.1 outlines what each stance represents.

## Box 14.1   Paternal and maternal stances

| Paternal stance | Maternal stance |
|---|---|
| External | Internal |
| Reality | Fantasy – innovation, creativity |
| Structure | Free floating |
| Time boundaries | Timelessness |
| Authority | Attachment-influence |
| Order | Thinking space |
| The fragmented world | Oneness |
| Diversity | Unity |
| Triad and beyond | Dyad |
| Collaboration – crossing boundaries | 'Groupishness' acting within boundaries |

The Object Relations tradition of psychoanalysis was an important shift in thinking that included the impact of human relations on infant and adult psychological development, while also acknowledging the innate and biological drives identified by Freud. However, the 'mamocentric' relationship between mother and infant (the relation to the breast) became the key focus and maternal attachment theory heavily influenced their organizational theories. Maternal containment provided a conforting emotional spaces that enabled thinking to occur; however, this was problematic as it took people into reflective spaces that could become regressive unless managed within a structure. In psychotherapy, this works as it is structured by the couch, the safe space, the clear roles and the precise 50-minute hour, i.e. time boundaries. In organizational life, however, maternal containment failed to link creative and reflective thinking to external reality. Turning to Jacques Lacan's work (a prominent French psychoanalyst) on the paternal metaphor, I realized that together with maternal containment they provided a psychological framework that could be used for developmental activity in organizations.

'The Law of the Father', therefore, refers to psychical internal organisation not a patriarchal, iron fist Law. Lacan is absolutely clear that the 'Father' and the power of the father are symbolic:
  'The Father is not a real object so what is he?...The Father is a metaphor [Lacan 1958]'
  Using Lacan's term the 'Parternal Metaphor' or the 'Name-of-the-Father' (Nom-du-Père), it is the 'Father' as signifier and not the real father I am referring to. (Western, 2005: 266)

The Paternal Metaphor can be appropriated to create a safe structured space that is necessary for maternal reverie to take place. Maternal reverie is the emotionally stable environment a mother/primary carer creates to enable an infant to learn and to think (Bion, 1962). After maternal reverie and thinking have taken place the paternal stance breaks into this space and introduces the external world, a wider systemic perspective, the reality principle and action. In developmental terms, the 'father' enters the idealized unity of the infant–mother bond. This enables the infant to realize that they are independent from their mother, and that others exist in the world separately from their mother. The infant can both observe others interacting (mother and father) and also experience being oberved (I am a person separate from mother and father) hence they begin to relate to the outside world.

Translated to organizational thinking, the paternal metaphor represents the external, structure, differentiation and reality, while the maternal metaphor represents the internal, unity, oneness, creativity, ideas and play. The paternal metaphor creates a containing structure and space, a place where the maternal metaphor takes over enabling the emotional space for play, creativity and thinking to occur. The paternal metaphor then breaks up this unified bond (mother–infant) to turn their creativity into an outward-facing activity in the 'real world'. This framework is the basis for all creative and developmental activity and is vital for effective leadership practice.

Too much a paternal stance creates an authoritarian culture, which focuses on action, structure and becomes rigid, there is no space for reflection and adaptive thinking. This underpinned the patriarchal business structures and leadership of the twentieth century. Too much a maternal stance creates an inward-looking organization, where the in-group are idealized and the outside world is denigrated and refused. Unity is prized at the expense of eliminating any difference or external threat to this idealized unity. A good example of an organization with too much of a maternal stance would be a utopian community that becomes cultish, the perfected community and identifies all external influences as evil or threatening. It is no coincidence that Hitler referred to Germany as 'the motherland', idealizing the unity and perfection of the German/Aryan race with disastrous impact.

These stances are not gender-determined; men and women take up either and/or both stances. However, how much of these archetypal psychic structures are biologically determined or socially constructed around gender is hotly debated. This frame work is the basis for developmental and thinking activity that is translated into social action (Figure 14.1).

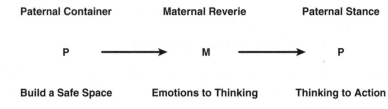

**Figure 14.1**   Learning development framework

Within the physical, emotional, and in this case spiritual container of the monastery, the monk is supported and encouraged to form the 'monk within' alongside others undergoing the same formation process. The monk's life is shaped and formed through partaking in daily spiritual practices, for example, prayer, work, reading the scriptures, and vitally important is the liturgy (which is the form and structure of the religious service and practice). It is the whole rather than any of the parts of this process which forms both the novitiate monk and the community. The monks call this holistic experience *'the life'*. In addition to this process there is spiritual direction, Thomas Merton explains:

> Spiritual direction does not consist merely in giving advice. The man who has only an advisor does not really have a director in the fullest sense. Since the spiritual life does not consist in having and thinking, but in being and doing, a director who only gives ideas has not begun to form the one he directs. (1966: 7)

The Spiritual director is a guide, a mentor, a 'loving father' in the monastic tradition. Their role is to be receptive and to support the monk in finding their path, not to teach that path, nor to develop the person, but to observe, reflect and guide the new monk through the formation process. The formation process is a communal process, in which an individual paradoxically sacrifices their individuality to the will of the rule, the abbot, and the community, in order to gain their individuality fully.

## So how does spiritual formation inform leadership formation?

Leaders are also formed through the context and 'community' in which they work. Just as a monk cannot exist without a monastic tradition or a supportive community, leaders also require a context and a community (albeit a temporary work-based community). Community and the social context form the monk, and so it is with leaders. The intensity is different and the desired end result is different but I am suggesting that the process is very similar. Leadership is not a learnt profession or trade or a taught set of skills, leadership is much more complex and goes deeper. Leadership is not just the property of the individual, and yet individuals are vital to leadership; whereas the monastic community has refined its formation process to minute detail: the layout of the monastery, the daily routine, the clear lines of authority, periods of study leave, the amount of solitary time mixed with community prayer and physical work. The context and process in which leaders are formed are very hit-and-miss affairs, both for the individual and the organization.

Therefore, a radical change of perception is required. Leadership formation suggests that leaders and leadership are 'formed' within a context and a process at the workplace, through the organization, its culture, systems and processes. The problem is that this formation process is largely ad hoc and unrecognized. I am suggesting that the process of leadership formation takes precedence over the notion of leadership development, and that contemporary leaders urgently focus on how they can support leadership formation through their organizational culture, structures and processes.

Leadership formation relates to a holistic process, working at a collective idea of leadership rather than focus on the development of individual leaders. This will take place in 'the life' of their particular workplace community.

A process of formation is needed whereby individuals and teams under guidance, a mentor or coach[1] would take some responsibility for their own formation, and the organization would share this responsibility.

As well as a holistic vision, a radical inclusivity is also required. The religious term charism refers to an individual's unique gifts, and also to an organization's gift to the world, so that the Fransciscan charism will differ from the Benedictine charism, and individuals will have their own particular charism. This idea of charism should replace the focus on charisma if we are truly to attain dispersed leadership in organizations. Charisma is limited to an elite few who have 'special qualities'. Charism relates to the special qualities each of us has, and which, if tapped, make all of us potential leaders. Successful organizations must create a context and processes for the holistic formation of all-potential rather than high potential leaders.

Creativity is at the heart of this approach, releasing creativity is a parallel process to releasing leadership talent. Richard Florida whose influential work on creativity and urban development, emphasizes the need to be inclusive:

> Creativity defies race, gender and ethnicity. It knows no race, it knows no ethnicity, it knows no gender, it knows no age, it knows no income-level, it knows nothing about appearance, it knows nothing about sexual orientation. Every single human being is creative, and we don't know where that creativity will come from. (Florida, 2003: 28)

Florida continues saying how creativity comes from the street as well as the university, and the business incubator. Entrepreneurs drop out of college, 'creativity comes from everywhere and anywhere', 'We have to have conditions that mobilize that energy. Ecosystems that allow us to tap and harness the energy of everyone, not just the top talent' (ibid. 3: 28). It is the current leadership task to create the ecosystem that supports leadership formation throughout an organization, it is the same ecosystem that will also support creativity.

## Creating the ecosystem and the process: the spatial leader

Spatial leadership is somewhat counter-intuitive, the leadership attempts to create the conditions that enable future direction, dispersed leadership and new innovations to emerge from all parts of the organization. They do not think of the organization as a static enterprise, with clear boundaries but as a spatial network that is fluid. The leadership take on the role of organizational architect, thinking spatially about how connections are to be made, how clusters of innovation might take place, how diverse parts of the organization might meet to exploit difference and potential new innovations. It also includes the design of buildings, locations, structures and processes.

These physical and psychic spaces become 'laboratories of experience' and allow a learning organization to develop, for creativity to flourish and leadership to emerge. These spaces also act as containers for anxiety, and as sites of community and of cultural audit. They become internalized into organizational culture. They are formal and informal, regular and irregular, virtual and real.

In the new Scottish Parliament, the architect Enric Miralles understood this process and designed Contemplation Pods attached to the Scottish MPs' offices, the idea being to create a physical thinking space (Figure 14.2). This physical space is observable on the outside of the building, so they are both practical and symbolic. Hopefully these spaces become internalized and create thinking spaces within us, reminding us for the need to stop, to reflect, to muse, to consider, to drift and to contemplate. They represent a symbolic and secular monastic cell.

Leadership Formation is too important to leave to chance, therefore I have identified three key principles:

1  Leadership Formation must be holistic and embedded in organizational culture.
2  Leadership Formation requires both an informal and a formal process.
3  Individuals, teams and organisations need *a form*, containing (paternal) structures and reflective (maternal) spaces, for leadership formation to occur, i.e. to discover and develop their specific leadership 'charism'.

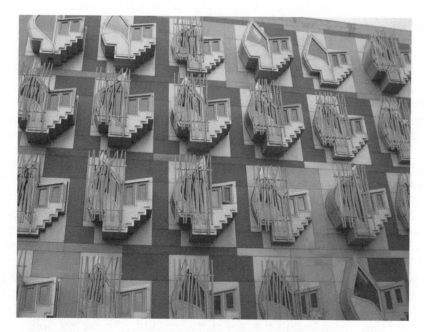

**Figure 14.2**     Contemplation Pods, Scottish Parliament Building

Leadership formation is not something that can be prescribed outside of a local context, each organization will have a unique process. The formal process is likely to include mentoring/coaching support, reviews, training and development opportunities, peer and team formation activities, opportunities for looking awry, i.e. stepping out of context, opportunities to support others (this reduces dependency and encourages leadership) senior leaders monitoring and sharing progress and challenges.

Leaders of organizations looking to implement a leadership formation process can ask these questions:

- How can we create the conditions, and contexts to enable informal leadership formation to occur?
- Where are the spaces in our organization for (non)thinking and creativity?
- Where are the contexts and networks to enable communication to occur across silos?
- Where are the spatial clusters to enable healthy competition, collaboration and new innovation to occur?
- How can leadership formation be engaged with local communities of practice?
- How can cross-disciplinary and cross-fertilization of ideas and sharing of experience and knowledge be encouraged?
- How do individuals and teams support leaders who are not given positional power?

- Are we alert to the potential for leadership to flourish in the most unexpected places?
- Do we have processes in place which supports leadership formation?
- Do we have mentors and current leaders available to support new leaders and leadership initiatives?
- How do we value and encourage dispersed leadership?
- How are leadership spirit and ethical leadership behaviour encouraged in our organization?

Leadership Formation steps back from the grandiosity and the hubris of the Messiah discourse, which aims at the transformation of organizations and followers. Transformation will be a by-product of Leadership Formation; seeking transformation before formation is premature, it reflects society's preoccupations with immediate gratification. You cannot buy leadership from a quick course, or popular manual. Leadership exists all around us, but so much of it presently goes unnoticed and is uncherished, at the expense of organizational success and social well-being. It takes time, the right conditions and the right support to nurture the 'leader within'. The leader within oneself, and the leadership within the organization, both need nurturing and sustaining. Leadership Formation will reveal many manifestations of leadership that are currently hidden, if we are open to new forms of leadership, like creativity, it will surprise us.

Today's leaders need to urgently address the question of how to prepare the way for the next generation of leaders; a way that enables leaders to engage ethically, with the whole ecosystem, and with leadership spirit.

# Note

1 Providing mentoring and coaching doesn't have to be an expensive layout. Utilizing peer-coaching, and mentoring from within the organization helps build a coaching community and coaching culture which supports the wider process of leadership formation. To bring in an external view, to support looking awry, it is good practice to use networks and collaborate with partner organizations to get cross-fertilization of ideas and experience. Many coaching and mentoring schemes fail as unregulated coaches act in an ad hoc fashion and nearly all coach training focuses on an individual's performance with some exceptions. Coaching and mentoring schemes to support leadership formation require a systemic approach to be taken, and this means educating, training and supervising the mentors/coaches. Coaches and mentors replace the idea of the monastic 'spiritual directors' and they should work in a similar non-directive manner.

# Appendix 1

## Leadership Approaches

Figure A.1 is a teaching tool I use to illustrate some of the many approaches to leadership. It is not a hierarchy but positions how different leadership approaches work together. They are not exclusive but in some organizations and sectors there will be a greater focus on some areas than others. The Eco-leadership discourse pays particular attention to the *Leadership Between* and *Leadership Beyond* approaches. Spatial Leadership is foundational for Eco-leadership to occur.

### Leadership Approaches

### Leadership Beyond

#### Eco-leadership
Ethical leadership emphasizing connectivity to organizational ecologies.
Focusing on networks and the connectedness of the whole system,
including stakeholders and the political and natural environment.
A reflexive, generative and dispersed leadership which
adapts to emergent patterns.

#### Signifying Leadership
Leading through symbolic interventions, narrative,
communication and through influencing culture.

#### Intellectual Leadership
Leading through thinking, creative ideas and innovation.

------------------------------------------------------------------------

### Leadership Between

#### Spatial Leadership
Leadership drawing on spatial awareness, and takes a role as
Organizational Architect, creating (non)thinking spaces, and contexts in
which diversity and creativity can flourish and ideas cross functional
boundaries. Creating matrix structures and conceiving of the organization
as connected networks rather than a fixed entity support this leadership.

------------------------------------------------------------------------

*(Continued)*

## Leadership Within

### Transactional Leadership
Motivating through transactions: pay, conditions, opportunities, compromises.
Personal and team material and non-material rewards to motivate fit into this transactional approach.

### Expert Leadership
Using expert and technical knowledge as leverage for leadership.

### Efficient Leadership
Leadership by technique to achieve efficient output, results focused leadership.
Setting boundaries, controlling, a rational approach. Efficient leadership often emerges during crisis and remains popular in some sectors e.g. manufacturing. While other leadership styles are often espoused, most CEOs' performance is measured by efficiency, and this leadership approach can become pervasive throughout the organization.

**Figure A.1**    Leadership approaches
*Source:* Western (2006)

# Appendix 2

## Lead2lead: A Case Study

### Critical Leadership Development

This successful leadership development activity (see www.lead2lead.com) was designed by myself and my colleague Jonathan Gosling to attempt to develop a pedagogy that trained leaders to look awry, to think systemically, to undertake depth analysis and to embed their learning on location. This later developed into a systemic organizational intervention, aimed at the ecology of leadership.

This work was built on a managerial exchange, a five-day work-shadowing programme, designed by Jonathan Gosling and Henry Mintzberg, on their innovative International Masters in Practicing Management program (see www.impm.com and Mintzberg, 2004a: 322). The course participants were paired up and each spent one week as visitor and one week as host. The visitor would shadow their exchange partner while at work.

We asked participants on this exchange programme to reflect on: 'What was happening to you? What was happening around you? ... Try and deduce patterns in your management style, clues as to how corporate and national culture affect you' (Western, in Mintzberg, 2004a: 323). I was asked to research and run this programme. Our research found that these exchanges were hugely successful, and that the participants who gained the most from this experience were those who managed to look awry at their own normative assumptions about culture and organizations. The most impressive changes came about when individuals gained insight into patterns and beliefs that were culturally bound which they previously hadn't questioned. Two examples are cited below drawn from a research paper 'Pairing for Leadership' (Western and Gosling 2003).

---

#### 'Management by thinking' or 'management by doing'?

This example comes from the manager of a British Telecom company visiting the owner/manager of a successful family-run bakery in India. He writes about how he feels he has lost sight of his own company's strategic goal and comments on his Indian colleague's determination to focus on strategy:

> He only attends the business for 4–5 hours a day. The rest of the time he is reflecting on the direction of the business and formulating his change initiatives and growth plans.

*(Continued)*

---

*(Continued)*

Contrasting this with his own work patterns and that of other Western managers, he continues:

> I spend approximately twelve hours a day at work and usually return home exhausted. On return to home I think about food, family, football and other non-work topics but certainly not strategy. I'm far too knackered. During my working week I attend to strategy for a small proportion of the time. Most of the week is consumed in operational issues and this week's latest greatest panic.

He continues to comment on observations of his Indian host:

> He has a clear agenda to encourage growth in individuals, to encourage them to take responsibility, to fulfil their potential. He is not focused on 'control'. He has also limited his work time at the business premises, leaving him with the necessary energy at the end of the working day to reflect on current issues and plan for the future. Undoubtedly the group is a success and it has reached this level of achievement as a direct result of new and changed strategies in the bakery industry.

Finally, he reflects on himself and his culture and makes a decision to modify his behaviour as a result of this experience:

> There is something very Anglo-Saxon about my own insistence on knowing everything that's happening in my ambit of responsibility and controlling any half-important activity. I see it about me at work in many of my colleagues also. And we compound the problem by working long hours and saving little or no energy for the equally important issues of strategy. If XXXXX (His Indian host) practises 'management by thinking', my personal bias is towards 'management by doing'... I hope to modify my own behaviour as a manager.

## Discovering America

An American visitor to Britain wrote this insightful comment after reflecting on what she learnt almost as a by-product of the exchange:

> Learning what it means to be an American, outside America and acknowledging that I am, in fact, an American.

This statement clearly indicates first of all the recognition of the self through the otherness of culture. Initially she is saying 'I recognize that I am different, that I feel different in another culture.' She then goes on to discover something which she knows at a superficial and personal level, 'I am an American', but that is rediscovered at a 'depth analysis' level. She realizes that she is not only born an American but carries with her American culture, values, expectations and this only becomes manifest when contrasted with another culture which does not carry these.

If a leader can discover their own social location, and the culturally bound normative assumptions they are working from, they can then ask other revealing questions. What does it mean to be seen as an American – and what does this mean when doing business in a global economy? Do we assume that this multinational organization, with its New York base, is expected to be culturally American throughout the world?

This moves us towards the Eco-leadership discourse, the leader taking account of the internal ecology of the organization and how it relates to its external ecology.

We then took the management exchange idea in a new direction and created the Lead2lead approach. The focus changed to observing leadership in action and to deepen the experience through improved preparation and debriefing. Our realization was that leaders, and people in general, find it incredibly difficult to step outside of their normative assumptions and whichever leadership discourse they were working from. But when they do, huge discoveries are made.

We approached this challenge by training the leaders prior to their visits in observation skills, in order to increase their ability to deepen their experience when shadowing and being shadowed. We trained leaders to observe the external world (sitting in a café or airport, for example, we called this *Primary Observation*) and relate this to their normative frameworks, to how they see and make sense of the world around them. We then trained them to observe the same place but to observe their reactions and feelings to what they saw (*Secondary Observation*). This had the impact of raising their awareness of the richness of the data they could access from within, and if they shared this with others, how together they could challenge their own assumptions, and discover new lessons about themselves and others, which they could use in their leadership practice. This set them up for the three-day shadowing exchange. During the three-day visit of their exchange partner they would keep a journal and give their partner feedback on what they saw and what they experienced. After both had undertaken this process, they were debriefed by external coaches to embed the learning and to look for ways to improve their leadership practice.

A further advance was to take this shadowing approach beyond an individual development remit and to design a systemic approach which would impact on the ecology of the organization. To achieve this, the leadership shadowing would be designed within an organization rather than between companies. Leaders would visit leaders for three days, across company boundaries, geographically and functionally, building new networks across companies, as well as developing a cadre of new leaders. We worked with HR teams and senior leaders to plan how to most effectively match leaders to create the most effective impact for individual learning, and for the company to maximize the benefits of creating new networks.

In one Lead2lead project we paired up 100 senior managers from all parts of a company going through a corporate merger. They were trained in observation techniques, to become more reflective, to look awry, to give feedback, and then to visit each other and observe each other's leadership practice (and to be observed). They gave each other feedback, shared stories, discussed company challenges, recognized strengths, and after this experience they all received one-to-one coaching from external coaches to undergo some depth analysis, to embed this learning, to make the links which support systemic thinking and to look at ways to implement and apply their learning experience.

An additional and powerful aspect of this approach was that the external coaches fed back the information to the central team who did a narrative analysis and together we collated themes. This was a cultural audit of the company not from expensive consultancy surveys, but from the embedded experience of the company's employees. We fed this information back to all those who undertook the training and discussed this with the company board.

This brief case study demonstrates the potential to develop leaders in their workplace, drawing on tacit knowledge, developing a greater individual awareness of their local ecology, of other parts of their organization, and the emotional as well as practical life of another leader and her/his team. We were always surprised at the impact this had on the extended team being visited. Observing a leader, in reality, meant observing a department or team. Being observed as well as observing another heightens the capacity to reflect on what is normally taken for granted. The whole organization picks up on this process, as most of them are involved in it, either directly or indirectly. Developing new networks and an ecological awareness of their workplace, and building reflexivity into systems through normalizing the practice of observation, all contribute towards developing leaders who move towards the Eco-leadership discourse.

This type of leadership developmental work helps alert leaders to their local ecology and shift their mindsets from functional thinking to holistic thinking. Further work is needed to develop the leader's ability to face a new paradigm.

# Bibliography

Aburdene, P. (2005) *Megatrends 2010: The Rise of Conscious Capitalism.* Charlottesville, VA: Hampton Roads.

Ackers, P. and Preston, D. (1992) 'Born again? The ethics and efficacy of the conversion experience in contemporary management development', *Journal of Management Studies,* 34(5): 677–701.

Ali, T. (2002) *The Clash of Fundamentalisms: Crusades, Jihads and Modernity.* London: Verso.

Allen, W. (1976) 'If the Impressionists had been dentists: a fantasy exploring the transposition of temperament', in *Without Feathers.* New York: Warner Books.

Altman, M. (2001) *Worker Satisfaction and Economic Performance.* Armonk, NY: M.E. Sharpe.

Alvesson, M. (2002) *Understanding Organizational Culture.* London: Sage.

Alvesson, M. (2003) *Understanding Organizational Culture.* London: Sage.

Alvesson, M. and Svenginsson, S. (2003) 'Managers doing leadership: the extra-ordinarization of the mundane', paper presented at Studying Leadership conference, Lancaster University, 12 Dec.

Alvesson, M. and Wilmott, H. (1992) *Critical Management Studies.* London: Sage.

Alvesson, M. and Wilmott, H. (1996) *Making Sense of Management: A Critical Introduction.* London: Sage.

Andermahr, S., Lovell, T. and Wolkowitz, C. (2000) *A Glossary of Feminist Theory.* London: Arnold.

Argyris, C. (1964) *Integrating the Individual and the Organization.* New York: John Wiley.

Aristotle (1985) *Nicomachean Ethics.* Indianapolis: Hackett Publishing Company.

Armstrong, K. (2000) *The Battle for God.* London: HarperCollins.

Armstrong, K. (2001) 'Cries of rage', *New Statesman,* 24 Sept.: 17.

Armstrong, K. (2002) 'Fundamentalism and the modern world: a dialogue with Karen Armstrong, Susannah Heschel, Jim Wallis and Feisal Abdul Rauf', *Sojourners Magazine,* March–April, 31(2): 20–6.

Aune, K. (forthcoming) 'Singleness and secularization: British evangelical women and church (dis)affiliation', in K. Aune, S. Sharma and G. Vincett (eds), *Women and Religion in the West: Challenging Secularization.* London: Ashgate Publishing.

Axtel Ray, C. (1986) 'Corporate culture: the last frontier of control', *Journal of Management Studies,* 23(3): 286–95.

Badarraco, J. (2001) 'We don't need another hero', *Harvard Business Review,* 79(8): 120–6.

Barker, R. (1993) '"Tightening the iron cage": concertive control in self-managing teams', *Administrative Science Quarterly,* 38(3): 408–37.

Barker, R. (1997) 'How can we train leaders if we don't know what leadership is?', *Human Relations,* 50(1): 343–62.

Barley, S. and Kunda, G. (1992) 'Design and devotion: surges of rational and normative ideologies of control in managerial discourse', *Administrative Science Quarterly,* 37: 363–99.

Barlow, J.A. (1981) 'Mass line leadership and thought reform in China', *American Psychologist,* 36: 300–9.

Barnard, C. ([1938] 1991) 'The functions of the executive', in M.B. Calas and L. Smircich (1991) 'Voicing seduction to silence leadership', *Organizational Studies*, 12(4): 567–602.

Barr, J. (1981) *Fundamentalism*. London: Xpress.

Bass, B. (1985) *Leadership and Performance beyond Expectations*. New York: Free Press.

Bass, B. (1990a) 'From transactional to transformational leadership: learning to share the vision', *Organizational Dynamics*, 18: 19–31.

Bass, B. (1990b) *Bass and Stogdill's Handbook of Leadership*. New York: The Free Press.

Bass, B. (1998) 'The ethics of transformational leadership', in J. Ciulia (ed.), *Ethics: The Heart of Leadership*. Westport, CT: Praeger.

Bass, B. (1999) 'Two decades of research and development in transformational leadership', *European Journal of Work & Organizational Psychology*, March, 8(1): 9–32.

Bass, B. and Avolio, B. (1994) 'Shatter the glass ceiling: women make better managers', *Human Resource Management*, 33(4): 549–60.

Bass, B and Steidlmeier, P. (1999) 'Ethics, character and authentic transformational leadership behavior', *Leadership Quarterly*, 10: 181–217.

Bateson, G. (1972) *Steps to an Ecology of Mind: Collected Essays in Anthropology, Psychiatry, Evolution and Epistemology*. Chicago: University of Chicago Press.

Bateson, G. (1979) *Mind and Nature: A Necessary Unity*. New York: Bantam.

Bauman, Z. (1989) *Modernity and the Holocaust*. Ithaca, NY: Cornell University Press.

Bauman, Z. (1993) *Postmodern Ethics*. Oxford: Blackwell.

BBC News (2006) 'Britain is "surveillance society"', 2 Nov. Available at: http://news.bbc.co.uk/1/hi/uk/6108496.stm

Becker, G.S. (1998) *Accounting for Tastes*. Cambridge, MA: Harvard University Press.

Bell, E. and Taylor, S. (2004) 'From outward bound to inward bound: the prophetic voices and discursive practices of spiritual management development', *Human Relations*, 57(4): 439–66.

Bellah, R.N., Madsen, R., Sullivan, W.H., Swidler, A. and Tipton, S.M. (1996) *Habits of the Heart: Individualism and Commitment in American Life*. Berkeley: University of California Press.

Bennis, W. (1986) *Leaders: The Strategies for Taking Charge*. New York: Harper and Row.

Bennis, W. and Nanus, B. (1985) *Leaders: The Strategies for Taking Charge*. New York: Harper and Row.

Bennis, W. and Thomas, R. (2002) 'Crucibles of leadership', *Harvard Business Review*, Sept., 80(9): 39–45.

Berggren, C., Adler, P.S. and Cole, R.E. (1994) 'Nummi vs. Uddevalla rejoinder', *Sloan Management Review*, 35(2): 37–9.

Bessette, J. (1980) 'Deliberative democracy: the majority principle in Republican government', in *How Democratic Is the Constitution?* Washington, DC: AEI Press. pp. 102–16.

Best, S. and Kellner, D. (1991) *Postmodern Theory: Critical Interrogations*. London and New York: Macmillan and Guilford Press.

Binney, G., Wilke, G. and Williams C. (2004) *Living Leadership: A Practical Guide for Ordinary Heroes*. London: Pearson Books.

Bion, W.R. (1961) *Experiences in Groups*. London: Tavistock.

Bion, W.R. (1962) 'Theory of thinking', in *Second Thoughts: Selected Papers on Psychoanalysis*. New York: Jason Aronson.

Bollas, C. (1987) *The Shadow of the Object: Psychoanalysis of the Unthought Known*. London: FAB.

Bollas, C. (1997) *Freely Associated: Encounters with A. Molino*. London: Free Association Books.

Bond, M.A. and Pyle, J.L. (1998) 'The ecology of diversity in organizational settings: lessons from a case study', *Human Relations*, 51: 589–623.

Bright, M. and Alam, F. (2003) 'The making of a martyr: from pacifism to jihad', *The Observer*, 4 May.

Brown, H. (1989) 'Organising activity in the women's movement: an example of distributed leadership', *International Social Movement Research*, 2: 225–40.

Bryman, A. (1986) *Leadership and Organizations*. London: Routledge and Kegan Paul.

Bryman, A. (1993) 'Charismatic leadership in business organisations: some neglected issues', *Leadership Quarterly*, 4: 289–304.

Bryman, A. (1996) 'Leadership in organisations', in S.R. Clegg, C. Hardy and W.R. Nord (eds), *Handbook of Organizational Studies*. London: Sage, pp. 276–92.

Bufe, C. (1988) *A Future Worth Living: Thoughts on Getting There*. Tucson, AZ: Sharp Press.

Bunting, M. (2001) 'Illiberal liberalism'. Available at: http://gospel-culture.org.uk/articles.htm (accessed 1 May 2004).

Burgin, V. (1996) *In/different Space: Place and Memory in Visual Culture*. Berkeley, Los Angeles: University of California Press.

Burgoyne, J. and Pedler, M. (2003) 'A practice–challenge approach to leadership and leadership development', paper presented at the Studying Leadership conference, Lancaster University, 12 December.

Burns, J. (1978) *Leadership*. New York: Harper & Row.

Burrell, G. (1997) *Pandemonium: Towards a Retro-Organization Theory*. London: Sage.

Butler, J. (1990) *Gender Trouble: Feminism and the Subversion of Identity*. London: Routledge.

Butler, J. (2004) 'Gender regulations', in J. Butler (ed.), *Undoing Gender*. New York: Routledge.

Calas, M.B. and Smircich, L. (1991) 'Voicing seduction to silence leadership', *Organizational Studies*, 12(4): 567–602.

Calas, M.B. and Smircich, L. (1995) 'Dangerous liaisons: the "feminine-in-management" meets globalisation', in L. Fulop and S. Linstead (1999) *Management: A Critical Text*. London: Macmillan.

Calas, M.B. and Smircich, L. (2003) 'To be done with progress and other heretical thoughts for organization and management studies', in E. Locke (ed.), *Postmodernism and Management: Pros, Cons, and the Alternative*, Research in the Sociology of Organizations, Vol. 21. Amsterdam: JAI.

Calhoun, C. (1995) *Critical Social Theory*. London: Blackwell.

Capra, F. (1996) *The Web of Life*. New York: Doubleday.

Casey, C. (1995) *Work, Self and Society after Industrialisation*. London: Routledge.

Castells, M. (1997) *The Power of Identity*. London: Blackwell.

Chesterton, G.K. ([1908] 2004) *The Man Who Was Thursday*. Bristol: J.W. Arrowsmith.

Churchman, C.W. (1968) *Systems Approach*. New York: Delta.

Churchman, C.W. (1979) *Systems Approaches and its Enemies*. New York: Basic Books.

Cole, S. (1931) *The History of Fundamentalism*. New York: Richard R. Smith.

*Collins Dictionary* (1992) 3rd edn. London: HarperCollins.

Collins, J. (2001) 'Level 5 leadership', *Harvard Business Review*, January: 67–76.

Collins, J. and Porras, J. (2000) *Built to Last*. New York: Random House Business Books.

Collinson, D.L. (2006) 'Rethinking followership: a post-structuralist analysis of follower identities', *The Leadership Quarterly*, 17(2): 172–89.

Collinson, D.L. and Hearn, J. (1996) 'Breaking the silence: on men, masculinities and managements', in D. Collinson and J. Hearn (eds), *Men as Managers, Managers as Men: Critical Perspectives on Men, Masculinities and Managements*. London: Sage.

Conger, J.A. and Kanungo, R. (1987) 'Toward a behavioural theory of charismatic leadership in organisational settings', *Academy of Management Review*, 12: 637–47.

Conlon, M. (1999) 'Religion in the workplace: the growing presence of spirituality in corporate America', *Business Week*, November.

Constance, R. (2003) 'Designing learning organisations', *Organizational Dynamics*, 32(1): 46–61.

Cooper, A. (1996) 'Bad deeds, naughty words', unpublished paper, Tavistock Clinic, London.

Coopey, J. (1995) 'The learning organization: power, politics and ideology', *Management Learning*, 26(2): 193–213.

Cuilla, J. (1995) 'Leadership ethics mapping the territory', *Business Ethics Quarterly*, 5: 5–28.

Deal, T. and Kennedy, A. (1982) *Corporate Cultures*. Reading, MA: Addison-Wesley.

De Beauvoir, S. ([1949] 1972) *The Second Sex* (trans. and ed. H.M. Parshley). Harmondsworth: Penguin Books.

Della Porta, D. (1999) *Social Movements: An Introduction*. London: Blackwell.

Derrida, J. (1982) *Margins of Philosophy* (trans. with additional notes by A. Bass). Brighton: Harvester Press.

Desmond, J. (1998) 'Marketing and moral indifference', in M. Parker (ed.) *Ethics and Organizations*. London: Sage.

Diana, M. and Eyerman, R. (1992) *Studying Collective Action*. London: Sage.

DiMaggio, P. J. and Powell, W.W. (1983) 'The iron cage revisited: institutional isomorphism and collective rationality in organisational fields', *American Sociological Review*, 48: 147–60.

Dineen, T. (1999) *Manufacturing Victims: What the Psychological Industry is Doing to People*. Toronto: Robert Davies Publishers.

Dor, J. (1997) *Introduction to the Reading of Lacan*. New York: Jason Aronson Inc.

Douglas, T. (1983) *Groups: Understanding People Gathered Together*. London: Tavistock.

Drucker, P. (1973) *Management Tasks, Responsibilities, Practices*. New York: Harper.

Dubrin, A. (2000) *Leadership. Research Findings, Practice and Skills*. Boston: Houghton Mifflin.

Du Gay, P. (2000) *In Praise of Bureaucracy: Weber Organisation Ethics*. London: Sage.

Dumm, T.L. (1996) *Michel Foucault and the Politics of Freedom*. Thousand Oaks, CA: Sage.

Dvir, T., Eden, D., Avolio, B. J. and Shamir, B. (2002) 'Impact of transformational leadership on follower development and performance: a field experiment', *Academy of Management Journal*. 45(4): 735–44.

Edwards, R. (1979) *Contested Terrain*. New York: Basic Books.

Elmore, R. (2000) *Building a New Structure for School Leadership*. Washington, DC: The Albert Shanker Institute.

Enteman, W.F. (1993) *Managerialism: The Emergence of a New Ideology*. Madison, WI: University of Wisconsin Press.

Etzioni, A. (1961) *Complex Organizations*. New York: Holt Rinehart and Wilson.

Etzioni, A. (1993) *The Spirit of Human Rights, Responsibilities and the Communitarian Agenda*. New York: Crown.

Etzioni, A. (1997) '"Community, yes, but whose?" A debate with Roger Scruton', *City Journal*, Spring: 79–83.

Etzioni, A. (2002) *Next: The Road to the Good Society*. New York: Basic Books.

Eysenck, H.J. and Hans, J. (1953) *The Structure of Human Personality*. London: Methuen.

Fanon, F. (1970) *Black Skin, White Masks*. London: Paladin.

Farish Noor, A. (ed.) (1997) *Terrorising the Truth: The Shaping of Contemporary Images of Islam and Muslims in Media, Politics and Culture*. Penang: Just World Trust.

Fiedler, F.E. (1967) *A Theory of Leadership Effectiveness*. New York: McGraw-Hill.

Fiedler, F.E. (1974) 'The contingency model – new directions for leadership utilisation', *Journal of Contemporary Business*, 3 (Autumn): 65–79.

Findlater, C. (2006) 'An evaluation of the *U-Process* for individual and collaborative realisation of emergent change', unpublished MA dissertation, Management Learning and Leadership.

Fitzpatrick, M. (2000) *The Tyranny of Health: Doctors and the Regulation of Lifestyle*. London: Routledge.

Fitzpatrick, M. (2006) 'Get off the couch', available online at: http://www.spiked-online.com/index.php?site/article/2094/.

Flood, R.L. (1999) *Rethinking the Fifth Discipline*. London: Routledge.

Florida, R. (2003) 'An introduction to the creative class', in S. Franke and E. Verhagen (eds), *Creativity and the City*. Amsterdam: NAI Publishers, pp. 21–40.

Foucault, M. ([1977] 1991) *Discipline and Punish: The Birth of the Prison.* London: Penguin.

Foucault, M. (1980) *Power/Knowledge: Selected Interviews and Other Writings, 1972–77*, ed. C. Gordon. London: Harvester.

Freeman, J. (1984) *The Tyranny of Structurelessness.* London: Dark Star Press and Rebel Press.

Freud, S. (1921) *Group Psychology and the Analysis of the Ego.* New York/London: W.W. Norton.

Freud, S. ([1930] 2002) *Civilisation and its Discontents.* London: Penguin.

Friedman, M. (1962) *Capitalism and Freedom.* Chicago: University of Chicago Press.

Frosh, S. (1997) 'Fundamentalism, gender and family therapy', *Journal of Family Therapy*, 19: 417–30.

Fulop, L. and Linstead, S. (1999) *Management: A Critical Text.* London: Macmillan Press.

Furedi, F. (2003) *Therapy Culture.* London: Routledge.

Gabriel, Y. (1999) *Organisations in Depth.* London: Sage.

Gastil, J. (1997) 'A definition of democratic leadership', in K. Grint (ed.), *Leadership: Classical, Contemporary and Critical Approaches.* Oxford: Oxford University Press.

Gay, P. (1999) 'Sigmund Freud', *Time Magazine*, 29 March. Available at: http:www.time. com/time/time100/scientist/profile/freud03.html.

Gemmil, G. and Oakley, J. (1992) 'Leadership – an alienating social myth?', *Human Relations*, 42(1): 13–29.

Gerlach, L. and Hine, V. (1970) *People Power Change: Movements of Transformation.* Bloomington, IN: Bobbs-Merrill.

Giacalone, R.A. and Jurkiewicz, C.L. (2003) *Handbook of Workplace Spirituality and Organizational Performance.* Armonk, NY: Sharpe Press.

Giddens, A. (1982) *Profiles and Critiques in Social Theory.* London: Macmillan.

Giddens, A. (1991) *Modernity and Self-Identity: Self and Society in the Late Modern Age.* Cambridge: Polity Press.

Giddens, A. (1992) *The Transformation of Intimacy: Sexuality, Love and Eroticism in Modern Societies.* Cambridge: Polity Press.

Gilbert, M. (2003) 'Norms', in W. Outhwaite (ed.), *The Blackwell Dictionary of Modern Social Thought*, 2nd edn. Oxford: Blackwell.

Goffee, R. and Jones, G. (2006) *Why Should Anyone Be Led by You? What it Takes to Be an Authentic Leader.* Boston: Harvard Business School Press.

Goffman, E. (1961) *Asylums: Essays on the Social Situation of Mental Patients and Other Inmates.* New York: Doubleday.

Gole, N. (1997) 'L'emergence du sujet islamique', in M. Castells, *The Power of Identity.* London: Blackwell.

Goleman, D. (1995) *Emotional Intelligence: Why It Can Matter More than IQ.* New York: Bantam Books.

Goleman, D. (2002) *The New Leaders.* London: Little, Brown.

Graham, B. (1968) 'False prophets in the church', *Christianity Today*, 12(8): 4.

Gray, J. (2003) *Al Qaeda and What it Means to be Modern.* London: W.W. Norton.

Greenleaf, R. (1977) *Servant Leadership.* New Jersey: Paulist Press.

Greiner, L. (1973) 'What managers think of participative leadership', *Harvard Business Review*, March/April, 51(2).

Grint, K. (1997) *Leadership: Classical, Contemporary and Critical Approaches.* Oxford: Oxford University Press.

Grint, K. (2005) *Leadership Limits and Possibilities.* London: Palgrave.

Gwyn, D. (1989) *Unmasking the Idols.* Richmond, IN: Friends United Press.

Habermas, J. (1971) *Knowledge and Human Interests.* Boston: Beacon Press.

Habermas, J. (1984) *The Theory of Communicative Action*, Vol. I. London: Heinemann.

Habermas, J. (1987) *The Theory of Communicative Action*, Vol. II. Cambridge: Polity Press.

Habermas, J. (1996) *Between Facts and Norms: Contributions to a Discourse Theory of Law and Democracy.* Cambridge: Polity.

Habermas, J. (1998) *The Inclusion of the Other*. Cambridge, MA: MIT Press.

Halperin, D.M. (2002) *How to Do the History of Homosexuality*. Chicago: University of Chicago Press.

Handy, C. (1997) *The Hungry Spirit: Beyond Capitalism – A Quest for Purpose in the Modern World*. London: Hutchinson.

Harding, S.F. (2000) *The Book of Jerry Falwell: Fundamentalist Language and Politics*. Princeton, NJ: Princeton University Press.

Hardt, M. and Negri, A. (2001) *Empire*. Cambridge, MA: Harvard University Press.

Haslam, S.A. and Platow, M.J. (2001) 'The link between leadership and followership: how affirming a social identity translates vision into action', *Personality and Social Psychology Bulletin*, 27: 1469–79.

Heifetz, R. (1994) *Leadership Without Easy Answers*. Boston: Belknap Press.

Helgeson, S. (1990) *The Female Advantage*. New York: Doubleday.

Hertz, N. (2001) *The Silent Takeover*. London: Heinemann.

Hill, C. (1985) *The World Turned Upside Down*. New York: Peregrine.

Hirschhorn, L. (1988) *The Workplace Within: Psychodynamics of Organisational Life*. London: Cambridge Press.

Hochschild, A.R. (1983) *The Managed Heart: The Commercialisation of Human Feeling*. Berkeley: University of California Press.

Horkheimer, E. (1987) *Eclipse of Reason*. Boston: Beacon Press.

House, R. (1977) 'A theory of charismatic leadership', in J.G. Hunt and L. Larson (eds), *Leadership: The Cutting Edge*. Carbondale, IL: Southern Illinois University Press.

House, R. and Aditya, R. (1997) 'The social scientific study of leadership: quo vadis?', *Journal of Management*, 23: 409–73.

Hrab, N. (2004) 'France launches global cultural war'. Available at: http://www.techcentralstation.com/012004d.html (accessed 15 July 2004).

Huey, J. (1994) 'The leadership industry', *Fortune*, February, 21: 54–6.

Huff, P.A. (2000) 'The challenge of fundamentalism for interreligious dialogue', *Cross-Currents*, Spring/Summer, 50(1–2): 94–102.

Hughes, T.P. (2004) *American Genesis: A Century of Invention and Technological Enthusiasm, 1870–1970*, 2nd edn. Chicago: The University of Chicago Press.

Hui, C. (1994) 'Effects of leader empowerment behaviors and followers' personal control, voice and self-efficacy on in-role and extra-role performance: an extension and empirical test of Conger and Kanungo's *Empowerment Process Mode*', unpublished doctoral dissertation, Indiana University, Bloomington.

Huy, Q. (2001) 'In praise of middle managers', *Harvard Business Review*, September. 80(8): 72–9.

Huy, Q. (2002) 'Emotional balancing of organizational continuity and radical change: the contribution of middle managers', *Administrative Science Quarterly*, March.

Jackall, R. (1988) *Moral Mazes: The World of Corporate Managers*. New York: Oxford University Press.

Janis, I. (1972) *Victims of Groupthink: A Psychological Study of Foreign Policy Decisions and Fiascoes*. Boston: Houghton Mifflin.

Jaques, E. (1955) 'Social systems as a defence against persecutory and depressive anxiety', in A.D. Colman and M.H. Geller (eds), *Group Relation Reader 2*. Washington, DC: A K Rice Institute.

Jaques, E. (1990) 'In praise of hierarchy', *Harvard Business Review*, Jan/February. 68(1): 127–33.

Johnson, P. and Duberley, J. (2000) *Understanding Management Research*. London: Sage.

Joll, J. (1979) *The Anarchists*. London: Methuen.

Jones, D. (2005) *iPod Therefore I Am*. New York and London: Bloomsbury.

Joo, B. (2005) 'Executive coaching: a conceptual framework from an integrative review of practice and research', *Human Resource Development Review*, 4(4): 462–88.

Judge, A. (1994) 'The dilemma of denial: leadership's shadow revisited', *Futures*, 26(10): 1086–105.

Jung, D.I., Bass, B.M. and Sosik, J.J. (1995) 'Bridging leadership and culture: a theoretical consideration of transformational leadership and collectivist cultures', *Journal of Leadership Studies*, 2: 3–18.

Kandola, R. and Fullerton, J. (1994) *Managing the Mosaic: Diversity in Action*. London: Institute of Personnel and Development,

Kanter, R. (1979) 'Power failure in management circuits', *Harvard Business Review*, July–August, 57: 65–75.

Kanter, R. (1983) *The Change Masters*. New York: Simon and Schuster.

Katz, A. (1981) 'Self-help and mutual aid: an emerging social movement?', *Annual Review of Sociology*, 7: 129–55.

Katz, R.F. (2006) 'Studying leadership: knowledge into action'. Paper presented at the 5th annual conference on leadership, Cranfield University School of Management, 14–15 Dec.

Kerouac, J. (1958) *The Dharma Bums*. London: Viking.

Kerr, S. and Jermier, J.M. (1978) 'Substitutes for leadership: their meaning and measurement', *Organisational Behaviour and Human Performance*, 22: 375–403.

Kets de Vries, M.R.F. (1991) 'The leadership mystique', in L. Fulop and S. Linstead (1999) *Management: A Critical Text*. London: Macmillan Press.

Kets de Vries, M.R.F. (1994) 'The leadership mystique', *Academy of Management Executive*, 8(3): 73–92.

Klein, M. (1959) 'Our adult world and its roots in infancy', in A.D. Colman and M.H. Geller (eds) (1985) *Group Relation Reader 2*. Washington, DC: A K Rice Institute.

Klein, M. and Riviere, J. (1974) *Love, Hate and Reparation*. New York: Norton.

Klein, N. (2000) *No-Logo*. London: HarperCollins.

Klein, N. (2001) 'Reclaiming the commons', *New Left Review*, 9: 81–9.

Kondo, D.K. (1990) *Crafting Selves: Power, Gender and Discourses in Identity in a Japanese Workplace*. Chicago: University of Chicago Press.

Kotter, J.P. (1990) *A Force for Change: How Leadership Differs from Management*. New York: Free Press/London: Collier Macmillan.

Krantz, J. (1990) 'Lessons from the field: an essay on the crisis of leadership in contemporary organizations', *The Journal of Applied Behavioral Science*, 26(1): 49–64.

Kropotkin, P. (1902) 'Mutual aid, a factor in human evolution', *Annuaire de la Science Agronomique*, 1(2): 148–9.

Kunda, G. (1992) *Engineering Culture: Control Commitment in a High Tech Corporation*. Philadelphia, PA: Temple University Press.

Kutner, B. (1950) 'Elements and problems of democratic leadership', in A. Gouldner (ed.), *Studies in Leadership*. New York: Harper, pp. 459–67.

Lacan, J. (1958) Seminar 15 January 1958, cited in J. Dor (1997) *Introduction to the Reading of Lacan*. London and New York: Jason Aronson.

Ladd, J. (1970) 'Morality and the ideal of rationality in formal organisations', *The Monist*, 54(4), October.

Lasch, C. (1979) *The Culture of Narcissism: American Life in the Age of Diminishing Expectations*. New York: Warner Books.

Lawrence, W. (1979) 'The presence of totalitarian states-of-mind in institutions', *Free Associations*. Available at: http://Human-Nature.Com/Free-Associations/Lawren.html

Lawrence, W. (1999) 'Won from the void and formless infinite: experiences in social dreaming', in W.G. Lawrence (ed.), *Social Dreaming @ Work*. London: Karnac Books.

Leitch, A. (1956) 'The primary task of the church', *Christianity Today*, 1(1): 19.

Lewin, K. and Lippett, R. (1938) 'An experimental approach to the study of autocracy and democratic leadership', *Sociometry*, 1: 292–300.

Likert, R. (1961) *New Patterns of Management*. New York: McGraw-Hill.

Lilley, S. and Platt, G. (1997) 'Images of Martin Luther King', in K. Grint  (ed.), *Leadership: Classical, Contemporary and Critical Approaches*. Oxford: Oxford University Press.

Lovelock, J. (1982) *Gaia: A New Look at Life on Earth*. Oxford: Oxford University Press.

Luke, J.S. (1998) *Catalytic Leadership: Strategies for an Interconnected World*. San Francisco, CA: Jossey-Bass.

Lyotard, J.-F. (1984) *The Postmodern Condition*. Manchester: Manchester University Press.

Maak, Th. and Pless, N.M. (2006) 'Responsible leadership: a relational approach', in Th. Maak and N.M.Pless (eds), *Responsible Leadership*. London: Routledge.

MacIntyre, A. (1985) *After Virtue: A Study In Moral Theory*, 2nd edn. London: Duckworth.

Marcuse, H. (1964) *One-Dimensional Man. Studies in the Ideology of Advanced Industrial Society*. Boston: Beacon Press.

Marx, K. ([1845] 1978) 'Theses on Feuerbach', in Robert C. Tucker (ed.), *The Marx–Engels Reader*, 2nd edn. New York: W.W. Norton.

Maslow, A. (1968) *Toward a Psychology of Being*. New York: Van Nostrand.

Masson, J. (1990) *Against Therapy*. London: Fontana.

Maturana, H.R. and Varela, F. (1980) *Autopoiseis and Cognition*. Dordrecht: Reidel.

Maturana, H.R. and Varela, F. (1987) *Tree of Knowledge*. Boston: Shambula.

May, A. (2000) 'Leadership and spirit: breathing new vitality and energy into individuals and organizations', *The Academy of Management Executive*, 14(2): 128–30.

Mayer, J. and Salovey, P. (1993) 'The intelligence of emotional intelligence', *Intelligence*, 17(4): 433–42.

Mayer, J.D., Caruso, D.R. and Salovey, P. (2000) ' Models of emotional intelligence', in R.J. Sternberg (ed.), *Handbook of Intelligence*. Cambridge: Cambridge University Press.

Maynard, M. (2006) 'Ford Chairman receives call from Bush', *New York Times*, 9 Sept.: B3.

McAdam, D. (1982) *Political Process and the Development of Black Insurgency*. Chicago: University of Chicago Press.

McCarthy, J. and Zald, M. (1987) *Social Movements in an Organisational Society*. London: Transaction Books.

McCarthy, T. (1978) *The Critical Theory of Jürgen Habermas*. Cambridge, MA: MIT Press.

McClelland, D. (1975) *Power: The Inner Experience*. New York: Irvington Publishers.

McGregor, D. (1960) *The Human Side of Enterprise*. New York: McGraw-Hill.

McLuhan, M. and Fiore, Q. (1967) *The Medium is the Massage: An Inventory of Effects*. New York: Bantam Books.

Meindl, J. (1995) 'The romance of leadership as a follower-centric theory: a social constructionist approach', *The Leadership Quarterly*, 6(3): 329–41.

Melucci, A. (1989) *Nomads of the Present: Social Movements and Individual Needs in Contemporary Society*. London: Hutchinson.

Menzies Lyth, I. (1960) 'A case study in the functioning of social systems as a defence against anxiety', *Human Relations*, 13: 95–121.

Merton T. (1966) *A Search for Solitude, the Journals of Thomas Merton*, vol.III, *1952–1960*. ed. L. Cunningham. San Francsico: HarperCollins.

Michels, R. (1915) *Political Parties: A Sociological Study of the Oligarchical Tendencies of Modern Democracy*. Glencoe, IL: The Free Press.

Miller, E. (1993) *From Dependency to Autonomy*. London: Free Association Books.

Mintzberg, H. (2004a) *Managers Not MBAs: A Hard Look at the Soft Practice of Managing and Management Development*. San Francisco: Barrett Kochler.

Mintzberg, H. (2004b) 'Enough leadership', *Harvard Business Review*, Nov.: 21–2.

Mitroff, I.I. and Denton, E.A. (1999) *A Spiritual Audit of Corporate America*. San Francisco: Jossey-Bass.

Monbiot, G. (2000) *Captive State: The Corporate Take Over of Britain*. London: Macmillan.

Moore, R. (2000) *The Light in their Consciences: Early Quakers in Britain 1646–1666*. University Park, PA: Pennsylvania State University Press.

Morgan, G. (1986) *Images of Organisations*. London: Sage.

Moskowitz, E. (2001) *In Therapy We Trust: America's Obsession with Fulfilment*. Baltimore, MD: Johns Hopkins University Press.

Naess, A. (1989) *Ecology, Community and Lifestyle*. Cambridge: Cambridge University Press.

Naisbitt, J. (1982) *Megatrends: Ten New Directions Transforming our Lives*. New York: Warner Books.

Nelson, R. (1989) 'Organisational–environmental isomorphism, rejection and substitution in Brazilian Protestantism', *Organization Studies*, 10: 207–24.

Nelson, R.E. and Gopalan, S. (2003) 'Do organisational cultures replicate national cultures?', *Organization Studies*, 24(7): 1115–51.

Nicholls, J. (1987) 'Leadership in organisations: meta, macro and micro', *European Journal of Management*, 6: 16–25.

Nietzsche, F. ([1899] 1996) *Thus Spake Zarathustra*. London: Unwin, republished Orion Books.

Northouse, P.G. (2004) *Leadership, Theory and Practice*, 3rd edn. Thousand Oaks, CA: Sage.

Oates, S. (1982) *Let the Trumpet Sound: The Life of Martin Luther King, Jr*. New York: Harper & Row.

Obholzer, A. (1994) 'Authority, power and leadership: contributions from group relations training', in A. Obholzer and V.Z. Roberts (eds), *The Unconscious at Work: Individual and Organizational Stress in the Human Services*. London: Routledge, pp. 39–47.

Obholzer, A. and Roberts, V.Z. (eds) (1994) *The Unconscious at Work*. London: Routledge.

Orwell, G. (1949) *Nineteen-Eighty-Four*. London: Secker & Warburg.

Ouchi, W. (1981) *Theory Z: How American Business Can Meet the Japanese Challenge*. Reading, MA: Addison-Wesley.

Ouchi, W. and Price, R. (1978) 'Hierarchies, clans and Theory Z: a new perspective on organization development', *Organizational Dynamics*, 7(2): 24.

Pantoja, D. (1999) www.next-wave.org/dec99/paradox_of_postmodern_leadership.htm

Parker, M. (1992), 'Post-modern organization or postmodern theory?' *Organization Studies*, 13: 1–17.

Parker, M. (ed.) (1998) *Ethics and Organizations*. London: Sage.

Peters, T. and Waterman, R. (1982) *In Search of Excellence: Lessons from America's Best Run Companies*. New York: HarperCollins.

Pfeffer, J. (1978) 'The ambiguity of leadership', in M.W. McCall, Jr and M. Lombardo (eds), *Leadership: Where Else Can We Go?* Durham, NC: Duke University Press.

Prasad, P. and Caproni, P. J. (1997) 'Critical theory in the management classroom: engaging power, ideology and praxis', *Journal of Management Education* 21(3): 284–91.

Pugh, D. and Hickson, D. (1971) *Writers on Organisations*. London: Penguin Books.

Putnam, R. (2000) *Bowling Alone: The Collapse and Revival of American Community*. New York: Simon & Schuster.

Puwar, N. (2004) *Space Invaders: Race, Gender and Bodies Out of Place*. Oxford: Berg.

Pye, A. (2005) 'Leadership and organising: sensemaking in action', *Leadership*, 1(1): 31–49.

Quaker Faith and Practice (1995) *The Book of Christian Discipline of the Yearly Meeting of The Religious Society of Friends (Quakers) in Britain*. Pub. London Yearly Meeting.

Rice, A. (1965) *Learning for Leadership*. London: Tavistock.

Rich, A. (1980) 'Compulsory heterosexuality and lesbian experience', *Signs: Journal of Women in Culture & Society*, 5(4): 631–60.

Rieff, P. (1966) *The Triumph of the Therapeutic: Uses of Faith after Freud*. London: Chatto and Windus.

Robertson, P. (1982) *The Secret Kingdom*. Nashville, TN: Thomas Nelson.

Rogers, C. (1961) *On Becoming a Person: A Therapist's View of Psychotherapy*. London: Constable.

Rose, N. (1990) *Governing the Soul*. London: Routledge.

Rosener, J.B. (1995) *America's Competitive Secret: Women Managers*. New York: Oxford University Press.

Ruggiero, G. and Sahulka, S. (eds) (1998) *Zapatistas Encuentro*. New York: Seven Stories Press.

Ryan, R. (2003) 'The writer as freedom fighter, the freedom fighter as writer', *New Formulation*, 2(1): 23–33.

Said, E. (1973) *Orientalism*. London: Routledge and Kegan Paul.

Salerno, S. (2005) *SHAM: How the Gurus of the Self-help Movement Make Us Helpless*. London: Nicholas Brearley.

Saul, J.R. (1992) *Voltaire's Bastards: The Dictatorship of Reason in the West*. Toronto: Penguin.

Schein, E. (1988) *Organizational Culture and Leadership*. San Francisco: Jossey-Bass.

Schwartz, T. (2000) 'How do you feel?', *Fast Company*, June, 35: 296.

Segal, L. (1994) *Straight Sex: Rethinking the Politics of Pleasure*. London: Virago.

Senge, P. (1990) *The Fifth Discipline: The Art and Practice of the Learning Organisation*. New York: Doubleday/Currency.

Senge, P., Scharmer, C.O., Jaworski, J. and Flowers, E.S. (2004) *Presence: Exploring Profound Change in People, Organisations and Society*. London: Nicholas Brealey.

Shamir, B., House, R. and Arthur, M. (1993) 'The motivational effects of charismatic leadership: a self-concept based theory', *Organization Science*, 4: 1–17.

Sherman, S. and Freas, A. (2004) 'The wild west of executive coaching', *Harvard Business Review*, 82 (11): 82–9.

Smith, D. (1997) 'Managers lack proper skills', *The Sunday Times* (Business Section), 14 September.

Smith, S. and Wilkinson, B. (1996) 'No doors on offices, no secrets: we are our own policemen: capitalism without conflict?', in L. Fulop and S. Linstead (eds) (1999) *Management: A Critical Text*. London: Macmillan Press, pp. 106–7.

Snow, N. (2002) 'Common sense', *Adbusters: Journal of the Mental Environment*, Mar/April, 40.

Sotorin, P. and Tyrell, S. (1998) 'Wondering about critical management studies: a review of and commentary on selected texts', *Management Communication Quarterly*, 12(2): 303–36.

Spears, L. (1995) 'Reflections on Leadership' in http://www.greenleaf.org/leadership/servant-leadership/What-is-Servant-Leadership.html

Starhawk (1986) *Truth or Dare*. New York: Harper Row.

Stephens, C., D'Intino, R. and Victor, B. (1995) 'The moral quandary of transformational leadership: change for whom?', in R. Woodman and W. Pasmore (eds), *Research In Organizational Change and Development*, Vol. 8. Greenwich, CT: JAI Press, pp. 123–43.

Steyrer, J. (1998) 'Charisma and the archetypes of leadership', *Organizational Studies*, 19(5): 807–28.

Stiglitz, J. (2003) 'The Mammon interview', *The Observer*, 12 October.

Stodgill, R.M. (1974) *Handbook of Leadership: A Survey of Theory and Research*. New York: The Free Press.

Sullivan, N. (2003) *A Critical Introduction to Queer Theory*. New York: New York University Press.

Swan, E. (2006) *Executive Coaching: Psychobabble or Spaces for Doubt?* Lancaster: Centre for Excellence in Leadership. Working Paper Series CEL.

Swan, E. and Cwerner, S. (2006) *Solutions from Within? Coaching as Personalised, Personal and Content-free Pedagogy*. Lancaster: Centre for Excellence in Leadership.

Taylor, F. (1911) *The Principles of Scientific Management*. New York: Harper & Row.

Ten Bos, R. (1997) 'Essai: business ethics and Bauman ethics', *Organization Studies*, 18: 997–1014.

Thapan, M. (ed.) (1997) *Embodiment Essays on Gender and Identity*. Mumbai: Oxford University Press.

Thibaut, J. and Kelley, H. (1959) *The Social Psychology of Groups*. New York: John Wiley.

Thomas, R. Roosevelt Jr. (1991) *Beyond Race and Gender: Unleashing the Power of your Total Workforce by Managing Diversity*. New York: American Management Associates.

Tichy, N. and Devanna, M. (1986) *The Transformational Leader*. New York: John Wiley.

Tjosvold, D. and Field, R. (1984) 'Managers' structuring cooperative and competitive controversy in group decision making', *International Journal of Management*, 1: 26–32.

Tjosvold, D. and Hui, C. (1998) 'Empowerment in the manager–employee relationship in Hong Kong: interdependence and controversy', *Journal of Social Psychology*, 138(5): 624.

Tjosvold, D. and McNeely, L. (1988) 'Innovation through communication in an educational bureaucracy', *Communication Research*, 15: 568–81.

Tolman, D.L. and Diamond, L.M. (2002) 'Desegregating sexuality research: cultural and biological perspectives on gender and desire', *Annual Review of Sex Research*, 12: 33–74.

Touraine, A. (1981) *The Voice and the Eye*. New York: Cambridge University Press.

Tourish, D. and Pinnington, A. (2002) 'Transformational leadership, corporate cultism and the spirituality paradigm: an unholy trinity in the workplace?', *Human Relations*, 55(2): 147–72.

Treacher, A. (2000) 'Ethnicity, psychoanalysis and cultural studies', *Free Associations*, 7(4): 113–26.

Trevett, C. (1995) *Women and Quakerism in the 17th Century*. York: The Ebor Press.

Trist, E. and Bamford, K. (1951) 'Some social and psychological consequences of long wall method of coal-getting', *Human Relations*, 4: 3–38.

Trotsky, L. (1940) *The Class, The Party and the Leadership*. Available at: http://www.marxist.net/trotsky/cpl/index.html (accessed 12 Sept. 2004).

Ulrich, D. (1984) 'Specifying external relations: definition of and actors in an organization's environment', *Human Relations*, 37(3): 245–62.

Vallance, E. (1979) *Women in the House: A Study of Women Members of the House of Commons*. London: Athlone Press.

Victoria, B. (1998) *Zen at War*. New York: Weatherhilt.

Von Bertalanaffy, L. (1968) *General Systems Theory: Foundations, Development, Application*. London: Allen Lane.

Vuola, E. (2002) 'Remaking universals? Transnational feminism(s) challenging fundamentalist ecumenism', *Theory, Culture & Society*, 19(1–2): 175–95.

Walby, S. (1997) *Gender Transformations*. London: Routledge.

Wallis, R. (ed.) (1975) *Sectarianism: Analyses of Religious and Non-religious Sects*. London: Peter Owen.

Watson, S. and Vasilieva, E. (2007) 'Wilderness thinking: a novel approach to leadership development', *Development and Learning Organizations*, 21(2).

Weakland, J. et al. (1974) 'Brief therapy: focused problem resolution', *Family Process*, 13: 141–68.

Weber, M. (1930) *The Protestant Ethic and the Spirit of Capitalism*. London: Allen and Unwin.

Weber, M. (1947) *The Theory of Social and Economic Organisation*. New York: Oxford University Press.

Weick, K.E. (1995) *Sensemaking in Organizations*. London: Sage.

Western, S. (2000) 'Plain living: provocative thoughts', *The Friend* (Quaker Journal), September: 4–7.

Western, S. (2005) 'A critical analysis of leadership: overcoming fundamentalist tendencies'. PhD thesis, Lancaster University Management School, UK.

Western, S. (2006) 'Look who's talking', *Coaching at Work*, 1(2): 31–4.

Western, S. and Gosling, J. (2003) *Pairing for Leadership*. Centre for Leadership Studies, Exeter University, Exeter. Available at: http://www.ex.ac.uk/rbp/Research/Discussion/PapersMan/Man2003/Man0314.pdf

Whitley, R. (1992) *Business Systems in East Asia: Firms, Markets and Societies*. London: Sage.

Whyte, W.H. (1956) *The Organization Man*. New York: Simon and Schuster.

Wickens, P. (1987) *The Road to Nissan: Flexibility, Quality, Teamwork*. London: Macmillan.

Wilkinson, B. (1996) 'Culture, institutions and business in East Asia', *Organizational Studies*, 17(3): 421–47.

Willmott, H. (1998) 'Towards a new ethics? The contributions of poststructuralism and posthumanism', in M. Parker (ed.), *Ethics and Organizations*. London: Sage. pp. 76–121.

Wollstonecraft, M. (1982) *Vindication of the Rights of Women*. Harmondsworth: Penguin Books.

Woodcock, G. (1977) *Anarchism*. Penguin: London.

Woodhouse, D. and Pengelly, P. (1991) *Anxiety and the Dynamics of Collaboration*. London: Routledge.

Yukl, G. (1998) *Leadership in Organizations*, 4th edn. Englewood Cliffs, NJ: Prentice-Hall.

Yukl, G. (1999) 'An evaluative essay on current conceptions of effective leadership', *European Journal of Work & Organizational Psychology*, March, 8(1): 215.

Yukl, G. (2002) *Leadership in Organisations*, 5th edn. Upper Saddle River, NJ: Prentice Hall.

Zaleznik, A. (1997) 'Real work', *Harvard Business Review*, 75 (Nov-Dec): 53–59.

Zaleznik, A. (1989) *The Managerial Mystique*. New York: Harper and Row.

Zaleznik, A. (1992) 'Managers and leaders: are they different?', *Harvard Business Review*, 70(2): 126.

Zinn, H. (1991) Declarations of Independence. New York: Harper Perennial.

Žižek, S. (1992) *Looking Awry: An Introduction to Jaques Lacan through Popular Culture*. London: Verso.

Žižek, S. (1999) *The Ticklish Subject*. London: Verso.

Žižek, S. (2002) *Welcome to the Desert of the Real*. London: Verso.

Žižek, S. (2003) *The Puppet and the Dwarf: The Perverse Core of Christianity*. Cambridge, MA: MIT Press.

Zohar, D. and Marshall, I.N. (2004) *Spiritual Capital: Wealth We Can Live by*. London: Bloomsbury.

# Index

Please note that page references to non-textual information such as Figures or Tables are in *italic* print, whereas page references to Boxes will be in **bold** print. Titles of publications beginning with 'A' or 'The' will be filed under the first significant word.